...and along came Alexis

MIROLAND IMPRINT 32

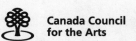

Guernica Editions Inc. acknowledges the support of the Canada Council
for the Arts and the Ontario Arts Council. The Ontario Arts Council
is an agency of the Government of Ontario.
We acknowledge the financial support of the Government of Canada.

...and along came Alexis

EMMA PIVATO

MIROLAND (GUERNICA)
TORONTO • CHICAGO • BUFFALO • LANCASTER (U.K.)
2021

Connie McParland, Michael Mirolla, series editors
Gary Clairman, editor
David Moratto, cover and interior design
Front cover photo: Joe Pivato
*The cover image is a part of the Whitemud Nature Reserve
near Alexis' home where she likes to 'walk'.*
Guernica Editions Inc.
287 Templemead Drive, Hamilton, ON L8W 2W4
2250 Military Road, Tonawanda, N.Y. 14150-6000 U.S.A.
www.guernicaeditions.com

Distributors:
Independent Publishers Group (IPG)
600 North Pulaski Road, Chicago IL 60624
University of Toronto Press Distribution (UTP)
5201 Dufferin Street, Toronto (ON), Canada M3H 5T8
Gazelle Book Services
White Cross Mills, High Town, Lancaster LA1 4XS U.K.

First edition.
Printed in Canada.

Legal Deposit—Third Quarter
Library of Congress Catalog Card Number: 2021933075
Library and Archives Canada Cataloguing in Publication
Title: ... and along came Alexis / Emma Pivato.
Names: Pivato, Emma, 1943- author.
Description: First edition.
Identifiers: Canadiana (print) 2021014078X | Canadiana (ebook) 20210140895 |
ISBN 9781771836784 (softcover) | ISBN 9781771836791 (EPUB) |
ISBN 9781771836807 (Kindle)
Subjects: LCSH: Pivato, Alexis, 1978- | LCSH: Pivato, Emma, 1943—Family. |
LCSH: People with disabilities—Biography. | LCSH: Mothers of children with
disabilities—Biography. | LCSH: People with disabilities—Family relationships. |
LCGFT: Biographies.
Classification: LCC HV1568 .P58 2021 | DDC 362.4092—dc23

This book is for my family
for together we walked this road
And for other families like ours
whose tales remain untold

Contents

Introduction 1

1   *It begins* 5
2   *The new normal* 9
3   *Those early nights* 13
4   *My secret guilt* 17
5   *Those early days* 19
6   *The Mayfield experience* 23
7   *Exploring the system* 29
8   *Family life with young Alexis* 35
9   *Patterning* 41
10   *The Gateway Association and 'the book'* 47
11   *Seizures* 53
12   *A second opinion; a second chance* 59
13   *Why does Alexis stop breathing?* 67
14   *The development of the GRIT model* 77
15   *Convincing Gateway to be our sponsor* 83
16   *Finding the parents, teachers and therapists* 87
17   *The GRIT program is launched* 93
18   *The early GRIT years* 97
19   *Masako Whalley and the vibrator era* 101

20	*Communication*	107
21	*Conditional Learning*	111
22	*GRIT grows—and grows and grows*	115
23	*A family crisis and a possible resolution*	119
24	*A new beginning*	125
25	*Emma, the school psychologist!*	129
26	*Further reflections*	133
27	*The men I married*	139
28	*Alexis Alone*	145
29	*Alexis and I both start school*	151
30	*The challenge of Academic Challenge*	157
31	*Juliana in the middle*	171
32	*After two years Alexis moves on*	183
33	*The Formation of Integration-Action Alberta*	189
34	*The dark side of pressured inclusion*	193
35	*Crisis and Rejection*	195
36	*Alexis and Lydia at St. Gabriel's School*	201
37	*Alexis goes to high school*	207
38	*Leaving school behind*	211
39	*Community Living at home*	215
40	*A critical event*	219
41	*My daughter's work*	223
42	*The Standing Frame Story*	229
43	*Other Useful Therapeutic Devices*	235
44	*Cognitive and social stimulation*	239
45	*The cart story*	245
46	*Impulse buying—pros and cons*	249
47	*The travelling bathroom dilemma*	253
48	*Let's start again—from scratch*	267
49	*The all-in-one wheelchair*	273
50	*Starting all over yet again*	283
51	*Feeding Alexis*	289

52   *Running 'the business'* 301
53   *God, friends and others* 307
54   *The mothers who won't quit* 313
55   *Has it been worth it?* 319

Alexis' father speaks out 323
Epilogue 327
Afterword 333

Acknowledgements 339
About the Author 341
Endnotes 343

Introduction

This is a story about a now 43-year long journey I have taken with my younger daughter, Alexis. We each brought along certain supplies for the trip. I brought a belief in fighting for the underdog that I acquired from my mother, and an interest in people that I picked up from my father. Alexis brought her innocence, her trust and her many challenges. Throughout the years of our partnership we have travelled along an uncharted road, and we have made many rich discoveries along the way.

My mother was a teacher who taught in various isolated country schools throughout Northeastern Alberta during the 1930's and '40's, travelling back and forth by horseback. She fought hard to help the weak students in her classes and instilled in me the belief that education was everything—not just as a means to an end, but as an end in itself. My father was a warm and friendly man with a strong musical bent who believed that you should work hard but then you should play hard. His main advice for me was to be good to others and help out wherever you can.

By the time Alexis was born both my parents had passed away. But it was with these memories of them in mind that I set out to build a meaningful life for my daughter. This was a goal that various friends, family members and medical professionals said I could never achieve. And in retrospect one could say they were right. Alexis' life is not meaningful in a conventional sense—but it *is* meaningful to her.

Creating a life with some meaning and value in it for Alexis has not been easy. But it has not been impossible either. I have been driven to write our story because the knowledge I have acquired along the way could help others. But, at the same time, I have been loath to do so. Profound brain damage comes in many forms and so do the families left to cope with it. Yet, the experience we have been through has been so rich that I feel obliged to share it.

To be told that my nine-month-old daughter was profoundly disabled filled me with horror and anguish to a level I had never experienced before. It literally came at me in waves until I thought I was being washed away. But at another level, the reflective part of my mind wanted to capture what I was feeling, to write it down before it was lost so that others who have felt this way could have their pain described and have someone to share their experience with at a gut level.

I remember thinking that throughout human history many have experienced such acute horror and worse in different circumstances. It is not unique to the disability world. At the time Alexis was born in 1978, the various human atrocities of the Vietnam War were still fresh in all our minds. To compare our own situation to the massive human tragedies of that era seemed inappropriate.

Alexis was born in a relatively safe country with various medical and social resources in place to help people like her. Some perspective was called for. But as a mother facing the reality that her child had been effectively destroyed before she was even born, I could not look at our loss and her loss in this way.

And so, as I slowly and painfully came to terms with the fact that Alexis and I were now part of the disability world, the two of us began our journey together.

Alexis at 17 months, sketched by fellow parent,
Bev Getz, from a photograph

CHAPTER 1

It begins

I **felt the** wind in my face as my stretcher raced towards the delivery room. *Strange,* I thought ... *like a TV show.* Where did that man beside me holding the IV come from? The nurse I knew. She was racing along my other side, her hand planted firmly on my stomach. But who was pushing the stretcher so fast—and why?

This labour was different. The hospital labour floor seemed full of screaming mothers-to-be. The nurses ran from one to another and the one attending to me when my own nurse went on break seemed very impatient. I tried to talk to her, to tell her it was time, but another scream came from nearby, too imperative to be ignored. When she got back to me it was almost too late. Hence, the frantic race down the hall.

My obstetrician was not waiting in the delivery room. There was no time for him to get there. I glimpsed an intern fumbling to put on his gloves. He finished just as the baby emerged and caught her awkwardly. She was white and limp and I saw the helpless look on his face. It seemed like a full minute passed before the nurse pointed out the oxygen mask and suction nearby. *Was she waiting on protocol?* I thought angrily. *Is protocol more important than my baby's life?*

The intern grabbed the mask and applied it firmly to the baby's face. Alexis turned from white to blue and the nurse then hurried her out of the room while the intern attended to me. It seemed a long time before they brought her back and when they did I was not given her to hold. She was all swaddled up but I managed to greet her and to touch her hand. I felt her weakly grasp my finger and at that moment I knew. *We'll get through this together, Alexis. We'll be partners,* I said.

My husband Joe and I debated heavily about having a third child. Our two older children were born while we were both still working on our Ph. D's and very preoccupied with our future plans. Joe was not in favour of further adding to our family, but I pushed for it. I thought we needed more challenge in our life.

To put the challenge issue in context, I once read a story in my high school reader that has stayed with me all my life. It was called "The Monkey's Paw" and the basic premise of that story is "beware what you ask for; you might get it in a way you would never expect!"

I had difficulty in even conceiving a third child. This was ironic since our other two children had come very quickly, despite our best efforts to delay that process. From early on in my pregnancy with Alexis there seemed to be problems. Shortly after she was conceived my then 3-year-old son had an asthma attack and was hospitalized in the emergency room and then in a ward. He looked so scared and pathetic lying there in an oxygen tent and having such difficulty breathing. I could not leave him. I did not want to leave him for a second. Yet at the same time I knew I was pregnant and the last place I should be at that critical point was in a hospital ward.

The staff assured me that it was a non-contagious ward but the very next day a little girl came in who had been hospitalized because of convulsions. In the hall afterward her parents told me that she had contracted Rubella and it was because her temperature had sky-rocketed that she had ended up having seizures. Rubella is particularly dangerous for pregnant women.

Within a couple of days, I had a red rash all over my hands and arms and I had a fever and started having stomach cramps and 'break-through bleeding'. My doctor recommended bed rest for the next few days and gradually the bleeding stopped. But I was exhausted throughout the entire pregnancy, and that was a very different experience than I had had with my two older children. However, my obstetrician reassured me. "Oh, you've got two young children at home; that is why you are tired."

When I was wheeled into the delivery room to have Alexis, my husband, Joe, was called and he arrived soon after. But he was not allowed to see the baby for another hour. We both worried about this when we talked later. In those first days in the hospital when I tried to breastfeed Alexis she could not nurse very well. A couple of days after we brought Alexis home, I was surprised when a community nurse came to the door to check on her. This had not happened with my older children and I suppose the experienced maternity staff at the hospital had sensed that something was not quite right.

After checking with me on what was happening and examining Alexis, the nurse expressed concern. According to what she was seeing and hearing she felt that Alexis was not getting enough to eat and advised me to supplement her with formula. I had never been told that with the others.

Alexis tended to choke on the flow from the bottle nipple, so I was advised to get a special kind of nipple used for nursing baby goats. Alexis also could not seem to tolerate regular formula and a soy-based formula was suggested. The next few months passed slowly, and we gradually fell into a more or less regular routine.

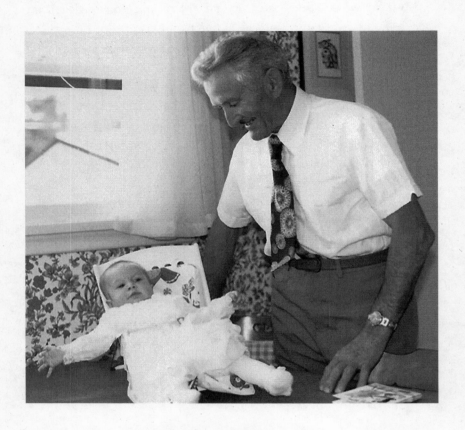

Alexis, 4½ months, with her nonno,
Toni Pivato: on the day of her baptism

CHAPTER 2

The New Normal

When **Alexis was** about three months old, I began to hear her babbling in her crib after naps and in the morning, as I had with my older two children. This time I vowed to capture those early sounds and I rigged up a tape recorder in her room that could be turned on remotely. But soon the babbling slowed down and then gradually stopped altogether. I wondered and worried about that. Could it be due to hearing loss? But no! She responded normally to other sounds. I was particularly thrilled about the way she would call out for us upon awakening and then stop once she heard us coming.

The bedrooms in our home were separated from the rest of the house by a long, hardwood-covered hallway that always creaked when you walked along it. Clearly, Alexis had formed a cause-effect relationship. When the hall creaked, she knew we were coming and stopped calling out. I took this as a tangible sign of normal child development.

But still I worried. There were other signs, like her early feeding difficulties, and her lack of interest in reaching for objects, and the fact that Alexis had always been so floppy. However, friends and family members, even my own husband, were not concerned and suggested that I was being too negative and over-reacting. *Maybe I am,* I thought. *Maybe I have post-partum depression and am seeing things too darkly.* But my brother agreed with me. Of course, he was rarely around and only going by what I told him over the phone, whereas Joe, my husband, was there every day and not seeing any problem.

After much back and forth in my mind I finally made an appointment with Alexis' paediatrician when she was seven months old. She was still not sitting up independently at that point and that definitely was moving beyond the stage of developmental normalcy. After a long wait in the hot waiting room of our paediatrician's office we were finally called in to see him. Alexis was sleeping soundly, slumped in her sac-like 'Umbroller' stroller. We had found it necessary to acquire this in order to go out with her, although our other children had managed fine as babies in a traditional, firm-backed baby cart.

The doctor performed the usual physical examination and found Alexis to be perfect with no obvious problems. Of course, he could assess nothing cognitively since she would not wake up and I explained that it was too hot in his waiting room and we had passed her usual naptime. He turned to me and said "I don't see anything wrong with her, Mrs. Pivato. But I know how you worry about these things. I am going to refer you to a specialist just for your own peace of mind." Then he jotted a name and contact number down on a prescription pad and handed it to me as he left the room.

Finally, at nine months—and very apologetically—I took Alexis to the specialist. I laid my pretty baby on his table, looking with pride at her beautifully proportioned body, her sweet face, and her big, beautiful eyes with their long lashes—and within moments all of that was destroyed. He examined her briefly and turned to me. "I don't blame you for being concerned, Mrs. Pivato."

Finally! I thought with relief. Somebody who believes me and doesn't think I'm neurotic! But wait. No! I don't want to be right. I want to be wrong and neurotic. Please don't let the next words come.

"Your daughter is functioning at a 2-month level instead of a 9-month level. She must be a great burden to you."

I looked at the examining table. Alexis was gone. And in her place was "a great burden."

"Is she retarded?" I asked.

"Oh, we don't use that word anymore. But the damage is definitely central and probably severe."

A mother's heart can only take so much. My head was filled with a strange noise. I heard only scattered words after that.

"... looks like Rubella Syndrome ... blind, and possibly deaf as well ...

full assessment in two months ... can have physio for a while but won't do much good."

I dressed Alexis and put her in her stroller. I had never noticed before how heavy and inert she was. I went out to the waiting room to join my husband and our other children, Janni, 4, and Juliana, 3. They looked different. My husband looked different, too—not like the man I had loved and married, but just a man caught up in the same twist of fate as me. And my children—how dare they play so light-heartedly? I contemplated ways to squelch and subdue them.

Joe did not blink when I told him. "It can't be that bad. I've *seen* her respond. Doctors don't know everything." And later—when it was, it really was that bad—his tune changed only slightly. "We'll manage; we'll cope; it's not the end of the world. Worse things have happened."

And we did manage, and we did cope, and we still do, thanks in good part to him, my brave, solid, loving husband who has always done way more than his share. But still, by any reasonable standard, what happened to Alexis, and therefore to our family, cannot be considered anything short of a disaster.

In any case, I was devastated—and continued to be devastated for a long, long time. Any parent hearing such news would feel a deep sense of loss and experience a long grieving process. But for me there was something else.

CHAPTER 3

Those Early Nights

I **felt ruptured**, torn apart. I have asked myself many times since if it was normal to feel that way—to feel like I had lost not only my daughter but also myself?

I remember that I felt betrayed, like I had measured up to my part of the bargain and the universe had not. I realize that such thinking is not logical but that is how I felt. For many months I could not sleep properly, waking at two or three in the morning and then curling up in the rocking chair in the living room with only a cup of tea for comfort. I would cry for hours, pleading, bargaining, even hallucinating at times. Yet in the daytime I was a different person, determined to do the best I could by Alexis, my other children, my husband and my career.

The next few months were a period of withdrawal. My adult ballet class was preparing for a performance in the spring. I could not stand the light-hearted banter and dropped out. Both my older children attended the community cooperative nursery school where I was vice-chairperson. I pulled them out and resigned from my position. This suited my son fine. It was clear by that point that he was exceptional in the other direction and found nursery school too constricting. But Juliana missed her playmates there and the school's interesting activities very much. A kind neighbour offered to take her to and from the sessions since her own daughter also attended and they lived nearby. I agreed and stayed away. I just could not bear to see all those normal children and happy families.

My son was taking Suzuki violin lessons. Every week was agony for me, huddled in the back of the school classroom where the lessons took place. I spent the hour rocking Alexis and trying to keep her quiet while simultaneously keeping Juliana engaged in a quiet activity and listening to Janni asking the instructor his endless questions. "Why do we hold it that way? Why not this way?" he asked as he turned the bow backwards. "Who made the first violin? Why does your violin sound different from mine?"

And the concerts! All those doting parents and privileged children! I felt totally alienated. I fought to keep going because once our son quit, somebody else would immediately take his place. I knew there was a long waiting list. Finally, I just could not do it any longer. At the end of the school year I withdrew him. I took Juliana off the fall registration list for cello and Alexis off the wait list for viola. Another dream shot. "If I can't have my family trio, I don't want anything!" I said to myself childishly.

I had taken to wearing several layers of clothing to bed at night and turning the electric blanket up. I huddled at the edge of the bed, isolated in my misery. Worst of all, I withdrew from my children. "Leave me alone! Can't you see that I'm busy with Alexis? Go play downstairs."

Our modest social life had always been sustained by my initiative. But now I stopped asking my husband if we could go out or entertain people. I called friends only to ask their opinion on Alexis about some behaviour or other, and just those who might have something useful to say.

The only thing I did not withdraw from was my academic work. It was the one part of me that was still intact, untouched by this grey cloud that hovered over all of us. My Ph. D. advisor kept a steady pressure on me—arranging weekly meetings with my committee where I had to report on my progress.

Joe had completed his Ph. D. in Comparative Literature the year before and was working full-time at the newly opened Athabasca University. Many evenings and weekend afternoons he took over with all three children while I retreated to my basement study to work on my own dissertation. But in my depressed and preoccupied state it still took me another 18 months to complete it.

The day of my oral examination in the spring of 1980 finally came. I rooted around in my closet to find clothes I had had no occasion to wear for a long time and steeled myself for the ordeal ahead, but it went more smoothly than I had feared. There were only a few minor issues to fix up before I could graduate. My general research area was child development and my dissertation topic was 'giftedness' and creativity theory.

Two of the committee members were intrigued by some of the work I had been doing in the area and offered to work with me on it further so we could co-publish a couple of articles. I remember clearly what I said in response. "Today is the last day I will be talking or thinking about giftedness and creativity theory. From now on my focus will be on disability theory. I'm sorry."

I was apologizing to them for abandoning my work after all the time they had spent listening to me talk about it over those many months, but I should have been apologizing to myself. I had invested much in this project and had already given one conference presentation that had been well received. I knew that I had stumbled onto a potentially fruitful line of inquiry that was not being pursued by others. But I also knew that I had neither the time nor the energy to work both ends of the spectrum at once and that my first duty had to be to Alexis and to learning whatever I could that might be of help to her.

Why did I feel so strongly about this? Others in the same position went on with their lives. Why couldn't I? And I was not just giving up a research interest. I was giving up all hope of an academic career. It was not as if I could start over at that point and become a credible disability expert.

But I knew why. I was doing this because it was my fault. If the diagnosis of Rubella Syndrome we had received was correct, then Alexis was like this entirely due to my negligence. During the many months since her birth I had been in what can only be described as a state of mourning and I had done much soul searching. I had asked myself again and again what I could bring to the table to help Alexis and where my own limitations as a human being would get in the way. During one of those long ruminations, I suddenly remembered with shock and horror an incident that had happened when I was 8 years old.

CHAPTER 4

My Secret Guilt

I **started life** on a small farm in northeastern Alberta. Poor land covered with Jack Pine, out of which a couple of fields had been carved. It was a largely forgotten place that in the 1940's still seemed to be from another era. My mother taught grades one to eight at a country schoolhouse five miles down the road. My father was ostensibly a farmer but his biggest claims to fame were his capacity to play his 8-string Norwegian violin quite beautifully and the fact that he was a genuinely nice and kind person. There were farmers in the area who were able to make a living on the land, but my father was not one of them. We depended primarily on my mother's income and that was always the case when I was growing up, although my father continued to work at one job or another.

When I was ready to start school, mother and I moved to Elk Point, a small town 20 miles away, where she had attained a position teaching grade eight. I remember how terrified I was on the first day of school. I had rarely seen other children before except for my younger brother. Never had I been in a place with so many people, so many houses. I was frightened of the teacher, the children, even the schoolhouse. In those days each elementary grade was housed in a different small building and indoor plumbing was yet to come to that small town. But we did have electricity, which was better than the kerosene lamps we had on the farm.

That first day of school I walked haltingly into the cloakroom to hang up my jacket and my little cloth school bag on the peg assigned to me. The other children milled around, talking away to each other and ignoring me. But then one girl turned and spoke to me. "Are you new?" she asked. We introduced ourselves and from that day onward we were friends. I was no longer alone, and I remember what a great sense of relief I felt.

Two years later, this same girl, Beverly and I were walking along side-by-side with the rest of our class to the town health clinic where we were to receive rubella vaccine immunization shots.[1] Our teacher had told us how important this was for girls so that when we grew up and had babies of our own they would not be damaged if we were exposed to German measles during pregnancy. Beverly and I were talking energetically about a recent interest and continued talking as we entered the clinic. Suddenly we noticed that all the other children had gone ahead and completed their shots and the teacher was rounding up the class for our return to the schoolhouse.

My first instinct was to tell her that we had lagged behind and missed our turns, but Beverly did not agree. She was afraid we would get into trouble and out of fear for our friendship I listened to her. We never did get those Rubella shots. Some years after Alexis was born, I ran into Beverly and told her what had happened. But she did not even remember that early school incident. She had never had any children and was not planning to, so for her it was not an issue.

CHAPTER 5

Those Early Days

As I have said, those early nights and days were very different for me. At nighttime all the demons escaped and raged freely through my mind. In the daytime they were firmly pushed down deep into my subconscious. I was still chronically sad but there were many things to be done each day that kept me externally focused. As I went about the business of caring for three young children, putting meals on the table and running a household, the thesis nagged constantly at the corners of my mind. Also, Alexis's seizures were diagnosed at about that nine-month period and some of them were pretty frightening.

The first thing I had done when I came home from that fateful appointment with the specialist when Alexis was nine months old was to attempt to reclaim her from his dire prognostications. I laid her down on the kitchen table in order to remove her snowsuit. November 9th, 1978 and it was winter in Alberta! Alexis turned her head from side to side, clearly recognizing that she was home and that she was on a strange surface—or so I thought. She seemed focused on something her brother was saying and at that point my faith in her came back.

"She hears! I *know* she hears—and she sees, too!" I shouted defiantly. Then I collapsed against the wall in tears and Janni and Juliana milled around me uncertainly, not knowing what to do. My husband looked at me with compassion but also with a measure of judgment. I *knew* what he was thinking. He was expecting me to pull myself together and to think of the children and my responsibilities toward them.

Later that evening we phoned his parents in Toronto and I told them the terrible news. Like my husband, they refused to accept that the situation was hopeless and offered their support, not that they could do much from such a distance. But still, their positive attitude helped to strengthen my own resolve. The next morning, I got to work collecting information and exploring program possibilities for Alexis. Because her disabilities were so severe the neurologist had suggested institutionalization, but Joe and I were not willing to consider place-ment outside the home and his parents were also against it.

Several years previously I had taken a course on 'exceptionality assessment', focused on both ends of the intelligence spectrum. I would have preferred to take the regular assessment course, but it was reserved for students studying to become practitioners. My own research area was theoretical, so I did not qualify. However, as I had reasoned at the time, this course on exceptionality assessment had academic value for me because I would learn more about the assess-ment instruments available to measure creativity and superior levels of intelligence, my dissertation area. The rest, the part about the assessment of individuals with intellectual deficits, I would learn well enough to pass the course respectably.

Our course professor, Dr. Donald Cameron, was exceptional, himself. Unlike many of his colleagues, he had no discernable ego, only a genuine and deeply compassionate interest in people with intel-lectual limitations. But he shared his knowledge at the other end of the spectrum very competently as well, and the course turned out to be a valuable experience for me in more ways than one. Three of my fellow students were to become lifelong friends—and strong and knowledgeable supports to me in the struggles that lay ahead.

One of those students was Ardene Anderson, a counselor in the Edmonton Public School System completing a master's degree in educational psychology at that time. Ardene was one of the first people I called the day after the terrible news we had received about Alexis. She told me about an infant stimulation program for children with developmental disabilities based out of Mayfield, one of the schools she worked in, and gave me the contact information. I phoned the school immediately, unusual behaviour for me since I generally like to procrastinate a bit before taking any definitive step. But I was being driven by a terrible sense of urgency. Two weeks later the program had a waiting list, so I guess I made that phone call just in time!

CHAPTER 6

The Mayfield Experience

Within one week of my call the home tutor from the Mayfield Early Education Program made her first visit. It did not go as well as I had hoped and in retrospect, I must acknowledge that she did her sincere best. But the extreme emotions I was experiencing at that time, an anguish of pain and loss comingled with outrage and wounded pride, could not have made me easy to work with. I will record here the way I felt then from the draft of an article I prepared a few years later (1985) when Alexis was seven years old.

How Can I Reach Her?
February 1985

My daughter is about as handicapped as it is possible to be—and still live. She has a serious seizure disorder, cannot even roll over, let alone sit up, has no functional use of her eyes, hands or mouth for communicating, and she also has numerous food allergies. Yet there is something about her face that won't let me give up on her.

Alexis started on a home-based infant stimulation program shortly after her official diagnosis of 'severe developmental delay'[2] at nine months of age. The teacher came in one morning a week to outline for me various motor activities and data collection methods I could use with my daughter to facilitate her development.

Each session began with this woman walking briskly over to Alexis who was lying on her stomach on the floor. She lay on a thin, flannelette-covered foam mattress pad to keep her from banging her teeth when her head dropped, as it frequently did. This was the position I had been advised by a hospital physiotherapist to keep her in in order to hopefully strengthen her neck muscles so she would eventually be able to hold her head up independently.

An "appealing object" would then be dangled in front of Alexis' nose and the teacher would say brightly, "Alexis, look!" Alexis' response was always very prompt. As quickly as her poor motor control would allow, she would turn her head away from the "brightly coloured toy." Undaunted, the teacher would then dart over to Alexis' other side and repeat this command. But again Alexis would turn her head away.

I observed this charade being repeated up to six times in a row, before Alexis became too tired to turn her head anymore and resorted to closing her eyes, rubbing her face in the mat and moaning.

"She is trying to block out an unwanted stimulus," I explained, in an effort to translate Alexis' response.

"That is a subjective interpretation of her behaviour!" I was told.

During the week between teacher visits, my assigned task as teacher substitute was to try this same exercise with Alexis, as well as many others—eye focusing, auditory stimulation, hand clapping, rolling—with no greater success. In addition, I was obliged to keep track of each trial on little charts for the teacher's records. I can remember few experiences in my life that have caused me such a deep and intimate sense of pain as the marking down of the sign for failure again and again and again on those charts. With every stroke, the prognostications I had been given by the medical experts came roaring through my head: severe, hopeless, no remediation possible, should not be maintained at home, pointless, pointless, pointless.

Alexis made no progress in the cognitive development portion of that program. Her sole achievement was in the area of toilet training, that I had initiated before she was a year old, much to the disgust of the teacher who considered it to be an "inappropriate task," too sophisticated for her. But I persevered. Alexis would fuss; I would say, "Alexis, want potty?" And she would then stop fussing. I would sit her down on the floor in front of me on her little plastic pot holding her close with my arms cuddled tightly around her floppy little body. She would then relax and frequently be successful in her efforts. On those occasions I would tell her what a good girl she was as I cleaned up. Then I would hold her in my arms and Alexis would cuddle right in and smile and chortle. Often, I would look into her sweet little face and see there an expression of pride and satisfaction in having pleased me (but of course I am "being subjective" again).

This toileting program, which was admittedly quite time and energy consuming, went totally against the teacher's grain. She assured me that I was imagining Alexis' success and that I was placing my own ego needs and sense of personal gratification ahead of the orderly and realistic development of Alexis' intellectual potential—which could best be advanced by faithfully following the program she had laid out for me.

These remarks stung deeply. They challenged my sense of professional pride in what I had been able to accomplish with Alexis. But what they did to my sense of self as mother was far worse than that. Still I persevered.

Asking Alexis to "do something," watching her sensitive face as she tried to do what I asked, seeing her look of pleasure when she succeeded and I praised her, made me feel close to her in a way that had not been possible before. Strong waves of love and pride and compassion washed over all the negative feelings of sorrow, resentment, frustration and self-pity that had marred my relationship with her since her diagnosis.

In those moments, my mother's sense told me there was some-body there, a real little person who was mine to develop and guard over. But other times, marking the sign for failure across endless rows of endless charts, I felt only anger and pity and even contempt for this child who took so much and gave so little. As a psychologist, I also felt considerable revulsion towards this exercise that was anything but a motivator for me, the so-called "primary care provider" in this child's life.

By the time Alexis was 15 months old she was completely bowel trained and had frequent bladder successes as well. I began to notice that, if she was seated in her highchair and I asked the potty ques-tion, Alexis would often respond by flinging up her right arm from the elbow. I was quick to share this observation with the teacher, always anxious to provide some evidence that Alexis' toilet training was not just "training the mother" or "habit-training at best," as she had so frequently said. The response I received was not what I had anticipated, however.

My relationship with her had always been marked by a measure of condescension on her part. It was clear to me that I was perceived as a 'difficult mother' with pretensions of professional competency in an area where I was neither particularly competent nor capable of objectivity. But all that changed now. I had gone beyond merely ignor-ing or undermining the program through my willful resistance to carrying it out effectively and was now actively sabotaging it.

This was her reply ... I perfectly well knew that 'hands up' was supposed to be reserved as a signal of positive response to the com-mand, 'Want up?' when Alexis was in her highchair. Furthermore, even if Alexis were capable of responding to the potty question, such a response was inappropriate. A far more suitable response would be for her to place her hand on her tummy in a downward pointing direction. Why didn't I try that?

I decided that this time I must stop being so stubbornly defiant and must give this expert the benefit of the doubt. At least she was agree-ing that I could work towards initiating a toileting communication with Alexis. I must take the risk that Alexis could make the transfer to the more appropriate sign.

For two weeks I tried diligently to establish the new sign while continuing to work on encouraging Alexis to raise both arms in response to the 'Want up?' question. However, there was no response from Alexis—only what appeared to me (undoubtedly, I was being subjective again) as a confused look. Finally, after discussing the matter with my husband, never much of a believer in experts where Alexis was concerned, I went back to the original communication. But it was completely extinguished and nothing I could do would revive it. Never since, have I seen that little arm come flinging up at the elbow in a meaningful way.

I have often gone over this sad chapter in Alexis' life. *Was* it just my imagination? *Did* Alexis really understand what I asked her? In retrospect, I think she did. And I think the little bond we had established between us, her eager efforts to please me and her satisfaction when she did, were real, indescribably precious and very, very fragile.

CHAPTER 7

Exploring the System

By this time, I had had some experiences with the medical system, not all of them positive. However, the Mayfield Infant Stimulation Program was my first experience with the education/rehabilitation system in my desire to understand exactly what deficits Alexis had and which of them it might be possible to remediate with enough effort. Prior to this program the only remediation suggestion I had received was the one about keeping her in a prone position so her neck muscles would strengthen as she reflexively tried to raise her head.

The Mayfield Program had its own consultant physiotherapist who had recommended an exercise to build Alexis' neck, back and stomach muscles. The goal was to strengthen them so she could at least learn to sit independently. This exercise did seem to help a little and I went through it twice a day with her, faithfully but grudgingly. But I kept wondering if there was more that could be done, if only I knew what that was.

The exercise consisted of placing Alexis on the floor in front of me on her back, with her knees slightly bent. I sat on the floor with my legs on either side of her, holding her feet down. I then grasped her hands and pulled her gently upwards towards a vertical (sitting) position. Her head lagged behind her as I did this and at a certain point I stopped and said to her "head up, Alexis." I waited like that until she responded positively, which she generally did within a few seconds.

After several weeks of doing this exercise routinely, Alexis reached the point where she could do all seven 'sit-ups' while correcting her head lag, and the therapist then raised the number to 10. That was when something very interesting happened. Each time we started the 8th 'sit-up', Alexis complained loudly. *Is this just muscle memory?* I remember asking myself, *or can she really count?* Whatever it was, I took it as further evidence that there really was somebody there!

Despite these odd moments of hope and inspiration, I soon realized that I did not want to spend my days doing this tedious and minimally rewarding work. And I particularly did not want to keep the little checklists of Alexis' successes and failures with the various tasks. As I have said, this list was comprised almost exclusively of the latter, and constantly recording 'fail' on these forms did not help me in coming to terms with our new family reality and accepting Alexis for who she was. Nor could I see how it would be helpful to others in my situation. I just did not believe that a mother should be asked to make daily evaluations of her child. It did not seem psychologically healthy to me; it undermined the important bonding process between mother and child, based, as it must be, on unconditional acceptance.

Time to explore other options, I thought. But first I did a little self-exploration. By that point I had made the acquaintance of several other mothers faced with the challenge of raising a child with severe and multiple disabilities. I could not help comparing myself to them. Some were so hurt and angry that they blamed the system and everyone who crossed their path for what had happened to their child. But others seemed to be quietly accepting this new path in life and just focusing in on how they could follow it most efficiently for the greater good of their disabled child and the rest of their family. Measured against them, I found myself neither as angry as the former nor as noble as the latter.

I wanted out from under but not at Alexis' expense. Was there any way I could make that possible? Could I have my cake and eat it, too? By this time, I had become aware of other programs for children like Alexis in the city—but they were centre-based, not home-based. Still, I thought I would give them a try.

The summer Alexis was eighteen months old she attended a new summer program for very young children at the Elves Special Needs Society. She had the benefit of a very special teacher, Louise Butler, who was later to play an important role in the provincial government department charged with distributing funding dollars and overseeing program quality in order to meet the needs of adults with developmental disabilities. At the time of her recent retirement she was Senior Manager of Disability Services, Edmonton Region[3].

Louise was, in those early days, a young teacher starting out at Elves, a special place designated for meeting the needs of preschool children with the most severe disabilities. Very fortunately for Alexis, Louise was assigned to her caseload. Through her patient instruction and gentle, caring personality, Alexis gradually became more social and focused, but she was frequently ill and unable to attend, unused as she was to being around other young children and their various germs.

The special summer program had been a good experience for Alexis and certainly provided a healing break for me. However, there was no room for her at that time in the regular fall program. In some ways I was glad about that. Seeing her go off every morning strapped into the back seat of a taxi in her trunk support like a potted plant just seemed wrong. I would not do that even to my developmentally normal preschoolers, so how could I believe it was okay for Alexis?

The months passed and at first, I was happy to have Alexis at home, but gradually I realized that I could not handle the situation indefinitely. Then a kind friend suggested a different setting, one where she assured me that the staff would faithfully carry out Alexis' exercise program and toileting regimen, as they had done at Elves. I decided to give it a try.

The people at the Activity Centre were warm and caring but Alexis did not seem happy and her toileting routine broke down. I visited one day and discovered the reason. In the interests of efficiency there were group toileting sessions, preschoolers arranged in a circle in a room all sitting on their commodes. Alexis could not function that way. She was used to privacy.

I took Alexis away from that public display and into a little space designed as a change room. I sat down on the narrow bench and held her in front of me on the tiny pot meant for babies that a staff member had given me, all that was available. Alexis sat between my legs so I could support her back as she balanced on the pot but still nothing happened—or so I thought. Finally, I gave up and removed her, only to discover to my horror that she had succeeded, but the deposit had landed outside the minuscule pot and skittered down the leg of my white pants! I cleaned and dressed her and cleaned myself up the best I could and then we went home.

That evening I discussed the situation with my husband and with his mother, Mary, who was visiting at the time. The toileting arrangements were one issue but there was also a second matter that was irritating me. When Alexis was at Elves, as I mentioned, she had what was called a key worker. Louise Butler worked with Alexis most of the time and Alexis developed a connection with her and felt safe and comfortable with her. That was not the philosophy embraced by the management at the Activity Centre at that time, however. They believed that it was better to rotate their staff members, assigning them to one child one day and a different one the next. Their reasoning was that this would prevent the child from becoming attached and overly dependent on one person, something that could easily become a problem given the high rate of staff turnover. And they also thought it was better for staff from both a professional development point of view and a morale point of view to have the opportunity to work equally with all the clients and not to be restricted to one. That way, when there were particularly challenging clients, they could all share the pain.

From my present perspective I can at least partially understand their reasoning. For many years now I have hired part-time people exclusively to work with Alexis. That way if one is sick another can often cover and if one leaves, no matter how good their relationship with Alexis is, there will still be others working with Alexis who have a good, if different, relationship with her. I have found through the years that each person brings her own gifts. However, in my state of mind at that time, I perceived it a personal insult that someone might not like to work with Alexis exclusively five days a week.

There was also a third reason for me reconsidering Alexis' placement at that time. I was missing having her at home and hurting to think of her learning new things in my absence. I thought she would be better off at home, having conveniently forgotten what a burden that had been, which had driven me to consider the Activity Centre in the first place!

I presented my arguments to my husband and mother-in-law, concluding that I felt we should withdraw Alexis from this day program. They, of course, agreed with me since my arguments had been precisely directed to draw them to that conclusion. But then I had another problem. The people at the Activity Centre had been very supportive of Alexis and respectful of me and had carried out her feeding, toileting and range of motion programs faithfully. I actually had little cause for complaint and did not feel like confronting them on either the group toileting issue or the key worker issue, so I was stuck.

It was then that my dear mother-in-law suggested a non-hurtful way out. "Blame it on us!" she said. "Your immigrant, traditionalist, Italian in-laws who just can't deal with the idea of their young granddaughter being away from her home all day and being cared for by somebody else." I grabbed at this ruse happily and was able to remove Alexis from the situation gracefully and with genuine expressions of gratitude on my part for the care they had provided for her. Only when it was all over did I stop to think how utterly outrageous it was to portray Joe's parents in that manner. My mother-in-law was an intelligent, open-minded woman and my father-in-law was a caring, family-oriented man. Neither of them would have ever dreamed of interfering in our lives like this!

CHAPTER 8

Family life with young Alexis

Janni was almost 4 when Alexis was born, and 18 months later he started grade one at a private school a fair distance from our home. It ended at 12:30 each day so Joe drove him there in the morning on his way to work and I bundled Alexis and Juliana into the car at lunchtime and picked him up.

Why did we send him to school at such a young age? Because he had too many questions, too much thirst for knowledge the very qualities I had been looking at in my dissertation work on giftedness and creativity. He needed the many enrichment activities I was ideally trained to provide—but could not. I was too overwhelmed and preoccupied in meeting Alexis' needs. Yet I was not willing to see him languish with insufficient social and intellectual stimulation. I had seen what had happened to my own precocious brother in a conventional school situation, how the boredom had set in, which led to apathy, and then to rebellion. I had also seen other bright, under-challenged children grow up believing that everything would be given to them, so there was no point in working because it all would come so easily. I most desperately did not want that for my son.

But there were no fancy educational programs for bright pre-schoolers in Edmonton, Alberta at that time ... and there was a firm cut-off for entrance into grade one for both the public and separate

(Roman Catholic) systems. No young child could start grade one if he or she would not be having a 6th birthday before March 1st of the upcoming school year. Janni's birthday was March 18th.

After some discussion, Joe and I registered our son at a private school based on what I can only assume was a 19th century English boarding school model. Pre-testing was an entrance requirement and he, of course, passed easily, but that was a poor measure of overall school readiness. He attended school in his little green and grey uniform with a bow tie and quickly learned that his role was to sit in his chair and listen. Questions, his forte, were firmly discouraged.

As the months passed, I saw the son I knew begin to wither before my eyes, but I did not want to admit it to myself. He had been a cheerful, eager, bright little boy with endless questions he was used to his parents taking joy in and answering patiently. That was not the response he was getting at school where he was being systematically squelched. There were other qualities that were more admired in that setting, qualities he did not have. These included athleticism, poise and self-possession.

Janni was small for his age and that did not help the situation. He was wiry and strong but also on the clumsy side. He was naïve and open and curious and idealistic. These qualities did not endear him to the strict, reserved school principal or to the teachers under him who were expected to follow the rigid curriculum he had laid out. For example, they did not use Canadian readers but rather photocopied versions of outdated English Rhodes Readers. These reminded me of the texts I had used in my own early school years from the late '40's and early '50s, only with English rather than North American terminology. 'Lorry' replaced 'truck' and 'bonnet' replaced 'hood', for example.

The teacher he started with might have formed a relationship with him but she soon became ill and had to be replaced. Teacher absenteeism and turnover became a general issue while Janni was in that school. But the bigger issue was that he simply was not ready, either socially or emotionally. The reality was that our family had been

through, and was continuing to live through, a significant trauma
and it had affected all of us in various ways, including him.

There was another issue as well that I did not want to look at too
closely during that time. My mother died when I was 22, and for all
the years of my life before that she was critical of me and idolized my
brother for both his startling good looks and his intelligence. Intelligence was everything to her and that distorted perspective affected
me in my own life. I felt like I was using Janni as a family flagstaff
to hold up my battered pride after producing a child as damaged as
Alexis. In some sense he had no choice but to be outstanding, and I
feared that my covert pressure would distort his own development.

All these issues swarmed around in my mind as I tried to make
up to him for what he was losing out of his young life, both at home
with everything subsumed to his sister's regimen, and at school where
all that he had come to value about himself was being downgraded
or ignored.

Something else that ate at me constantly was the 'fun' issue. My
father had always said that a person should work hard and then play
hard. He had a strong sense of play and despite our somewhat bleak
family situation he had always seemed to me to be a happy person.
My mother was the opposite. She had absolutely no sense of play and
her entire modus operandi seemed to be to work and worry and then
to relieve the tension this built up by exploding in anger, usually at
me—or so it seemed.

I wanted for my children what I had not had for myself—some
of this sense of play. On the road to the school Janni attended at that
time, we passed a ski hill and many days I looked at it longingly. I
had enjoyed skiing very much before my marriage, but Joe was never
interested. Occasionally I went off with a friend in those early years
but after Alexis was diagnosed Joe was very much against it. It would
have been irresponsible, given Alexis' care needs, if I had broken a leg
and become incapacitated for any length of time, was his reasoning.
I understood the logic but still felt a strong sense of resentment over
this further loss in my life.

But, as I passed this hill day after day, I wondered if there was a way to regain that giddy sense of freedom that I had felt soaring down a hill in the days when I skied. It was something I still dreamed about at night sometimes. One day I drove up to the hill and stopped. I got the children out and we stood at the top. The conditions were perfect. They wanted to just slide down on their backs and I did not stop them. I even slid down myself in my leather coat. It provided a slippery surface but the experience left permanent marks on it. Not smart!

After that we stopped periodically at the hill on the way home from Janni's school at lunchtime. I bought the older children a plastic fold-up sheet toboggan and they soared down the hill together on it while Alexis and I watched from the top. But I wanted her to have the experience, too. It was March and we were having an early melt. The snow cover on the hill would not be there much longer. I should mention that Alexis would have been about 2 years and 2 months old at this point.

When we moved into our new home in Windsor Park, Janni was just a baby, 3 months old. The previous owner was a geology professor at the University of Alberta and the director of the Boreal Institute, and he left behind a one-person arctic pack sled. It was like an ordinary sled but slightly higher with steel runners and steel side rails.

In those days the Glenrose Hospital Orthotics and Prosthetics technicians still crafted trunk supports to hold children as disabled as Alexis securely in their wheelchairs. Whenever she was in the car, she was secured in this trunk support for transport. When Alexis was about one-year old Joe brought out the sled from our garage one day and figured out a way to attach the trunk support securely to it. That way I could go for walks with her in the winter by pulling her on the sled, something that would have been impossible in her wheelchair or baby cart. Whenever the children and I visited the ski hill I always pulled Alexis along in the sled in this manner as we walked to the top of the hill.

On this particular day, with the sun shining and the snow melting I felt compelled to have Alexis experience the sense of freedom and joy her brother and sister were feeling, sliding up and down that hill. There was a small amount of room for one person to kneel on the sled behind the trunk support, but it was not enough room for me, so Janni was designated. I positioned the sled at the top of the hill, and he got on the back. I talked to him seriously about how he had to steer it and how careful he had to be with Alexis sitting in front, unable to protect herself, and he understood the responsibility being placed upon him. But while Janni was wiry, strong and quick, coordination was not one of his strengths!

Life is never simple, and Juliana took that moment to object vehemently to being left behind and to question why Janni had been chosen over her to guide the sled. My grip must have loosened slightly as I turned to reason with her and the force of gravity on the slippery, melting snow jerked the sled out of my hands. The sudden jolt caused Janni to fall backwards off the sled and Alexis went careening down the hill alone.

The three of us tore after her but there was no hope of catching up. The sled moved swiftly and surely like it had a mind of its own. Near the bottom of the hill it slued to the left, heading down a lower hill next to the ski building. There was a large plate glass window on the facing wall and the people inside the building stared out in horror at this tiny child speeding towards them on a collision course. A steep cut-bank next to the window had been carved out by the melting snow and the sled nosed down it and collided with the base of the window. Alexis, securely strapped in her trunk support with the additional supporting structure that Joe had devised, never moved. And one person there told me later that when the sled hit the building, she had an excited smile on her face.

I retrieved Alexis, explained our actions as best I could to that sea of judgmental faces, and we all went home. Alexis napped longer than usual that afternoon and I had the satisfaction of knowing that I had managed to share with her one of the key experiences in my life, that wonderful, free sense of soaring down a hill!

Alexis, age 4, hanging upside down
so she could use her arms freely

CHAPTER 9

Patterning

By the time Alexis was 2½ I had exhausted all available preschool-aged intervention opportunities for Alexis. All that was left was to somehow cope alone or else to hire people privately and train them myself. About this time, I became involved with Margaret George, a B.C. woman who had carved out a niche for herself teaching basic patterning techniques to families with children with developmental delays in B. C. and Alberta.

Patterning is a now debunked theory that ontogeny recapitulates phylogeny. That is to say, the way the child develops in the womb and in early life mimics the original evolutionary process of life itself—from poorly differentiated amphibious creatures to the highly individualized animals we call human beings. Before humankind walked upon this earth, their progenitors swam in the ocean, then crawled along the ground and later walked on four limbs until finally, our direct ancestors, the great apes, reached the bipedal stage. The notion underlying patterning was that if the developmentally delayed child could be put through a crawling program, followed by a creeping program his or her brain would gradually develop the missing links that would lead to assuming an upright posture.

The patterning program was very intensive and to make it feasible parents solicited volunteers. I knew of only one other family involved with patterning at that time and they worked directly with the originators of this program in Philadelphia. They travelled back and forth with their daughter every six months to have her retested and her program revised and upgraded to meet her needs. We had neither the financial resources nor the family circumstances, with two other young children to consider, for this level of commitment and we were just grateful that Margaret George could offer us at least a version of the full program.

Janet (name changed) was a year older than Alexis and very different in terms of the bodily effects of her cerebral palsy. Instead of being hypotonic (low toned and floppy) like Alexis, she was hypertonic (high toned and very stiff with some resulting bodily distortions). Her parents worked with her obsessively to a degree that left me feeling like a slacker. All day long a parade of volunteers came to their home where they were met by Janet's mother and welcomed with various teas and baked goods.

Janet's parents believed that if they worked hard enough and followed the Doman-Delecato program faithfully enough they could undo at least some of the damage that had been visited upon their daughter through her unfortunate birth circumstances. But years later I ran across Janet out shopping with her father one day at our local mall and I was sad to see her stretched out in a semi-horizontal position in her wheelchair, apparently unable to sit upright any longer.

At the time, though, when I was first hearing about patterning and talking to the positive, supportive person who represented its face in Alberta for all of us who could not jaunt back and forth to Philadelphia, I believed we needed to try it, and in retrospect I am certainly not sorry that we did. The program Margaret George outlined for us was really a combination of sensory and sensory-motor stimulation exercises and the physical movements meant to recapitulate our development as a species. The latter were the most demanding, as we needed to go through them four times a day with three assistants involved each time. The sensory work was only done twice a day and was something we could do ourselves without outside help.

Alexis had been declared cortically blind by both the diagnosing neurologist and a neuro-optometrist we subsequently consulted. At my request, an ophthalmologist also examined Alexis. He found her eyes to be structurally normal and responsive to light, but it was clear that she did not track or even bother to keep her eyes open much of the time. He deduced that Alexis' apparent lack of vision must therefore be due to cortical damage at or below the optic chiasma, the structure in the brain where the nerves at the back of the eyes come together and cross over, since both her eyes appeared to be equally affected.

What Margaret George advised us to do, based on her knowledge of the Doman-Delecato model, was to run a penlight back and forth across each closed eyelid several times and to repeat this exercise five times a day. We also acquired a 'light box', a backlit screen programmed with various lines and patterns to encourage the user to eye-track back and forth across it. We would place Alexis in front of it in a completely blackened room in our basement where the only point of visual focus was the box and then gently guide her head back and forth in sync with the various tracks moving across the box.

By the time Alexis was 8 years old, thousands and thousands of trials later, she was finally willing and able to keep her eyes open except when she was very tired. In the evenings she would often still eat with them closed but for the most part they were open. Could she see any better? I don't know. But she did respond appropriately to light and no longer exhibited the 'blindisms' observed in many unsighted people. That was worth something because, as I have said before, Alexis was a very attractive child with lovely, large eyes and long, lush, curly lashes, upon which strangers often commented. I say 'was' because Alexis later lost the lushness in these lashes as well as the thickness in her hair due to the effects of the various anti-convulsive medications she was placed on through the years. These medications also affected her complexion, leaving it rough and bumpy in places.

As for the rest of the program, we had varied successes with it. Alexis had to feel, to smell and to taste different objects in order to have any hope of recognizing and cataloguing them in her mind. Each day, twice a day, we filled two 2-quart sealers with very hot and very cold water. Then we had her touch them, one after the other, multiple times while repeating 'hot' and 'cold'. For her to experience the different tastes we placed on her tongue sugar, salt, and lemon juice successively. Then we used a large clean aluminum turkey baster to squirt bitter air into her mouth. We identified each taste sensation as we went along—sweet, salty, sour and bitter—and did not hurry the procedure so she would have time to absorb and integrate the various sensations to the best of her ability and make what she could out of them.

At the time we were doing this we tried to gauge Alexis' reactions to the different tastes through her body language since she has no way of communicating formally. I do not know if it is through that early work with her that her taste bud nerve connections developed sufficiently so that she could appreciate different taste sensations. But I do know that Alexis very much appreciates the different tastes in the foods we have prepared for her through the years and responds better to some than to others. As my mother-in-law used to proclaim in her accented English when she watched Alexis eating, "Alexis likes tasty stoff!"

An interesting example of Alexis' capacity to appreciate different tastes occurs in the context of what Joe and I have come to describe as "the turkey wars"! Joe declares that he hates turkey and never wants to see it on our table. I maintain that I love it and expect to have it for Christmas. We finally found a way out of this impasse a few years ago by bypassing Christmas dinner at home altogether and going out to a fancy Christmas buffet that includes turkey as well as meat, fish and seafood. That way we can both be satisfied.

As for Alexis, every year I carefully prepare a delicious turkey dinner for her at the restaurant. We carry our mini food processor with us for this purpose. I tell her how good turkey is and devote all my efforts to feeding her slowly and carefully, so she does not choke and mar her experience. But every year, after a few bites, she turns her nose up in disgust and resists eating any more. Meanwhile, Joe is looking on and smirking! He then gets up and prepares her a meal with fish, mashed potatoes and vegetables that do not require use of the grinder. He feeds it to her, and she eats happily so I always lose that particular battle of our ongoing war!

For hearing we exposed Alexis to a variety of different sounds, but it was quickly evident that hearing was not a problem for her since she clearly liked some sounds better than others. For smell we had her sniff a variety of different spices, perfumes and other benign substances. For health reasons we did not have her sniff things like the acetone in nail polish remover or bleach or other unpleasant smelling substances, but I think in retrospect that perhaps we should have done at least some of that. I doubt she was able to recognize the difference between cloves and nutmeg, for example, but she would have been quick enough to differentiate between spice and bleach!

The core of the Doman-Delecato program was a graduated series of crawling exercises. The idea behind putting Alexis through the crawling movement was to train her how to use her arms and legs together and in harmony, i.e. left leg with right arm and vice versa. The trouble is that Alexis has no strength in her arms while her legs were, and still are, quite powerful. We braced her heels with our hands, as she lay flat on her stomach on the floor of our long hall, encouraging her to use them as leverage to push herself forward. She did this but her arms never moved so she more or less skated along on her face!

The patterning challenges did not end there. Other activities we were obliged by the program to put Alexis through made the crawling seem tame. One of these involved hanging her upside down from an overhead rod and encouraging her to then roll a large beach ball with her hands. We were fortunate enough to acquire a pair of hand-made deerskin booties in Alexis' size that laced tightly onto her feet. The only thing really unusual about them was the huge thick ring sewn into the sole of each bootie. These rings then looped through two hooks attached to a sturdy overhead rod and in this way, Alexis was suspended upside down.

What happened then was that her arms hung free of the constraints of gravity. Thus, she was able to move them back and forth and when they connected with the large beach ball on the floor beneath her it rolled away. It was the only time in her life we have ever seen Alexis have any meaningful use of her hands. And we saw that she recognized this and enjoyed the sense of power and control it gave her! The cost, though, was the seizures that inevitably followed this activity. We put them down to the pressure exerted on her by all the blood rushing to her brain in that position.

Yet another exercise involved helping Alexis to climb hand over hand along the rungs of a ladder suspended horizontally above her head. Our hands were necessarily clamped over hers to guide her along and to keep her from falling. She was small enough at that time that we could manage this feat but one day an occupational therapist was visiting and saw us going through this exercise with Alexis. She pointed out that with Alexis' low muscle tone there was little support for the ligaments, and it would be very easy to dislocate her shoulder, so we had to stop doing that particular exercise.

Despite the rather mixed successes we were experiencing Joe and I persevered with the patterning program for a year and a half. During that time, we invited approximately 150 different people into our home to assist us and some of them were very unusual. One lady was a 'born-again' Christian who insisted on speaking in tongues as she assisted with the swimming/crawling exercise, thus embarrassing me, irritating our other volunteer helper, and confusing Alexis who became even less capable than usual! Another worked as one of our paid assistants and was exceptionally good with Alexis, but shortly after leaving us she had a psychotic break and was diagnosed with schizophrenia.

We followed the patterning program for Alexis as faithfully as we could for about 18 months until all of us but Alexis left for my husband's sabbatical year at the University of Toronto. I am grateful to this day for all the volunteers who helped us, but I was not sorry to see it come to an end. Dealing with all those people on a daily basis was exhausting!

CHAPTER 10

The Gateway Association and the book

1 **981 was declared** the International Year of Disabled Persons and in Canada, as well as in many other countries, funding became available to support initiatives focused in this area. Alexis was then three years old. Early in 1980 I had joined what was then called the Gateway Association for the Mentally Handicapped[4]. Dr. Cameron had told me about it when I had spoken to him after Alexis' diagnosis at 9 months of age, but it took another year before I was able to admit to myself that her disability was such that our family qualified as members.

After attending the first monthly meeting I knew I had made the right decision. Here were other parents determined to give their disabled children the best chance in life and prepared to do battle if necessary, to ensure that would happen. I listened to their separate stories and was filled with respect for them and awe at the roads they had travelled. At a monthly meeting of the Gateway Association I suggested to Joan Charbonneau, the Gateway president at that time, and the other members of the board, that we apply for a 1981 provincial grant that was part of the celebration for that special year.

I had the idea to put together and publish a book of family stories and I wanted to meet with any of the local families willing to participate in order to discuss the project further. If there were not enough families locally who would share their stories, I thought that

47

we could also advertise through the various disability associations across Alberta. I would ask families to talk about their experiences of what it was like to have a child with a mental handicap (the language of the time) and what the impact on the family was.

I volunteered to collect and edit the stories and see the process through to the finish if Gateway would be the funding applicant. My reasoning was that this would be a useful resource for new mothers who found themselves in our position. At that time, I was chair of the Gateway Family Support Committee and it was our role to visit every new mother in the hospital who gave birth to a child with a developmental disability and to provide her with moral support and an information packet. I also suggested that a book of stories like this might be useful in the Rehabilitation Practitioner program being offered at that time by the recently established Grant MacEwan Community College, now the MacEwan University. That program was offering one- and two-year diplomas for students interested in working directly with individuals with developmental disabilities.

The response to my suggestion was positive. A funding application was duly made and funding received sufficient to pay for the cost of printing and illustrating 500 copies. Bev Getz, a fellow Gateway member and the mother of a boy with Down syndrome, produced beautiful charcoal drawings depicting 10 of the children involved. The colour photograph on the cover of the first edition was of one of the quilts designed by an artistically gifted woman with Down syndrome who was part of our Gateway community.

I prepared a call for contributions that was sent out to all the family support associations involving people with developmental disabilities across Alberta and soon the stories started to trickle in. The working title I came up with was "*What have you done to our Lives?—Alberta stories about the impact of a mentally handicapped child on family life.*" However, that did not meet with the approval of the new Gateway president who took over at the end of that year. She found the first part "too negative." I thought I was just asking an obvious question.

My strength and my problem in undertaking this whole process was that I was very close to the situation. I knew what that pain, that shattered hope, felt like to these parents when their children came into the world facing all these problems. As the stories began to arrive, I was both honored and humbled by what I read. Yes, we had all had those same initial emotions. But here were people in many different life circumstances who were coping with this momentous event in their lives in many different ways, mostly very bravely and positively.

When the book was finally ready to go to press, the new Gateway president also objected to the compromise title I came up with: *Different Hopes, Different Dreams,* on the grounds that it emphasized differences instead of similarities. A number of syrupy alternatives were suggested for my consideration but at that point I dug in and refused to make any further changes.

I don't know if it was then or earlier in my life that my hatred of political correctness set in[5]. All I know is that my logical mind was screaming *let us please call it like it is!* Nobody cheers when they are presented with a child with developmental disabilities. Nobody pretends it is just a little bump in the road. *The whole road has changed!* We, as parents, come to terms with it. We make the best of it. We love our children, however damaged they may be. But we do not pretend they are the same as other children who do not have their problems. We hope and dream and set our minds to creating the best life possible for them, but these hopes and dreams are not the same as the ones we hold out for our other children not so affected.

The original edition of *Different Hopes, Different Dreams* was published in 1984 with an expanded second edition following in 1991. I spent the best part of a year primarily preoccupied with putting the first edition together. I met or talked by phone with each of the families who agreed to contribute, helping them in many cases to map out the material they would be including. Then, when the stories were finally submitted, I was quite often faced with a massive editing job. I tried very hard to respect the original tone of the stories and not undermine any of the author's intentions, while eliminating redundancies and grammatical errors, and shortening the stories when it was necessary or appropriate to do so. In one case, at the request of the mother I even wrote the story, changing all identifying details so it could remain anonymous. In short, I did a great deal of work on this book, so much so that I vowed to myself I would never edit another book again!

I regarded the submission of these stories from families whose lives had been transformed by this event, and who were often still grieving, as a very serious and sober trust, and that is why it took so much time and effort to produce a book of good literary quality without losing or diluting the essence of what made the individual stories so poignant and authentic. But once the book was finally in print this same Gateway president referred to it as a "collation." I took that to mean that in her eyes it was one step up from a scrapbook! However, that is not how it was evaluated in the various positive reviews of it that appeared after it was published.

When I had finally completed the book to the best of my ability, the next and last step was to prepare the preface. During my doctoral study years, one of the projects I had worked on was with Dr. J.P. Das, researching the association between early childhood malnutrition and mental retardation. This was happening long before Alexis was born and he was one of the first people I contacted once she was diagnosed as 'severely developmentally delayed', the cautious terminology in use by the medical community at that time in 1978. I had asked Das, as he liked to be called, to write the introduction for the book and he agreed and gave me a very adequate one. I still have a copy of it.

The only problem was that Das used the word 'retarded' in it and refused to remove it. In the face of the strong feelings against this term by the advocacy movement I had no choice but to seek elsewhere for someone to provide the introduction. The term 'retarded' was still in use in the *Diagnostic and Statistical Manual of Mental Disorders*, DSM-III at the time, and even later in DSM–IV so I can understand why Das felt it was perfectly legitimate, in fact appropriate, to use that term. But I can also understand why the other parents got their backs up over the use of the term, 'retarded'. It had acquired a negative connotation, conjuring up images of drooling idiots and dull, animal-like creatures—except animals are not really dull. They just perceive the world differently.

Strangely enough, nobody objected to the second part of the book title; *Alberta stories about the impact of a mentally handicapped child on family life*. We were not yet into the People First movement at that point. But the burgeoning advocacy movement in Edmonton had sanitized the word 'retarded' out of use, replacing it with 'handicapped', a term co-opted from those with physical disabilities. Such disabilities were seen as much more socially acceptable than cognitive disabilities or, for that matter, mental illness. As Aristotle said so long ago, the capacity to reason is what makes us human. Still, the whole business of what it is to be a human as opposed to an animal has left me wondering, and in 2011 I wrote an article on this subject.[6]

At the beginning of this whole process, I had been promised by the director of what was then known as The Canadian Association for the Mentally Handicapped, Jacques Pelletier, that they would publish it since no other book of the type I was proposing was currently available. However, when I submitted the final manuscript to him he arranged a meeting with me and explained that no story should be longer than three pages, five at the very maximum. People would not be interested in reading beyond that point. I explained that I had already edited them down as much as I could without destroying their essential elements, along with any literary value they might have—but he was adamant.

Jacques was particularly dismissive of a 20-page contribution describing the tragic near-drowning death of a three-year-old girl, and how her mother had fought to bring her back to some kind of a life. This was an incredibly poignant and very well written story by a former English teacher. She was also a good friend of mine and I knew how much it had cost her to write it when she was still reeling from this second incredible loss to her daughter who had been born with serious brain damage but was still able to use a communication board before the accident. I explained that I could neither remove the story nor alter it any more than I already had—and on that basis we parted company.

This was a serious decision and a damaging one from a marketing perspective. By publishing the book locally, we could not hope for the kind of distribution we could have attained with the Canadian association. However, to do what I had been asked to do would, in my mind, have been to betray all those families who had shared their deepest, saddest and most reflective thoughts with me.

I am happy to report that 35 years later I am still receiving an annual public lending rights payment from the Canadian government, reflecting the fact that *Different Hopes, Different Dreams* remains in various public libraries across Canada. And I have been told that it has also been cited as a reference work in several university and college courses.

CHAPTER 11

Seizures

Of all the challenges in Alexis' life, her seizures have been the worst. I know of many families dealing with epilepsy but none who face our special challenge. Alexis simply stops breathing at times.

Her epilepsy was first identified when Alexis was 9 months of age. For several months before that I had been noticing peculiar periods where she seemed to be "not there." When I finally described this behaviour to her paediatrician, he ordered an EEG. The results indicated a "left prefrontal epileptogenic focus" and Alexis was prescribed an anti-convulsive medication, Phenobarbital, on a PRN basis, i.e., to be administered to her whenever I noticed these odd "away" spells.

We did not notice these quiet seizures unless we were in the same room with her at the time and looking directly at her. Even then, I used the Phenobarbital sparingly. Like the other parents in our situation at the time, I was very suspicious of the side effects of these "drugs," as we referred to them.

Around that time another issue came to the forefront. Since she was an infant, Alexis had demonstrated food intolerances and increasingly they were of an undetermined nature that made control difficult to impossible. These manifested as bouts of what we just referred to as 'upchucking'. Her cheeks would turn red and become very itchy and she would then bring up food heavily permeated with a thick mucus. Yet this material did not smell like vomit.

To get some control over her food intolerance problem I made an appointment with a medical doctor who also practiced alternative medicine. Alexis was about 18 months old at the time. He suspected that Alexis was not metabolizing some key vitamins appropriately and prescribed high daily doses of linoleic acid plus some other vitamins. This did not seem to help and in fact the upchucking even increased so I took Alexis back to her regular paediatrician. He also speculated that Alexis might have a metabolic disorder and referred her to Dr. Donald McCoy, at that time the head of paediatrics at University Hospital in Edmonton and a specialist in this type of disorder.

When I described Alexis' symptoms to him, Dr. McCoy agreed with the paediatrician's diagnosis and suggested that he take an "arterial blood sample" to send to Toronto Sick Children's Hospital for analysis. I, by nature naïve and trusting, agreed. The sight of three nurses holding Alexis down while she screamed in agony as they tried again and again to insert a huge needle into the centre of her chest will always stay with me. But whether or not they actually succeeded in getting the sample is something I cannot remember for some reason.

When I saw Dr. McCoy after that ordeal for Alexis was over, he told me that he was referring Alexis to Toronto Sick Children's Hospital for further assessment and that he would contact Handicapped Children's Services[7] himself to arrange for our costs to be covered. So, if that was the price Alexis had to pay for this referral and for our first contact with that major support agency, I guess in the end it was worth it.

Alexis and I flew to Toronto quite soon thereafter, when she was 21 months old, and she remained in the Sick Children's Hospital for two weeks under constant observation and with further testing being done. The specialists there did not find any evidence of a metabolic disorder, but they did discover that she had a swollen spleen and the vitamin regimen she had been placed on in Edmonton was immediately discontinued. What the hospital staff there most importantly found out was that Alexis was having almost constant 'Absence' seizure activity. I was told that she was experiencing literally hundreds of petit mal seizures a day. These were exhausting her and disorganizing her brain so much that she was not able to learn even what she was capable of learning.

This finding also explained the history I had provided, i.e., that Alexis regularly woke up during the night screaming, and then had to be held and comforted afterwards for a long time before she could sleep again. The constant seizure activity combined with her chronic lack of restful night-time sleep would likely explain why she seemed so dazed and tired all day.

I was amazed and sickened to hear this news and I castigated myself for not having paid closer attention and figuring this out by myself. But, as the neurologist assigned to her case explained, it is not the kind of seizure activity that would be evident to anyone not well versed in this area and that is what makes Absence seizures so dangerous. Left unchecked they do gradually cause further brain damage.

A second EEG was administered to Alexis at that time and the results indicated that the original left prefrontal epileptogenic focus had now spread to the right prefrontal area as well. That was bad news indeed. In a young brain, plasticity allows for many functions to be transferred across hemispheres in the prefrontal, frontal and median parts of the brain connected by the cerebral commissure when one side is damaged. But now both prefrontal lobes were involved.

Alexis was placed on the anti-convulsive drug, Valproic Acid (Epival) and, for the first time since she was five months old, she began sleeping through the night without waking up screaming several times. For more than two years the Epival kept her seizures under reasonable control but then the situation deteriorated again.

Cluster seizures consisting of myoclonic jerks appeared, interspersed with her Absence seizures. And these often triggered generalized (Grand Mal) seizures that would cause Alexis to sleep afterwards for long periods of time. Sometimes she had such multiple and severe seizures that she would stop breathing and turn blue. How long she slept after these incidents seemed to depend upon how quickly and efficiently I had been able to administer mouth-to-mouth resuscitation to keep her oxygenated until her lungs started working again.

The Epival Alexis had been taking since she was 21 months had helped significantly to control her Absence seizures and Generalized seizures, but it could do nothing to prevent the increasingly disruptive 'Myoclonic Jerks' she was experiencing at that point. They, in turn, seemed to undermine the control Alexis had previously enjoyed over the other seizure activity.

Myoclonic seizures can arise as part of a mixed seizure disorder such as Alexis was experiencing. They are likely the result of the brain damage she sustained from oxygen deprivation at birth. Her high upper palate is a classic sign of this birth hypoxia. The myoclonic jerks are a form of tonic-atonic seizure activity: sudden muscle stiffening alternating with a complete loss of muscle tone, resulting in what are colloquially referred to as 'drop' seizures.

Alexis' long sleeping spells after the more serious seizures were particularly frightening since she normally did not sleep much at all. I wondered if she was actually asleep at these times or just unconscious from oxygen deprivation. I worried that these severe seizures would cause further brain damage and turned to the medical profession for help.

The neurologist I was referred to at that time diagnosed Alexis with 'incurable hypsarrhythmia'.[8] When found at a later age than infancy it characteristically leads to further cognitive decline. Alexis was 4 years old when we began to notice the myoclonic jerks.

This specialist recommended that we place Alexis on corticosteroids as the only sure way to control her particular type of myoclonus. But, knowing the kinds of secondary damage that medication can lead to, I was unwilling to have Alexis try this approach. He then suggested brain surgery but even with my layperson's knowledge I knew that could not work. The seizures were already too widespread and varied in type to be controlled through a highly localized excision of brain tissue. I began to wonder if this doctor was seeing Alexis as a little girl with a big problem or as a test subject with an interesting condition for experimental purposes!

"My husband and I will never agree to surgery," I told him firmly, knowing that Joe would feel exactly as I did. He looked at me in disgust and it seemed to me that he lost interest in Alexis at that point. As what he termed "a poor third alternative" he suggested that we switch Alexis from the Valproic Acid she had been on since 21 months of age to Phenytoin, an anti-convulsive known by the name, Dilantin. This is the medication of choice for controlling myoclonic jerks, a form of partial seizure affecting the motor area of the brain.

The Dilantin did stop the seizures from generalizing but had no control over the Absence seizures and little control over the myoclonic jerks. Furthermore, within a month to six weeks I noticed that Alexis' eyebrows were beginning to grow together and I thought I saw the beginnings of a moustache. Hair growth and gum swelling are the two major, observable side effects of this particular anti-convulsive medication. When I went back to him with Alexis, the neurologist laughed at my "cosmetic concerns', as he termed them, and reminded me that Alexis would not know the difference anyway. I could not accept this response because Alexis was a truly beautiful child and it seemed to me that her looks and her sweet, trusting personality were all she had going for her.

CHAPTER 12

A second opinion;
a second chance

I **had gone** to this neurologist because the paediatrician I was then seeing with Alexis had always emphasized to me how little he knew about anti-convulsive drugs. Now, in despair, I turned to him for help. He was gentle and compassionate and basically agreed with my reservations about this medication. At my request he arranged to have Alexis seen by another neurologist, Dr. Gauk, then the leading paediatric neurologist in Edmonton.

Dr. Gauk could be very blunt and insensitive but he did know his business. I suspect that his rough manner was a cover-up for the fact that he really cared about these children. After the Chernobyl nuclear accident happened in 1985, he and his physician wife spent long periods every summer in the Ukraine caring for the children who had been affected. When I brought Alexis back to him for help with her seizures, he took one look at me and said, quite cheerfully, "Hi! Where have you been all these years with her?"

"Recovering from our initial encounter," I replied, without acrimony—for this was the very specialist who had diagnosed Alexis at nine months of age. He examined Alexis and then quickly skimmed over the summary of the seizure record that we had always kept very carefully and that her previous neurologist had not even deigned to consult.

"On the basis of your excellent record I would say that Alexis is having absence seizures and series of myoclonic jerks. We will put her on Rivotril (Clonazepam), a Valium derivative that is often effective in cases like this. However, she has such variation in seizure activity that I can't guarantee it will work but it's worth a try."

The introduction of Rivitrol produced results that were nothing short of dramatic and in a very short time Alexis' seizures were under almost complete control. Because of this, Joe and I were able to make our long dreamed of trip to Italy with our two older children in the summer of 1982, after making careful arrangements for Alexis' care. She was 4½ at that point and Linda Sharpe, her GRIT assistant during the program's first few months of operation, had just returned to her hometown of London, Ontario after completing her university degree in Edmonton. I contacted her to see if she would be willing to care for Alexis at her family home there while we were away, and she agreed eagerly. Thus, as discussed in more detail later, Alexis had a happy summer swimming in their backyard pool and enjoying the sunny Ontario weather.

Those six weeks in Italy were a wonderful hiatus for our family that really seemed God-given. I say this because in the fall Alexis' s seizures started up again with even greater ferocity. By November some of these seizures were so bad that she would stop breathing for up to 10 minutes at a time and I would have to do continuous mouth-to-mouth resuscitation. Then, one night, when these bad seizures were at their greatest frequency, happening an average of once a day at that point, along with multiple, less severe seizures, I suddenly realized there was a pattern to this seizure nightmare.

Since Alexis was 3½ we had been involved in the patterning program with her, previously discussed. Checking through her progress records I noted that every time we had changed the patterning format or increased its intensity the seizures had worsened. Then, after a few months they would abate. For example, this last bout of bad seizures had begun the very week we had changed from homo-lateral to cross patterning, from moving the limbs on one side of the body together vs. moving alternate arms and legs. And an even more

severe bout of seizures occurred when we instituted 8 rounds of patterning a day and the seizures only reduced to a tolerable level when
we cut back to 4 rounds daily.

I then contemplated what limited knowledge I had of patterning
theory and realized why increasing the medication only made the
problem worse. Patterning, by stimulating the damaged areas of the
brain and thereby facilitating the development of new neural pathways, is supposed to help the affected person to "work through" a
seizure disorder. However, anti-convulsive medications work by
blocking the irregular electrical discharges through these pathways.
Thus, to my layperson's mind, it seemed to me that the two processes were actually working against each other, creating more stress
for Alexis and hence increasing and worsening her seizures.

This little epiphany on my part did nothing to help Alexis' seizure situation, however. I was not prepared to give up the patterning
entirely since we had seen some definite developmental gains that no
other intervention had provided. And I certainly could not stop the
anti-convulsive medication given how serious Alexis' seizures were.
Instead we just carried on allowing Alexis to continue having these
terrible seizures without any further medical intervention.

Why did we do this? Somewhere along the way we had discovered what many other parents in our situation already knew: running
back and forth to the doctor or hospital when these bad seizures
occurred was generally futile for us and traumatic for Alexis. The
experts did not seem to have any more answers than we did and
could only prescribe more and more drugs, which then created their
own sets of problems. They left Alexis in an increasingly dazed condition and did little to bring the seizures under control. But then
something happened that forced us to seek medical assistance.

At five years of age Alexis had her first bout of status epilepticus,
a life-threatening condition in which the seizures do not stop without
medical intervention. We called for an ambulance and she was transported to hospital where a large dose of Valium (a tranquillizing
medication) was administered intravenously and that *did* stop the

seizures. But the price was two days with so little awareness that Alexis' regular seizure medication could not be administered orally so she had to remain in hospital.

A third EEG administered at that time indicated that she now had "multiple epileptogenic foci throughout the brain." I was told that her seizure disorder was 'intractable', meaning it could never be fully controlled and even partial control could not be attained with the use of only one seizure medication because of the various types of seizure activity she was manifesting.

There was no doubt in my mind that the ongoing lack of overall seizure control plus the bout of status epilepticus had resulted in further brain damage.

We could see the behavioural changes resulting from this further erosion of brain tissue for ourselves. Prior to this latest incident, Alexis had always appeared to be more left-handed than right, although because of her delayed development it was difficult to tell. However, afterwards she began favouring her right hand, and her left hand remained retracted with her fingers curled up. There was also a further reduction in her capacity to manipulate food and a loss of the ability to handle larger pieces of food in her mouth, i.e. anything but finely diced food. It seems likely that further brain damage including brain stem damage might have occurred at that time and it was shortly after this that her spells of non-breathing worsened.

In 1988 when Alexis was 10, she had her second bout of Status Epilepticus and she definitely experienced more brain damage on that occasion. Throughout all these years various neurologists tried out various combinations of anti-epileptic medications with her but none succeeded in bringing the seizures under complete control and she continued to have them on a daily basis. They began to vary more in type and intensity but the Absence seizures, the ones first identified in Alexis, remained a constant.

During Alexis' teenage years a new type of seizure emerged: temporal lobe seizures that brought on bouts of whininess followed by periods of intense screaming. This behaviour was not typical of

Alexis who was generally patient and trusting, often exhibiting, through her body language and vocalization, signs of happiness and contentment. After these 'screaming seizures', as we called them, were over Alexis seemed sad and even fearful, as if she was afraid of the seizure happening again—and sometimes it did.

By the time she was 17 we were no longer forewarned by these periods of whininess. The intense screaming spells just seemed to appear out of nowhere and to last longer than had been the case previously. The neurologist she was seeing at that time placed her on a new medication called Lamictal (Lamotrogine) and her seizure activity abated significantly, only to slowly build up again as time passed.

By her late twenties, the screaming spells were becoming increasingly uncontrollable, and had morphed into 'cluster seizures'. That is to say, Alexis would scream uncontrollably and thrash around violently for up to a minute and then suddenly stop moving and remain quiet for up to 30 seconds. But there would be a scared look on her face as if she was just waiting for the next bout. And then it would come—up to five or six seizures in a row like that. All we could do for her at those times was to transfer her quickly to bed and try our best to protect her feet from getting hurt as she lashed out fiercely with them. Finally, the 'seizure run' would be over and she would either fall into a deep sleep or she would suddenly look at us and smile as if nothing had happened. It appeared as if the violent seizure activity had erased her recent memory.

During her twenties and thirties, we were able to take Alexis to Mexico 13 times for two weeks in winter at a time. We also took her to the mountains for a week 14 summers in a row. But by her late thirties it became apparent that it was no longer safe to take her on these long trips anymore—not safe for her or for us.

During one of her Mexican trips Alexis had one of these severe screaming spells in the middle of the night. It was so loud and protracted that the security guard came over to see what the problem was and after that trip I took Alexis back to the neurologist to see if a medication change might help.

She was placed on the new miracle drug of the day, Keppra, medically known as Levetiracetam. It is most effective in treating tonic-clonic (Grand Mal) seizures and myoclonic seizures. Once again, after the introduction of this new medication, there was a dramatic reduction in seizure activity, but the effect gradually wore off and we went through several very bad years with these screaming spells, so bad that it was difficult to retain staff.

Still, we persisted in these annual trips to Mexico with Alexis. But I think we realized that they were coming to an end one year when, after intense negotiating, I managed to acquire the front (bulkhead) seats for us on the plane taking us home from Mexico. On these trips I always feared that if we had regular plane seats and the client in front of Alexis put his seat back and she then had one of her violent seizures she would bash her head against the seat. I even got a letter from her doctor each year explaining this problem and requesting that we be given the bulkhead seat at the front of the cabin with no seats in front of it. This is where families with small babies are characteristically allowed to sit.

On this particular return flight from Mexico, however, the West-Jet airline official I dealt with was not cooperative, citing safety concerns, but finally, after much negotiating on my part, it was agreed. We got on the plane and put Alexis in the middle seat with Joe on one side of her and our assistant on the other side. I was sitting in the row behind. But it was then that Alexis had one of her major screaming spells. I gave her the emergency Valium that I always carried to break the seizure run and settle her and she gradually quieted and drifted towards sleep. However, the rather officious flight attendant who seemed to have placed herself in charge informed us that we would have to leave the plane.

I did my best to explain to her what had happened and how the situation was now under control and Alexis would likely sleep all the way to Edmonton. I gave her the name of Alexis' neurologist and the contact information and asked her to call him for verification but she refused, stating that she had called their company neurologist who advised that Alexis should leave the plane. I explained that we did not have her seizure medication for the following day, and it was a new medication we would not be able to easily acquire in Mexico. Her response was that that was poor planning on my part, and I should have brought extra.

Before we knew it we were back on the tarmac in the broiling sun, and we waited there for an hour before a van came to take Alexis and us to the hotel. Unfortunately, I had to give Alexis her noon medication and to do so I gave her several spoons of some food I had brought from the resort. But in that strong sun the bacteria had multiplied, and Alexis contracted violent diarrhoea for the first time since that early summer when she had attended the preschool program at Elves. The people at the hotel were very nice and understanding when we finally got there but that night was one of the worst nights of our lives. And to top it all off, I was so rattled to be bounced off the plane and so angry seeing the people who had been seated behind us just chomping at the bit for their chance to grab the front seats that I forgot my purse under the seat and it was only returned to me a day after our return to Edmonton.

At this point in her life, early forties, the screaming spells are not as severe as they used to be, even though her current neurologist has actually been slowly reducing Alexis' anti-convulsive medications over the past three years because he felt they were reaching toxic levels of concentration.

Why then have her seizures in general appeared to be tapering off? One neurologist told me many years ago that the affected seizure circuits in the brain tend to "burn out" after a while, with the concomitant brain damage. Alexis' apparent reduction in seizure activity seems to have been accompanied by a general reduction in her level of cognitive awareness. She appears to be less responsive and less capable than previously in various ways.

CHAPTER 13

Why does Alexis stop breathing?

Alexis' seizures are always upsetting to her and to us— but the seizures that cause Alexis to stop breathing or to breathe shallowly and intermittently for significant periods of time are the ones that are really frightening and challenging to deal with. These "blue lip seizures," as we call them, can appear with no associated motor activity. Her lips turn blue, her pupils may or may not be enlarged and her hands may or may not be sweaty. If we don't notice immediately and intervene her lips can turn purple and then black and her extremities darken. It is only when she is uncharacteristically quiet and still, that we become aware something is wrong—and that is the really scary part.

One well-regarded Edmonton neurologist suggested that Alexis' spells of non-breathing or minimal, intermittent breathing may not be seizure-related at all. He speculated that they might be caused by a faulty connection in the part of the brain controlling breathing, a neuronal misfiring. He even suggested that the seizure medication Alexis takes might actually be making the breathing problem worse because of its sedating effect on the parasympathetic nervous system that controls all autonomic bodily activity, including breathing.

Alexis has experienced hundreds of non-breathing incidents through the years. Most last from 1 to 5 minutes but a few have gone on for as long as 10 to 20 minutes. Until Alexis was about ten, these bouts of non-breathing could be dealt with by mouth-to-mouth re-suscitation (artificial respiration) until such time as she was able to resume breathing independently. However, after her second bout of Status Epilepticus, this simple form of resuscitation no longer worked. That is to say, it would temporarily oxygenate her, but she would not start breathing again on her own without further interven-tion, or at least not for a very long time.

A major non-breathing incident occurred the summer she was nine. I was with Alexis at what was then the Eaton's department store at Southgate Mall in Edmonton. My goal was to buy her some new clothes for the upcoming school year, particularly pants. Finding the right ones was always a problem because I wanted them to be stylish, yet easy to get on and off while at the same time pulling up high enough in the back so that the incontinence pad she wore beneath her underwear would not be revealed.

Children's clothing was on the second floor and, as I headed for the change room with some hopeful finds in terms of trousers, I spied a nurse sitting in a small alcove nearby with some medical equipment, including an oxygen tank. I had never noticed that before in any store but assumed she was there because they had many elderly customers who might suddenly require some basic medical assistance. *That's handy!* I idly thought, and then placed Alexis on the floor in the change room so she could try on the new pants I had selected for her.

A particularly nice pair of pants I had chosen was elegantly slim in the legs and therefore a little tricky to get on. As I wrestled with them, I could not help but think how ridiculously heavy and inert Alexis' legs had become. She was still quite flexible at that early point in her life and usually responded better when I was dressing her. After struggling away for a couple of minutes I looked in exaspera-tion at her face, about to say something—and I was completely shocked by what I saw. Her whole face was a mottled grey and her lips were completely black!

The pants were half on and half off at that point and I quickly pulled them off so I could lift her. In the process one long sock was pulled down to her ankle and I saw that Alexis' leg was navy blue all the way up to her knee. I then saw that her arms were equally blue up to her elbows. I raced out calling for the nurse to get her oxygen tank and she came running. She did her best to handle the situation, holding the facemask firmly against Alexis' mouth and nose and turning on the oxygen—but nothing happened.

Alexis' whole face was blue black at that point. I jerked the mask away and began artificial respiration, forcefully breathing into her mouth as strongly as I could. "Not so hard!" the nurse warned me. "You could rupture her lung!" I tempered my efforts but was gratified to see the colour of her face changing and it was clear that Alexis was starting to breathe on her own. The nurse gently pushed me aside then and again administered the oxygen. This time Alexis was able to breathe it in and the horrible blue-black colour soon disappeared. She fell dead asleep at that point and I sat on the floor trembling for many minutes before I had the energy to lift her into her cart and leave the store.

Alexis' body was so limp I had to prop her in the trunk support in the car with one hand while I fumbled to secure the straps with the other. Somehow, I got her home, although I was shaking so badly that I could hardly drive. Fortunately, Joe was there and met us at the door. He saw the look on my face and Alexis' limp body and quickly took her out of the trunk support and carried her to bed. After telling him what happened, I went to bed myself, drained and exhausted.

I slept deeply but then I dreamed. I dreamed of my mother ... at her funeral. I saw her lying there asleep in her rich green dress with the bright gold broach glittering at the bodice. The dress was her favourite colour, but it was very small because she was very small, only 68 pounds when she died, a nurse at the hospital told me. The cancer had eaten away all the rest of her.

I am sure she would have liked the dress I bought for her to say goodbye in—but not the broach. Broaches were more to my taste than hers. In her jewellery box I had surveyed the array of beaded metal necklaces she always wore, and I knew she would have chosen one of them instead. But I had not been able to stand the thought of those beads biting into the back of her neck for all eternity.

I remember staring at her for long minutes in her coffin, all the usual expressions smoothed away from her face, and wondering who she really was inside. I remember her coal black lips and snow-white skin. I remember kissing her forehead and being so shocked by how cold it was, cold and hard and white and smooth like marble.

Then in my dream she changed into Alexis with the same coal black lips; Alexis trapped inside her own living death. I wondered what my mother would have thought, what she would have said. I remembered then what the three different neurologists had said about Alexis. Death could happen at any time, any time at all.

⤙

Another memorable, non-breathing attack occurred about six months later. Joe was away and I had two guests for dinner. Just as I was about to make coffee and present dessert Alexis stopped breathing. This time nothing seemed to work in terms of getting her going again and finally in desperation I placed her on the floor, leaned over her and did my untutored version of full-fledged CPR, cardiopulmonary re-suscitation. It still did not work until I frantically pushed from her heart area up to her left ear. And after several such thrusting movements she began to breathe properly.

I put her to bed after that to give her a chance to recover and turned to my guests. I apologized for my delay in serving dessert when I knew they both had other commitments later that evening and need-ed to leave. They stared at me stupefied and made no effort to move. In fact, they never did honor those commitments. It was then that I realized how this mundane reality of ours must look to outsiders. Victor Frankl, referring to his death camp experience during World War II in his book, *Man's Search for Meaning,*9 observed that human beings can get used to almost anything until it becomes just the new normal for them.

What I think I discovered that night was that dysfunction in the vagus nerve was the root cause of Alexis non-breathing spells, and that stimulating it would allow normal breathing to resume. The vagus (10th cranial) nerve innervates both the lungs and the stomach and has partial control over heart functioning. I believe it was through the strong thrusting movements from Alexis' left chest to her left ear that I was able to trigger it into functioning again so Alexis could breathe.

However, a formal understanding of what I was doing to get Alexis to breathe independently only came to me after the fact when I described Alexis' non-breathing spells to an epileptologist at a neuro-psychology conference I was attending in Texas. How I arrived at that particular solution long before this interchange had less to do with the conventional CPR training that I had undergone than with a combination of trial and error, motherly instinct, scattered bits of neuro-anatomical knowledge and a particular early childhood memory.

What I had recalled was the pump on our farm and how my father used to pour a cup of water down the well shaft before he could pump water up. This is called a feedback loop and in academic parlance there was much talk about such loops in the early '80's. I imagined myself breathing life into Alexis and her breathing back at me, and me nudging her brain with those chest-to-ear thrusts and her brain then nudging her heart and lungs.

This is as much as I can understand about why Alexis has these non-breathing spells, these 'blue lip' seizures. They are a mystery no neurologist has ever been able to explain satisfactorily. All we can do is cope with them and try to minimize their impact on Alexis' brain functioning. In the early years, mouth-to-mouth resuscitation was enough, and we had resuscitation masks available for the assistants who worked with Alexis. But once that approach no longer worked, the situation became more complicated and more frightening.

Joe and I, and all of Alexis' assistants have been trained in conventional CPR. This was, and is, a mandatory part of staff training for all provincially funded PDD[10] agencies, including ours. But conventional

CPR is neither necessary nor appropriate for Alexis with her young, healthy heart. Heart function is not her problem. The modification I developed many years ago—brisk upward strokes from chest to left ear—worked. But teaching Alexis' assistants the correct way to do it and ensuring that they did not panic in the process was both arduous and dangerous. It was also a lot to expect from people with minimal training and experience in the area of severe disabilities. We needed something better before the day came when I was not home, the system broke down and Alexis either suffered more brain damage from prolonged oxygen deprivation or died.

What we needed, I decided, was a home oxygen supply and a bagger to force the oxygen into Alexis' lungs when she had these spells. It seemed to me that we should be able to create the necessary feedback loop by using this approach to trigger the vagus nerve back into full functioning, and with a lot less trauma for both Alexis and the rest of us! I contacted 'Alberta Aids for Daily Living'; the provincial government branch in charge of providing equipment to assist people with disabilities, and I explained the problem. A respiratory technician soon came to the house to assess Alexis' need, but we were told that she did not qualify. Her heart and lungs were healthy, and her oxygen level was at 96, well within the normal range.

I explained about Alexis' non-breathing spells but of course she did not cooperate by having one while the technician was there. The woman reiterated that the provincial guideline for providing such support was a chronic low oxygen level. We offered to pay for the machinery and oxygen refills if they would provide them but even that did not seem to be possible. I was of course angry and disappointed by this outcome, but I could understand that there had to be rules in place to prevent misuse. Alexis' situation was so unusual that she simply fell between the cracks.

I then reached out to various officials and advocacy groups within the disability system. The advice I received was to contact our MLA, our provincial member of the legislative assembly, which I did. He listened very sympathetically and the very next day the same technician who had visited us phoned back. She had arranged for a provider to sell or rent the necessary equipment and ongoing oxygen supplies to us and to give us the necessary training and support to use them effectively.

Once we had the oxygen tank in place and learned how to use it, the difference to Alexis' life and our lives was amazing and I was very sorry that I had not pursued that avenue years earlier. We had just fallen into the habit of coping with Alexis' non-breathing episodes ourselves since none of the experts seemed able to help us with this issue. In fact, it was debatable as to whether or not they really believed me when I explained how bad and long-lasting Alexis' non-breathing spells were. There is often cyanosis with generalized motor seizures as well, but in those cases, it is brief and intermittent, a few seconds of lip darkening here and there. That is nothing like what Alexis experienced and still continues to experience at times.

Once the oxygen and bagger were available it was relatively easy to keep Alexis well oxygenated during these spells. The challenge was to train new staff to use the machine efficiently and to remember to turn off the oxygen supply afterwards. Many tanks have been wasted because the oxygen was only partially turned off and Joe frequently runs back and forth to the provider to replenish the supply. The other challenge was to have a source available when Alexis was away from home and for that we purchased a portable oxygen tank and separate bagger.

We were not permitted to carry the oxygen tank with us on the plane to Mexico, however, but, since I was with Alexis constantly during those holidays and could do my own version of CPR efficiently, we could cope. Also, in that relaxing atmosphere she seemed to have fewer non-breathing spells. We did carry it with us when we travelled with her to the mountains, along with a portable lift and other equipment. That way Joe and I could go out for a bit on our own and leave her in the care of the staff member we had brought along without worry.

In the past few years we have not been able to take Alexis on these long holidays. She no longer seems to have the strength and stamina to tolerate all the changes to her routine and accommodations that are involved, and we no longer seem to have what it takes to care for her under these less-than-ideal circumstances. At home everything is designed to meet her needs and keep her comfortable. We cannot replicate that elsewhere.

There is another element to consider as well, a very sad one. While her two bouts of status epilepticus, the first when she was five and the second when she was 10, resulted in some deterioration in functioning, Alexis' ongoing vicious seizures and non-breathing spells appear to have further eroded both her strength and her cognition. She is much less energetic during the day than she was when younger, and she sleeps a great deal more. Afternoon naps are now a requirement for her, and she is still exhausted by 9:30 at night and does not want to get up before 8:30 in the morning. Even then she is often grumpy and tired.

As Alexis is less alert and responsive than she once was, she can tolerate less noise and disruption than previously. On a good day we can take her out for a couple of hours and my friend Kathy's son, Rajan and his assistant visits her two days a week. Apart from that she has her daily long walks, winter and summer, and eats all of her meals outside in her gazebo whenever the weather allows. She also explores various city amenities—when Joe or I can drive her in our wheelchair van and when she has the energy, but that is about it for her social life. That is a very different situation than it was 20 years ago when she was out every day to a different venue, often for extended periods of time.

However, there is an upside to this change—for Alexis and for Joe and for me. The eager university students we hired to work with Alexis when she was younger no longer seem to be interested in dealing with someone with so many limitations and such a strict and homebound routine. Therefore, we have increasingly been hiring older women who have come to Canada from many different countries and are willing and able to do what is required for our daughter.

I have spoken before about our "lost language and cultural opportunities" because of our need to focus on our responsibilities towards Alexis. However, in at least one sense we have had a richer multi-cultural experience than most because of these people in our home working with Alexis and interacting with all three of us day after day. One could say that through our interactions with them, often for years at a time, we have come to understand and appreciate the living culture of people from many different parts of the world— and one might further say that in some ways this has been more satisfying, and perhaps more relevant, than the usual tourist fare of surveying the dead culture of the past through monuments, museums and art galleries in these same countries.

Music is another bonus that Alexis has given us. Because she is home most of the time, because she can't see and depends primarily on hearing for gaining her external awareness of the world and any sense of its richness, and because she appears to have a genuine appreciation for good music it is always playing in the background. When I get up and greet her and her assistant in the morning music is already emanating from our five-disc cd player and I am still hearing it when I retire for the night. And I don't mean just any music either! It is carefully curated by Joe and through the years friends and family members have gifted Alexis with CDs from a variety of North American musicians as well as from their various travels to different parts of the world. This music ranges broadly from classical to folk, country, jazz, blues and popular. Also, her brother-in-law, Marc, an accomplished pianist, sends her CDs every Christmas of his own compositions as well as of other artists in alternative music genres who have impressed him. Our staff has enjoyed Alexis' extensive cd collection as well, and because of her clear preference for male tenors we have learned much about the range of their performances through the years. So it could be said that we have all had our own enriching musical education!

The Development of the GRIT Model

By January of 1981, when Alexis turned three, I was working on the book, *Different Hopes, Different Dreams,* at the same time as I was trying to figure out the next step in Alexis' rehabilitation process. With all early intervention options for Alexis exhausted I doubled down on an idea that had been fomenting in my brain for some time. It was now clear to me that mothers could not carry out a home-based program for these young children with so many challenges on their own. It was also clear that sending them off to centres at such a young age was not appropriate. What was needed was a home-based program with the proper daily supports provided.

If there was money to support centre-based programs for preschool children with severe disabilities, I reasoned, there should be money to support home-based programs as well. It was not right to expect very young children facing such challenges to be shipped away from their homes every day in a stranger's vehicle. Most mothers would not even do that with their unimpaired children at such a young age. Furthermore, because the number of children requiring such a specialized program was small these centres were few and far between and the children often had to travel long distances.

The Edmonton Public School System had set up a home-based alternative to the centre-based programs. But the Mayfield Early

Intervention Program provided supervision only and not direct support like the centre-based models. I found this model still lacking, knowing from first-hand experience what a major trauma it was for families to be confronted with the reality of a severely disabled child. I was convinced that turning mothers into teachers and putting them in the position of not only training but evaluating their pre-school children on a daily basis was totally alienating and disruptive to the parent-child bonding process.

Based on these ideas, I decided it was time to put my Child Development credentials to use, the ones that various medical and disability experts had dismissed as having no relevance to the deviancy model of developmental delay then currently in vogue. I did a little research and discovered that there existed a special government branch whose primary concern was early childhood services. Its director was Dr. David Jeffares who had been instrumental in establishing the Alberta Education Early Childhood Program. *Maybe this is someone who will listen to me!* I thought. I found his number, telephoned and was able to make an appointment with him almost immediately.

As soon as I entered David's office and saw him sitting at his desk, I had the strong feeling that here was someone I could relate to. I explained to him my plan for a rounded developmental program for these children that would address not only their cognitive and physical rehabilitation needs but also their social, emotional, communication and self-help needs. I shared with him various situations I had seen where the behaviours I had observed had more to do with environmental limitations than actual disabilities. I described children with no formal communication abilities and minimal physical capacity just staring into empty space and twiddling their hands in the air aimlessly, "self-stimming" as it has come to be called, a term I have always considered to be particularly odious.

I talked about our children being children first and disabled second, about their critical need for early intervention and how important it was that this be provided in their home environment. We talked for more than an hour at that first meeting and his response to my ideas was totally different from what I had come to expect. I was used to being perceived and dismissed as a rather over-zealous pie-in-the-sky mother. But this time I was being listened to respectfully not only as if I were a fellow professional, but one with insider knowledge as well.

Dr. Jeffares was even responding with his own ideas and suggestions for how to get my imagined program off the ground! He was quite certain that existing PUF (program unit funding) grants could be tweaked to accommodate the exceptional needs of young children with multiple and severe challenges whose parents wished to keep them at home with the appropriate supports in place instead of sending them off every day to a centre-based setting.

All I had to do, according to him, was to further refine my program model and then find enough parents interested in it to make it financially feasible to hire a teacher and supporting therapists. Also, the children enrolled had to have been qualified as 'multiply and severely disabled', the language of the time, and they had to be 2½ years of age by September 1 of the program year in which they were enrolled. And there was a third task I must undertake: either get an existing program to take us under their wing for administrative purposes or else go through the process of incorporation so we could stand on our own. No government funds could be allocated to unincorporated bodies.

I went home that day knowing that I had my work cut out for me but feeling lighter and happier than I had felt since Alexis was diagnosed. Maybe there was hope after all! As I saw it, I had two problems. The first was further program development. I knew by the way Dr. Jeffares had responded during the interviews that the basic concept I had presented was in line with his expectations, as were the rough outlines of the program. But fleshing it out in language and content was another matter. And the hard fact was that I did not have the special education background and accompanying language to do this on my own. But I knew people who *did* have these skills.

For language and style and government regulations I asked Dr. Alex Hillyard for advice. I knew him through the advocacy work I had been doing and his position at that time was as director of the school-based program just starting out for older children with this level of disabilities. He offered several helpful suggestions that were of assistance to me in further developing and refining my proposal but one I found to be problematic.

The program, as I had devised it, was to be divided into 8 developmental areas: gross motor, fine motor, feeding skills, toileting skills, auditory awareness, visual awareness, communication and socialization. When I explained that all the children would be placed on a regular toileting regimen, he raised his eyebrows. "What makes you think they all have that capability?" he asked, or words to that effect.

I told him how successful we had been with Alexis and that we would never know if we did not try with the other children. From the few young children I had met to date who might fall into this category of 'multiple and severe', Alexis seemed to me to be one of the most impaired so why should we not assume that if we toileted the other children regularly they could accomplish what she had accomplished.

He did finally see my point but was critical of my language. "We don't use the term 'toileting' anymore," he explained. We talk about self-care and personal needs he went on to explain. That was my first introduction to the world of euphemisms in the disabilities arena, but it was not to be my last.

My second need was to organize my program content-wise so that it would be acceptable to the education experts who would be evaluating it while at the same time being pertinent to the very unique group of individuals it would be serving. For help with this I turned to my friend, Colleen Hermanson, whom I had also met in Dr. Cameron's course. Colleen had done her graduate work in the area of exceptionality, specializing in children with multiple and severe disabilities and she was already working as a teacher in a class for school aged children with that level of disability. At 10 o'clock at night when our children were all in bed and the day's tasks done, I would call her, and we would talk for up to an hour at a time about the pros and cons and possibilities of various aspects of the program.

Colleen not only gave me invaluable advice. She also gave me a level of unqualified support that I badly needed at that time in order to have the strength and courage to carry on. Those late-night talks made the whole process real for me and kept me going. Gradually, we chewed through the details and finally I was ready to present the formal written proposal to Dr. Jeffares.

CHAPTER 15

Convincing Gateway to be our Sponsor

T here was still one matter I needed to clear up before I could bring in the proposal, however. I already knew that developing the program and finding the children to fill it was all I could manage. I could not also handle all the paperwork involved in incorporating and satisfying the government that we were sufficiently well organized administratively to meet their standards. The obvious answer as I saw it was to get what was then called 'The Gateway Association for the Mentally Handicapped' to take us over.

It was late in 1979 when I joined Gateway, and that organization was only four years old at that point. It had been formed by a group of parents breaking away from the Winifred Stewart School, founded by the woman for whom it was named in 1953. She had wanted a place for her own son, Parker, who was born with Down Syndrome, to receive the training he needed to be able to function in society.

There was little support from either the government or the general public for such a project in those days, but Dr. Stewart persevered. She found other parents with children facing similar challenges, lobbied the government and worked on developing a suitable educational program for this group of children. In order for her school to come into being and continue functioning, the parents involved had to participate in fund raising activities and in administering the program largely on their own, with the actual educational program being provided by volunteer teachers in the early years. Winifred was, and is still recognized today, as a very exceptional lady who had a lot of courage and foresight in fighting the battles of her day. In 1972, Dr. Winifred Stewart was inducted as an Officer into The Order of Canada.

But the Gateway parents of the '70's were a different generation than the parents of the '50's. They took the right of a publicly funded and professionally administered educational program for their children for granted. What *they* wanted and lobbied hard for was to have their children educated in regular public or 'separate' (Roman Catholic) schools, not in a segregated setting. And they wanted to put their efforts toward advocating for their children to be included in regular society, not into administering programs and fundraising. They were quite adamant on these points and I knew that.

They were also at that time a group of older parents with older children whose intellectual limitations fell mostly within the moderate range. These parents were no longer concerned with early education programs and had no connection, apart from myself at that point, with parents whose children were facing the kinds of challenges Alexis was facing. Yet somehow I needed to convince them that they should take on the program I was proposing.

I asked the then Gateway president, Joan Charbonneau, if I could make a presentation at an upcoming Gateway board meeting. As I mentioned previously, I was chairperson of the Gateway Family Support Committee at that time and was well known to the group as an active, contributing member. However, not all of these parents appreciated my enthusiastic championing of an in-home early education program for children with severe disabilities. The original group of Gateway parents had struggled hard to get what they had for their children and it was understandable that some of them resented a 'Johnny-come-lately' piggybacking on their efforts. So, I would have to proceed carefully. On the plus side, I felt that I had an ally in Joan, who had made it clear to me that she admired and respected what I was trying to do.

One thing I knew was that before meeting with the Gateway Board I needed to find a name for my proposed program to make it real. Yet another late-night conversation with Colleen was devoted to resolving that issue. In my mind I was thinking that MASH would be a good name as an acronym for Multiple and Severe Handicaps. It seemed perfect to me, carrying some of the panache that went with the popular MASH TV program involving a group of army doctors at a front-line field hospital during the Korean War.

Colleen, usually so soft spoken and diplomatic, was in this case very blunt. "People will think you are referring to mashed potatoes. That is *not* the image we want to portray about our students!" She countered with GRIP as an acronym for Gateway Residential Intensive Program. I agreed with her that if I were going to ask Gateway to take us on there should be some recognition of their affiliation with it in the program title. But I felt that 'GRIP' as an acronym was kind of pointless. "What *kind* of grip?" I asked. "A grip on *what*? It did not have that special something I was looking for. Then, I had it!

What about GRIT? Gateway Residential Intensive Training program, *the GRIT program?* Colleen thought about it and her only reservation was that the word 'program' was not part of the acronym. But GRIT was the image I wanted to get across after all we had been through trying to get this venture going—and GRIT it would be. It must have struck a chord with people because now, almost 40 years later, the program is still called GRIT! But it has been functioning independently of Gateway for many years and the GRIT acronym now stands for 'Getting Ready for Inclusion Today'.

I made my pitch to the board as clearly and eloquently as I could. My first point of argument was their name: Gateway Association for the Mentally Handicapped. It suggested to me that they were mandated to serve all people with mental handicaps, not just a select group, so how could they justify ignoring our needs just because we made up such a small minority? My second point of argument was that I was offering my services as volunteer coordinator. I would take full responsibility for organizing and running the program, so it need not take away from their advocacy work.

My third point was a little trickier to make. I tried to get across, in a nice way, that I had been fully supporting Gateway's advocacy work not only with the family support work I was doing but also, and perhaps even more importantly, with the book of parent stories across Alberta I was putting together. These stories would provide various perspectives on what it was like to raise a child with developmental disabilities and the book would be seen as a Gateway initiative. Gateway had in fact received provincial grants to support its publication and, as I had pointed out in the grant application I had prepared, it would serve as a useful tool for our family support committee in meeting the needs of new mothers—and possibly might even be used as a resource for special education teachers in training.

I was trying to say, without actually saying it in so many words, that they knew me and could trust me, and even maybe owed me a bit for what I had already brought to Gateway. But that kind of schmoozing is not a very highly developed skill in my repertoire, so I left the room not really sure how I had come across. It was a long time before I was called back in, during which time I could hear agitated voices but finally the moment came. The president informed me that my proposal had been accepted. Gateway would throw their support behind this new program—on one condition: their treasurer would handle the books.

If they thought that I would object to that they were mistaken. I was delighted. To tell the truth I had not even given any thought to how that would be done, and it certainly wasn't any strength of mine! All *I* wanted to do was organize the program, work with the children and oversee the resource experts. I agreed immediately and expressed my gratitude for both their acceptance of the program, and for the offer of their treasurer to handle the financial bookwork. I walked away from that meeting very happy and relieved. Only much later was I to find out that the vote had been a very close one indeed!

CHAPTER 16

Finding the Parents,
Teacher and Therapists

T he program model was in place. The administrative
oversight was in place. All that was left now was to find the
children. At this time, I knew only one other parent who had
a child as severely disabled as Alexis. Tammy Springer had recently
joined Gateway. She was a very vocal and involved member and she
was excited about the concept behind the GRIT program, but her
severely disabled daughter, Kymberlie, was too young to be eligible.

I still received notices of Mayfield Early Intervention Program
meetings since we were on the list and I had the temerity to ask the
administrator if I could come to their next meeting and speak for a
few minutes about our proposed new program. Miraculously, she
allowed me to do so and I began by pointing out the obvious draw-
backs of a centre-based program. Then I gave my spiel about mothers
not wanting to be worn out by teaching and alienated by evaluating
their disabled children when they were still struggling emotionally
with the whole reality of their situation. What we were proposing
was an in-home program where the mother would be part of the
team but spared much of the daily work. Since this was, more or less,
a direct judgment of the Mayfield Early Education program, I was
surprised they did not shut me down at that point. I finished quickly
anyway, sensing the discomfort in the room, and sat down to a faint
round of applause.

The meeting ended and I was feeling quite demoralized, believing that I had not done a very good job of getting my point across. However, both Tammy Springer and a person I had not previously met were in the audience and Tammy came over to introduce Kathy Talwar to me—or so I thought. But instead Tammy just grabbed the pile of brochures that I had prepared and gave half of them to Kathy. "Quick! You take the front door and I'll take the back door. Don't let anybody get away without one!" she said. And they did just that! This was one of a handful of beautiful experiences I had in my days of close involvement with the GRIT program that I will cherish in my heart to the end of my life. Below is the keynote statement from the brochure that Tammy and Kathy handed out at that time:

> *It takes grit and determination to raise a child*
> *with multiple and severe disabilities.*
> *If you have the determination, we have the GRIT.*

Two days after meeting Kathy at the Mayfield presentation she phoned me to ask for some advice about feeding her son, Rajan, which was proving to be very difficult. Tammy's daughter, Kymberlie, was functioning at a higher level physically than Rajan so Tammy could not help her with these feeding issues. Kathy told me that she had desperately wanted to find someone with a child as severely disabled as her son and it sounded like I was that someone. I invited Kathy over, and she watched me feed Alexis and picked up a few pointers.

As I worked with Alexis, feeding her carefully to make sure she did not aspirate, Kathy and I talked. She was thrilled about my ideas for an in-home program handled by a developmental assistant and overseen by a teacher and therapists. But unfortunately, Rajan was also too young to participate. I asked Kathy if she knew any other mothers in our situation who had slightly older children.

Kathy told me that she had met a mother at a Glenrose Hospital therapeutic swim session for very developmentally delayed children, and she felt sure that this woman's son would qualify. But she couldn't remember her name—Donna or something like that. She thought she might have written the mother's phone number down but wasn't sure if she still had it. However, when Kathy returned home from our visit she did find the number and immediately called me back.

The mother's name was Debbie DeFord (now Appleby) and her number at that time was 454-6984. I remember it to this day because I was to call it many, many times in the coming years. I also remember our first phone-call. I wasted little time on social preliminaries; as I have said, I was not very skilled in that art at the time. Once I established that Debbie did indeed have a son of qualifying age with disabilities as severe as those of Alexis, I launched right into the details of the program I was proposing. She was immediately onside. We must have talked for an hour during that first call and by the time we were through I felt that my whole world had shifted. Here was someone who understood exactly what I was going through and whose thoughts and passions on the subject were the same as mine.

From the very beginning, Debbie and I became a kind of tag team and we soon began to see ourselves as a new edition of Mutt and Jeff, a widely published newspaper cartoon by Bud Fisher that ran from 1907 to 1983.

Debbie told me that I could put people off with my zealous monologues, big words and poor eye contact. I told her that I was not interested in sentiment, trivia and pointless socialization. She told me that if I wanted to work with people and get them to buy into the program, I better develop some of those skills. I told her that she spent too much time jabbering away on the telephone and allowing people to drop in whenever they felt like it for no good reason. And on it went.

That was our private relationship. But, in our public presentations at hospitals or schools or to other parents on behalf of Gateway or to promote the program, I do remember how we protected and supported and covered for each other. I came to understand what the phrase "I've got your back" meant. I also discovered that Debbie was more than generous with her time and efforts to help get GRIT off the ground and, later on, to keep it running. The vast differences in our circumstances made this generosity on her part all the more impressive.

I had a husband whose income easily supported the family. In addition, he did his share and more in terms of housework and childcare, including caring for Alexis so I could attend numerous evening meetings and make daytime presentations to various groups and individuals. Joe's position as an English professor for Athabasca University, a distance-learning institute, meant that he could flex his hours and work from home when he needed to. This was ideal for our situation. Although Alexis often woke up at night because of her seizures, she did go back to sleep after they were over, and she had calmed down.

Debbie's husband and circumstances were quite different. Although Barry was a charming, warm and sociable man who always made one feel very comfortable in his presence, he had a problem with alcohol and was unable to give Debbie, their son, Kent,[11] and a second son, Barry Jr., born when Kent was six, the financial and emotional support they needed.

Kent, who was physically more capable than Alexis, and could also see, albeit with some visual field limitations, had the kind of brain damage that caused him to engage in self-destructive head banging behaviour periodically throughout the day and routinely in the middle of the night. Fortunately, Debbie's parents lived nearby and helped as much as they could with Kent. The only reason she was able to attend the many meetings and participate in the presentations she did was because of them.

Of all the parents I met then and through the years since, only one other had family circumstances as severe as those faced by Debbie at that time. Yet she was the one who was always there for me, prepared to do whatever was necessary to keep the program running smoothly. But before we could even worry about that we had to find more parents with children of qualifying age so there could even *be* a program!

There were no online media options back in 1981 so getting the word out was not easy. Actually, it would have been easy if the two hospitals that functioned as a clearinghouse for all Edmonton and area children with this level of disability had been willing to pass on our information to their parents, but they were not. It was quite clear that they did not see our program as a serious and responsible alternative to the programs that already existed.

Debbie's efforts to spread the word through radio talk shows and community league boards were not yielding any takers, but the principal of my older children's school told me of a friend who had a child as disabled as Alexis and I met with that family. (I have described them earlier.) They were very rigidly adhering to the Philadelphia patterning program and did not want any interference with it. Also, their daughter was a year older than ours, meaning she would basically only qualify for the first six months of program operation. Still, after some talk, I managed to persuade them that they could carry on their program without any interference, and all that would change is that they would have an assistant to take some of the burden off them. This was certainly not a family on whom I could impose my toileting ideas, or therapy ideas, or any other ideas, and I do not remember now how the teacher and therapists fared in working with them, but at least we got them on board.

Marcine Hagen had also been present at the Mayfield meeting the night of my presentation and a couple of weeks later she called. Marcine's main concern was that sending her daughter to a centre-based program would involve a long bus ride that she did not feel her Kimberly could handle.

Ann Jones was the fifth and last mother to contact us about joining GRIT that first year. Her daughter, Kara, was higher functioning intellectually than the rest of our children but still faced multiple challenges. Because of her intellectual functioning level, she had been able to remain in the Glenrose Rehabilitation Hospital special school program, but Ann was not satisfied with it. According to what she told me herself, the Glenrose people finally got fed up with her and suggested that she join our renegade program, giving her the contact information we had provided to them. I suspect it was less a compliment to us than a way to get rid of a difficult mother!

And that was it. All five families who enrolled in GRIT that first year were rebels who refused to buy into the existing system. And the five of us were buoyed up by the moral support of Kathy and Tammy. As I came to know these parents better, and to hear and understand their separate stories, it all added to my certainty that I was on the right track. But at that point we got no more phone calls and I realized that if we were going to be able to access services for that second term, January of 1982, we had no more time to wait. We had already missed the fall term because of the difficulty in finding the parents.

From the beginning I had asked Colleen to become the GRIT teacher, but since the deadline was approaching for us to begin operations in the New Year, and since we had only five children enrolled at this point, we could not offer her a full-time job. And even if we could she would have been unwise to leave her secure position with the school board for such an uncertain venture.

It was a dilemma, but Colleen offered a solution. If it was all right with the parents, she would take the position on and visit each of the five families after school once a week. I checked with the parents and they all agreed to accommodate this schedule. Getting a well-trained and experienced teacher specialized in the area of severe disabilities like Colleen back in 1982 guaranteed our children the best possible program, and as an additional asset it also lent to our fledgling program credibility it would not otherwise have had.

Once Colleen was on board, she made it her business to hunt down the physical and occupational therapists we would need, as well as the vision and auditory specialists we would have to have available on a consultant basis. Colleen deserves a lot of the credit for getting the GRIT program off the ground—but she has never been one to worry much about credit!

CHAPTER 17

The GRIT Program is launched!

I **was finally** ready to go back to Dr. Jeffares with all his conditions met.

I should mention that there were times along the way when I stumbled and second guessed myself and became so overwhelmed with other things happening in my life, most notably Alexis' increasingly violent seizures and sleep disrupted nights, that I was hardly a model of organization and efficiency. Dr. Jeffares himself stopped by our home on his way to work to pick up the final proposal when it was ready and for the necessary photocopying and distribution. His steady belief in the project and the quiet encouragement he offered in our occasional phone calls did much to keep me going.

The fateful day came when we were to meet with him as a group and I rallied the parents. We were to meet at his office together so he could see for himself that everyone was onside and shared the same vision. Unfortunately, the Jones family had another engagement they felt they could not break despite my desperate urging, and apparently, I forgot to notify another family. That was the patterning family, and I am not sure they would have come anyway. They studiously avoided all our activities and generally made it quite clear that they had absolutely no interest in our program except to have access to a daily assistant paid for by the government for the few months left for which their daughter would qualify.

Thus, it was only three mothers who turned up in Dr. Jeffares' office, a rather measly and pathetic showing. I worried that he would not go ahead but made the case as forcefully as I could stressing Colleen's qualifications and those of the other specialists that she had been able to find, who were ready to assist us in meeting our children's needs. I could see the doubt and disappointment in his face and cursed myself for not being a better salesperson and a more efficient organizer.

However, the funding was based on individual grants, so under these circumstances it was less of an investment on the government's part than if we had had a larger number. Also, we had taken so long to get everything in place that the program could only begin February 1st. A six-month experiment involving only five individuals, the results of which would need to be evaluated before we could be permitted to go ahead, must have seemed to him a reasonable risk. He sold it to his superiors as a pilot program and within a couple of days we got final approval!

By that time, it was early January and what we needed to do then was to hire the assistants who would be working with the families. Each of the mothers advertised for her own child's assistant and did the interviewing. They were well aware of the program requirements and certainly we could not ask Colleen to be involved as she was busy with her full-time job in the Edmonton Public School System.

We found our own assistant for Alexis and she seemed perfect. We hired her privately and began training her. But mere days before the program was to start, she phoned to tell us she had fallen in the snow in the parking lot and broken her leg. Now when I think about it, I wonder if it was really true, because in the past 40 years I have heard lots of face-saving excuses from people who really did not want to take the job after meeting Alexis and hearing our requirements.

In any case, after all I had been through to that point, just on the very cusp of success, I was left without an assistant—and without her the whole process would be meaningless for us. I desperately searched for another, culling through applicants whose resumes I had not pursued. Luck was with me and I found one who I quickly came to realize was going to be even better than our original candidate, although she did not have the same technical qualifications. I think it was then that I stopped believing in qualifications.

Linda was interested, enthusiastic, energetic, intelligent, and she had good habits of neatness and personal hygiene. Those are the criteria I have used in hiring assistants for Alexis to this day. She turned out to be just what we needed. One of the reasons I had not considered her application more seriously in the first place was because she was planning to return to her family home in London, Ontario after the university year finished and I would have to get a new assistant at that time. But as it happened, that actually worked out very well for us, as I will explain later.

CHAPTER 18

The early GRIT years

The first 6 months of program operations were very exciting for me, and for all of us involved in GRIT. Colleen did her job as teacher with great tact and professionalism. The individual schedule of daily activities she devised for each child was meticulous but not rigid and the dream I had been holding onto for so long of a balanced developmental program for Alexis and others similarly challenged came true. Another part of my vision had been the notion of a flattened hierarchy where each member of the team: teacher, therapist, mother and assistant, had her role to play but all were considered equal in importance.

What we quickly realized was that the critical figures in the program were the assistants. They were the ones best positioned to critique the program and to find out through their daily work with the child what was missing and where improvements could be made. No less important was parent input. Only they could tell us what went on outside of program hours that might have implications for the effectiveness of the program. Colleen, as the de facto leader, set the standard for respectful interaction and encouraged equal participation. No one was allowed to ride roughshod over another's ideas and that included me, the program coordinator.

In order to increase the effectiveness of the therapist time available to us we had weekly group therapy sessions at my home. The therapist would work with each trio of child, mother and assistant, one group after another while the rest either practiced or visited, mostly the latter. Although not the original reason for setting it up in this way, the arrangement introduced a strong socialization component for the children and increased group identity and cohesion for the mothers and therapists.

Every month we had an administrative meeting at the Gateway office attended by me, as program coordinator, the mothers, Jim Whittle, the Gateway treasurer, and the new Gateway president. Debbie DeFord (now Appleby) was the official chairperson and she did an excellent job. I reported back to Dr. Jeffares at intervals because I knew he was anxious to hear how we were getting along.

The program was suspended for the month of August to allow for staff holiday time. In my eagerness to get going and keep going I had not initially been in favour of this arrangement but later saw the wisdom of it. Also, it gave us time to prepare for the new program year in September and seven new children were already registered for that, including Kymberlie Springer. Rajan Talwar had to wait still another year to join GRIT but his mother, Kathy, remained a stalwart supporter.

September rolled around much too quickly and we were in our second year of operation. The GRIT program had now grown from five to thirteen children, necessitating the hire of a second teacher since Colleen was still working with us on a part time basis. Much water passed under the bridge in those first 18 months of program operation and occasional mistakes were made, including by me at times. Unfortunately, I was not to enjoy the same relationship of mutual trust and respect with the new Gateway president as I had had with her predecessor, Joan Charbonneau. Sometimes the monthly meetings became a little acrimonious because of her desire to be in control and to second-guess me for just about every decision I made. But I was always impressed by how effectively Debbie was able to bring us back on point and restore order—and protect me in the process!

One apparent mistake that Debbie and I made was in agreeing to take on three children living outside of the Edmonton city limits but we were able to get past it by pointing out that the funding we were receiving was provincial, not municipal, and nothing in our program title suggested we were restricted to Edmonton. Also, the Edmonton Public Schools catchment area for serving school aged children with multiple and severe disabilities[12] included all of North Eastern Alberta so, in a sense, a precedent had been set. And GRIT has continued to operate in that way ever since.

Those were very happy days but at the end of July 1984, they came to an end for us, as I will discuss in more detail later. Our family was leaving in August for my husband's sabbatical year at the University of Toronto and a new coordinator was hired. Naturally, she had to be paid for the services I had been providing gratis up to that point, so arrangements had to be made with the Department of Early Childhood Services to add more money to our budget.

As in all organizations, administration gradually became more top heavy and full day programs now became half-day programs and followed the school schedule with a longer summer holiday and weeks off at Christmas and Easter. But, other than that, the original model has largely prevailed, and has even been copied in some other places.

A group of eager parents knew what their children needed, worked to get what they wanted, and in the process changed the system for young children facing severe and multiple challenges by providing them with opportunities for growth and learning they had never had before. Almost as important, it gave parents some needed peace of mind and made their family situations more bearable.

CHAPTER 19

Masako Whalley and the Vibrator Era

Masako, now Masako Miyazaki, was head of the Occupational Therapy program at the University of Alberta and an active researcher in the area of stroke therapy. She also had prior experience working with children affected by cerebral palsy, and we parents knew her and were working closely with her in the early eighties.

Masako told us that her approach was eclectic, and went on to explain what she had discovered to date that seemed to have some remediation value for her stroke patients, and might work for our children as well. She talked to us of the new neurological evidence emerging at that time of 'collateral sprouting', i.e., regeneration of axons in the central nervous system, in some animal studies that had been done, for example, on the visual system of cats.

She went on to explain to us that vibration is one of the first senses to be integrated in animals, and that the proprioceptive system is one of the first to be developed. When these two senses are linked together clinically it has a dramatic effect on balance. And that is where her use of the vibrator came in. She told us of the successful results she had seen in stroke patients when using the vibrator as a part of their program of therapy and about the spontaneous recovery of certain functions she had witnessed. But she cautioned that this therapy would not be effective with all vibrators but only those whose pulsation rate fell within certain narrow parameters.

"What can this vibrator therapy do for our children?" we asked. Masako explained that it could reduce the intensity of seizures, improve balance and, in a new variation she had recently discovered, increase lip and tongue control so that feeding our children would be easier and there would be less risk of aspiration.

In those days we had very few ways to help our children, so this was exciting and hopeful information for us. We clamoured to know when we could start and where we could acquire these magical vibrators. There was only one place, she told us. When we got there, we needed to speak to the tall man who always wore a 3-piece pinstriped suit. We should ask him for the 'non-doctor vibrator' and the therapeutic mouthpiece to go with it. We could mention her name as he was used to dealing with her.

The place we needed to visit was simply called "The Love Shop." It had newly opened on Jasper Avenue, in the heart of downtown Edmonton and was the first of its kind in our city. The parents looked at me helplessly. One suggested that I go there and purchase a set for each of them and they could then reimburse me. After all, I was the one urging them that we all acquire these as a necessary tool in the developmental program we were carrying out for our children.

I refused, wondering myself how I would be able to muster up the nerve to enter into that forbidden world—but I did. The tall (very tall) thin man was there in his 3-piece suit, and he greeted me most graciously and professionally. I acquired the two separate items as quickly as possible, transferred them to a shopping bag from another store I had brought along for that purpose and, after checking outside to make sure nobody I knew was in the vicinity, slunk out.

How did they work? In Alexis' case, at least, they proved to be worth the embarrassment of acquiring them and soon became just another tool in our repertoire. The mouthpiece was particularly effective. It attached firmly to the vibrator and before every meal we would run it over Alexis' tongue and all over the inside of her mouth and lips for several minutes.

Alexis soon acquired greater control over her tongue than previously and was also able to close her lips more effectively when eating. It was as if her tongue, formerly inert and sloppy in her mouth, came to life and Alexis seemed delighted with the result, moving it around and all over her mouth even between meals, apparently just for the fun of it. We took to calling her 'Mrs. Tongue'!

The seizures were another matter. Alexis' seizures were violent, intractable and sometimes dangerously silent. Her lips could turn blue or even black and we would not notice immediately if we weren't looking directly at her. It was only when we had an ominous sense of her stillness that we might look. What could a vibrator do in such a scenario? Mouth to mouth resuscitation was the only effective response. However, for her more moderate seizures the vibrator did appear to reduce their intensity to some degree, and we carried it with us everywhere we went—even to church!

The other parents also reported gains with the use of the vibrator, more so in some cases than in others. Gradually a whole series of vibrator stories began emerging. The first, and one of the funniest, was Debbie's own trip to *The Love Shop*. Debbie always liked to pretend that she was more worldly and sophisticated than me, but basically she was every bit as prudish if not more so. She resisted acquiring the vibrator for her son, Kent, as long as possible and I had to nag her several times to get on with it. Finally, when she had run out of all possible excuses and could put it off no longer, she went.

Debbie later described to me and the other parents her experience there. She entered the store and was immediately overwhelmed by the forest of strange objects she encountered. This so completely flustered her that she forgot the name of the vibrator she was to ask for and even forgot that it was called a vibrator. All she could remember was the word, 'doctor'. But when the man in the 3-piece pin-stripe suit approached her she did remember that he was the person she was supposed to talk to.

"I want to buy a Doctor Dildo," she blurted, when he looked at her inquiringly.

"Aah. You must be one of the GRIT parents!" he replied cheerfully.

Debbie just nodded her head mutely and he provided her with the vibrator and then asked if she wanted the therapeutic mouthpiece as well. She nodded again, paid for the second required item and then left the store as rapidly as possible.

"I have never been so embarrassed in my life!" she told us, glaring at me.

We were in general a motley crew, wrapped up in caring for our children with little time left to consider such peripheral matters as elegance and style. But one of our parents, Sandra, always presented herself in a very professional way, both in her dress and her general mien. She purchased her initial vibrator from a different clerk and used it extensively for her daughter on whom it seemed to be more effective in terms of increasing balance and reducing seizure severity than for most of the rest of our children. Brain damage comes in many forms and the results of this treatment were therefore unpredictable. In any case, about a year after acquiring her first vibrator, Sandra found it necessary to make a second trip to *The Love Shop*.

"I want to buy a new Non-doctor Vibrator," she informed Mr. 3-piece. "We wore out the first one." Nobody else in our group had ever witnessed this person looking in any sense discomposed but this time he was, according to Sandra. Only then did she realize what she had said. She must have lost some of her own poise at that point too, and I would have liked to be there to see it!

There were other stories, but like so many of the events that happened during this period, I did not record them, and they have slipped from my memory. However, one last story I will always remember. It happened early in the second year of our operation when we had 9 new members enrolled. They were all required to buy the vibrator sets but this time I could not just expect them to do so.

Three of the families lived outside of Edmonton. Another mother, a foster parent, was an older lady, and two other families were newcomers to Edmonton from different ethnic groups. Meanwhile, our teachers and therapists wanted to get on with launching the new programs for the children and an important component for the feeding program in particular was missing. This problem was weighing on me as my husband and I planned a brief weekend trip to Vancouver together where he was speaking at a university conference.

We arrived for the conference in the evening and settled into our hotel on Broadway in downtown Vancouver. The next morning, after Joe left to give his conference presentation at the university, I looked out the hotel window only to discover that there was a Love Shop right across the street! Suddenly I had an idea. Perhaps I could buy the 7 or 8 sets of Non-Doctor Vibrators here if they stocked that many. Then I would not have to worry about anybody I knew seeing me going in or out of the store in Edmonton! But I just could not get up the nerve to go into the Love Shop alone.

When Joe returned from the conference that evening expecting me to be ready and waiting to go out to dinner, I stated that I wanted to go into the Love Shop first and check out the vibrators and I needed him to accompany me. He was not impressed that I could not manage to come away for a modest, two-day holiday with him without worrying about the program or that, having had the entire day to myself, I had not managed to perform this task independently—but he finally agreed.

We entered the shop and I looked around anxiously for a man in a 3-piece suit, but there was only an overweight young woman there looking bored and chewing gum. I wandered around timidly until I spied the Non-doctor Vibrator, but this time it was part of a kit with the therapeutic mouthpiece included. I looked at the price and immediately became excited. The kit was labelled at $29.95. This was $10 less than the two pieces together were in Edmonton!

"Pardon me," I said to the clerk.

She looked at me with raised eyebrows as if I had no right to interrupt her from her placid gum chewing. "Ye-e-s," she drawled.

"Is the therapeutic mouthpiece included with the vibrator for this price?" I asked, pointing at the $29.95 price sticker.

"The what?"

"The therapeutic mouthpiece," I replied, pointing at it.

"*That's* not a therapeutic mouthpiece!" she replied. "*That's* an anal stimulator."

I stood there in shock for a second and saw that another couple who had come into the store after us were now staring at me. Still, I had a responsibility and needed to pull myself together. "But the price?" I managed to croak. "Is that the price for both pieces?"

"Yes?" she said, a question in her voice.

"I'd like eight sets if you have them, please."

She collected the items, I paid her, and we returned to the hotel. Joe's only comment was: "How do you plan to fit all those into your suitcase?"

"I have to phone Debbie!" I replied.

"Can't it wait until we get home tomorrow? What is the point of paying long distance charges and an extra hotel fee on top of that?"

"No, I need to phone Debbie right now," I replied. As he could see that I was visibly shaking Joe conceded the point and I called her.

"Debbie, Debbie," I said when she answered.

"What?" she replied, concern in her voice.

"I bought the vibrators, eight sets. But you will never guess what we have been putting in our children's mouths!" And I told her what the clerk had said.

"Everybody knew that but *you*, Emma," was her response.

So, I guess in that case the joke was on me!

CHAPTER 20

Communication

At the time I was putting together the GRIT model, none of the key players in the area except Dr. Jeffares took my Child Development credentials very seriously. I think this was because, consciously or not, they were still operating in terms of a deviancy rather than a developmental model. They were focused on remediation, and the Skinnerian methodology being used, particularly with nonverbal individuals, seemed grounded more in animal psychology than human psychology.

Why do I say this? One of the first suggestions I was given by 'the experts' was to use 'truncated speech'. That is, I was to use as few words as possible in my efforts to build communicative bridges with my daughter. Just as we teach a dog to sit, beg, heel, and shake a paw, or ask an infant: want up? drink? go potty?, so I was to speak in similar terse language to my daughter so as not to overwhelm her.

There is, of course, a certain logic to this because Alexis most likely has a very limited capacity for filtering, abstracting and general understanding, so complex language would only confuse her. However, what is not taken into account with this mechanistic approach is the emotional component or, more specifically, the lack of one. It is not to say that there is no value in this approach. There certainly is. But what I have found through the years to work best with Alexis is empathy and body language.

Just holding her, kissing her cheek, telling her we love her while rubbing her arm gently has seemed to register more effectively in terms of establishing and maintaining a genuine connection between us than terse, two-word questions. Since her physical limitations provide her with no way to respond directly, a lot of guesswork is involved, but communication has always come through some bodily response. Here are some examples.

When Alexis needs to go on her commode and I am feeding her, I note when she stops eating or puts her head down. I ask her: "Do you need to go to the bathroom, Alexis?" Out of that statement I am quite sure she can pick out the key word, 'bathroom', because, when a word is relevant to her needs, I have noted that she will suddenly become still for a second. Then, if I take off her tray and start moving her wheelchair in the direction of her bathroom area, I have often noted that she will smile and look happy and relaxed. If, instead, I turn in the other direction towards her bedroom because I think she needs to rest she will start fussing if I have guessed wrong. Once she is on the commode and functions successfully, I cannot help but say "good girl!" I say this in my natural, genuinely pleased voice and not in a formulaic manner. And she always grins when I react this way, so I know we are communicating meaningfully at those times.

What is important in the scenario just described is that Alexis feels valued, respected and understood. She knows that she is safe, that people are taking her needs seriously, and are there to care for her and make sure she is all right. She therefore feels secure, and I think that she also feels she has a place in this world and certain rights. I know this because of the different ways in which she responds to different people.

When Alexis' assistants are on her wavelength, I see her relaxing and I hear her contented sounds. When they are not but are trying hard, new assistants usually, I see her more tense but still somewhat patient, perhaps making minor complaining noises. But when they have been there awhile, and either cannot or will not make the connection, I hear the complaints becoming louder.

Sometimes I see on her face a look of patient resignation as if she understands they will only be there a few hours and she needs to make the best of it because they mean well. Often these are people able to connect with her and bring value to her life in some ways but not in others. But when none of this is the case, on unfortunate occasions when I have hired someone who talks the talk but does not walk the walk, Alexis complains loudly, looks very unhappy when they arrive, gets stressed and seems to have more seizure activity than usual, or acts very tired and goes to sleep unnecessarily, presumably to escape the situation.

When the latter situation arises, I have to act and find a way to get rid of that person. Since it generally happens during the probationary period this is not a legal problem. But it is a moral one. I try to find a way to make it about their best interest, not about their failure, about how much happier and more effective they would be in using their skills and compassion through working with someone who could communicate their needs verbally.

I noted very early on that it was when Alexis felt safe and secure, i.e., she could trust that her needs would be met, that we were able to begin communicating meaningfully. She would make her little sounds and I would respond as appropriately as I could. To this day her father and I can tell by her sounds alone, even though we are upstairs, and she is on the main floor, what type and intensity of need she has.

CHAPTER 21

Conditional Learning

It was through the lens of early child development theory and through my own experiences of mothering two older children that I approached the mothering of Alexis. First and foremost, I needed her to feel safe and secure. That is the basis of all communication and of all subsequent pro-social behaviour. I held her and nursed her and changed her and talked to her just as I had with my other two. But the difference was that when she was too weak and tired to nurse I gave her a bottle, and when she started to choke I responded quickly and helped her to clear her airway, and when she had a seizure I held her after and rocked her until she calmed down. This is normal, innate mothering behaviour. 'Bonding theory' is simply an analysis of this behaviour.

But I could not sit with her and entertain her all day with two other children to worry about, a house to run, a husband to communicate with and an unfinished thesis constantly nagging at me. Not to mention the elephant in the room. It is boring to spend day after day entertaining your child. The caring part is not so hard, but the entertaining part is more difficult. What do you do and how do you do it—particularly in a situation like this where no advance scouts have laid down the track for you?

Knowing all this and knowing that I could not do it myself I had no choice but to devise the GRIT program. I knew that love and empathy and patience were not enough. There were no saints available for hire. For this to be more than protracted babysitting that would inevitably become boring and unsustainable, not to mention unproductive, there needed to be a program in place—a structured program. And there I could buy into some of the behavioural or cognitive behavioural philosophy.

Long before I started GRIT, I knew that some form of conditioning was required to bring Alexis into the human world of communication and interaction. Early on I observed that Alexis could benefit from a simple form of conditional learning. She showed me this by the way she learned that her cry would lead to creaking sounds in the hall and the creaking sounds would lead to a presence (sometimes me and sometimes her father) who would look after her needs. I know she made this connection because it did not take long before the creaking sounds alone were enough to stop her crying.

This example, minus the floor creaking, could be described as a form of Operant Conditioning (i.e. Alexis operates on her environment in a particular way, in this case by crying, and then a predictable, positive result occurs when someone comes to attend to her needs. However, Alexis and others who share her profound level of disability do not have the physical and/or cognitive capacity to operate on their environment at will, other than in this very limited sense. For her and her cohort a more promising answer lies in classical conditioning.

We see an example of classical conditioning in the way Alexis was able to pair floor creaking with the immediate arrival of a helpful presence. However, for classical conditioning to have any real effect in this case it would have to be part of a closely structured schedule. That became the other principle building block of the GRIT model. First it was a developmental instead of a deviancy approach; and second, it was based on a learning theory grounded in classical conditioning and build around a closely structured daily schedule that would encompass all aspects of normal development.

With advice from Colleen I concluded that the best way to do this was to break the day into 15-minute chunks of 8 basic areas of skill development, repeated as needed throughout the day. These areas were initially gross motor, fine motor, language, vision, hearing, sensory (touching, smelling, tasting), cognition and self-help skills. Each child had different strengths and weaknesses, however, and the schedule was adjusted to meet their needs.

There was a third major component to the program as well that I will simply call being-ness. The assistant worked with the child 7 hours a day, although in some cases the mothers preferred a half day schedule of 3½ hours, either morning or afternoon, because of their child's need for long daytime naps. The role of the assistant was to be constantly attentive to the child. There was minimal paperwork and no other administrative duties involved so this was possible. The mother was obliged to be in the home while the assistant was there except in special circumstances. She would prepare the child's lunch and provide what other assistance might be needed.

I have no hard data to support what follows. Although baseline measures of development were taken by Colleen at the start of the program, the introduction of the program itself brought with it so many confounding variables: new assistant, new teacher, new therapists, a huge change in schedule, that it is impossible to say what factors resulted in the gains that we observed in the first six months.

All I can say in retrospect is when I first met a number of the original 13 children, they appeared withdrawn and unaware, focused in on themselves and not on the world around them. Some just flapped their hands idly in front of their faces in an autistic-like manner, yet only one of them was actually diagnosed as autistic. But it did not take long after the program began for this behaviour to change. The assistant came in every day and for the most part cheerfully focused on the child. I could not be in 5 places, and the next year 13 places, at once, of course, but we did have frequent meetings and I also received regular feedback from the teachers, Colleen, and in year two a second teacher, Anne Price. They visited each family weekly, dividing the families up between them. Additionally, I learned much in our weekly group therapy sessions.

What do I think happened? And this I do base on feedback— feedback directly from the mothers as well as a careful system of charting and graphing organized by Colleen. First of all, having the assistant there to take away much of the burden and responsibility of the mother during the days changed the whole atmosphere in the home. It became more peaceful, orderly and inviting. Secondly, with someone talking to them and attending to their needs all day the child began to respond. Thirdly, with the structured program that was laid out the child began to predict what would happen next and with prediction comes a sense of control and with that sense of control comes a greater willingness to invest. We all know this through our own personal experiences in life.

Perhaps most importantly of all, just witnessing someone working in a patient and engaging manner with their child—and reinforcing him or her every time they responded appropriately—functioned as a powerful role model for the parents and helped them to see their son or daughter as a child first and as disabled second. What I think has often been overlooked in other programs designed to help this population is how deeply hurt and saddened parents are by the tragic loss of the normal child they were looking forward to, and how long it can take to come to terms with that trauma. The assistant's positive attitude and respectful engagement with the child on a daily basis did much to normalize the situation.

CHAPTER 22

GRIT grows and grows and grows

A fter I saw and heard of the children's developmental gains throughout the program, however incremental they were, I knew that I had been right to work so hard to establish an intensive, home-based program with a paid assistant to follow through on the suggestions of the program experts (teacher and therapists). But there was still work to be done and we carried on with videotapes to chart the children's progress and with various presentations, workshops and seminars to describe what changes we were finding.

Debbie worked with me on some of these talks. For example, we did a presentation together on the GRIT program in 1983 at the 3rd International Conference on Mental Retardation in Toronto. And sometimes Colleen and I presented, as we did at the Psychology Association of Canada Annual Conference in Banff in 1984. Joe and I even presented together, and still do on occasion. An early instance was in 1985, at an Obstetrics and Gynaecology Conference in Edmonton. We described the path we had travelled with Alexis and explained why the GRIT program had been developed and how it worked.

Many times I worked on my own, trying to get across to various audiences and in various venues the learning model developed for GRIT, the gains we had observed, and why I thought they were happening. In 1986, in collaboration with three GRIT parents and one assistant, we analyzed the assessment results available to date from the early GRIT students and prepared a 100-page research paper on the program, solicited by the Alberta Department of Health. I also published a couple of papers in Entourage, the journal for what was then called The Centre for Mental Retardation. The name is now the G. Alan Roeher Institute. And I talked about the program to any interested participant I could find at other conferences I attended for my own professional purposes.

In all these ways we managed to stimulate interest in the GRIT model and, as I have learned through recent discussions with the current GRIT director, people still come from other places, and sometimes even other countries, to find out more about how this unique program operates, and how it meets the needs of young children once regarded as untreatable.

What was this 'research' we were describing? How valid was it? Really, all we could do was a series of single subject studies. While the children all shared the common label then in use for funding purposes of 'multiply and severely disabled', they were all different in terms of their specific types of brain damage and resulting behavioural manifestations. That is to say, they all had different strengths and challenges.

In our second year of operation there were even a few children who were not in wheelchairs, but they all had some level of physical and/or sensory disability in addition to their severe intellectual impairment, and most had seizure disorders of one sort or another. Therefore, and quite apart from the small sample size, no group study was feasible. All we could do was measure each child against his or her baseline according to the pretesting we did when they entered the GRIT program and then evaluate their gains on an individual basis.

Even at that time, in the early '80's, there was a fair amount of anecdotal information available on children facing such a high level of functional limitation and we felt confident that the gains that our children were making, according to both our observations and the ongoing testing we were doing, were considerably beyond what would have been expected without the GRIT intervention. But how and why this was happening was another question.

There were a number of factors that continued to cloud our results. Not all parents and assistants were equally knowledgeable and/or diligent in terms of maintaining the records on which the assessment process depended. Also, the negative behaviours of some of the children got in the way of measuring their actual level of functioning, as did severe seizure activity that often led to a temporary regression. Still, we had to go on measuring to the best of our ability and presenting our results in as credible a manner as possible so we could continue to receive provincial funding.

We must have been doing something right. In 2017 I attended a party celebrating the 35th anniversary of the GRIT program and, along with Dr. David Jeffares, spoke to the past and current parents in attendance. It was heartening to learn that at that point more than 1000 children had benefitted by attending this program. David and I both spoke about the process we had gone through to get the program started and approved, and we compared what we had done then to the things that were happening now with GRIT.

That GRIT has continued to flourish as it has owes much to a strong team through the years and, in particular, to its two, long-standing executive directors: Catherine McLeod who ran the program from 1990 to 2005, and Barb Reid, from 2005 to the present time. Interestingly, Barb was there at the beginning, back in 1982, as the developmental assistant for Kimberly Hagen during those first two years. She returned to GRIT in 1995, becoming the program coordinator, and later a teacher before taking up her present position. By the time she returned the Gateway Association no longer operated GRIT. It became independent in 1992 and its official name was changed to 'Getting Ready for Inclusion Today', although everyone continues to refer to it simply as 'GRIT'.

Under Catherine's leadership GRIT was further professionalized, with monthly 'professional development' workshops for all staff and annual conferences. GRIT's core values: community inclusion family-centreed practice, learning through play, and learning organization, were formalized, and access to the multi-disciplinary team involving relevant specialists outside GRIT was consolidated. GRIT also became a founding member of the Edmonton Regional Consortium (ERC), supporting parent leadership and advocacy for inclusive education.

Under Barb's leadership, GRIT expanded beyond early childhood education to create two more program streams with an increased focus on evidence-based research to guide professional practices. 'GRIT Plus' was established to meet the unique needs of preschool children with autism. ASAP (Access, Support and Participation) was extended provincially to support licensed day cares to be inclusive of all children. GRIT's program philosophy, service delivery model and research outcomes, have been shared through presentations at both provincial and international conferences. While the program is dependent on government funding, active and successful fundraising efforts have been critical in sustaining the development of several new GRIT initiatives. In 2013, GRIT was the recipient of the Human Rights Champion award from the John Humphrey Centre for Peace and Human Rights.

CHAPTER 23

A Family Crisis and a Possible Resolution

I n July of 1984 Alexis officially graduated (aged out) of the GRIT program. Starting that September, she would need to go into a school program, and the one I had selected for her was the one where my friend, Colleen Hermanson, had her classroom. This was as close to ideal as it could get in the Edmonton of 1984. Colleen had already been her teacher throughout Alexis' 2½ years on the GRIT program, so orientation was not an issue.

What *was* the issue was Joe's looming sabbatical year from his university and how we would handle it as a family? He had chosen to spend the year working at the University of Toronto as a research associate in order to complete his book, *Contrasts: Comparative Essays on Italian-Canadian Writing*. I knew that the completion of this work was important to him and that he needed to be in Toronto to do it, but he did not want to be away from the family. And yet we could not go as a family because we would be unable to receive any support for Alexis in Toronto comparable to what we had in Edmonton.

We had been mulling over this problem for several months but in March of that year a new and more threatening problem arose. At that time, we had a three-bedroom home in Windsor Park, near the University of Alberta—and we had three children. Our bedroom solution was to put bunk beds in one room for the girls with Alexis in the top bunk protected from falling out by a sturdy railing. This worked quite well except for one issue: lifting her over the top of the railing since the railing was immovable.

For a long time, I had had nagging back issues because of lifting Alexis on and off her commode, in and out of her bed and the tub, and adjusting her in her wheelchair or on her commode because she has always had a tendency to slump forward. But in March of that year something in my back just gave way. I had pain and numbness all the way from my lower back to my big toe on my left side and I was barely able to walk. My doctor referred me to a neurologist for an urgent appointment and this is what he had to say.

"You have an L4/L5 dislocation, Mrs. Pivato[13], and it is very serious. You have two choices. You can either have an operation to fuse the vertebrae, in which case you will never be able to lift again. Or you can have complete bed rest for a month and absolutely no lifting for a year. Which option would you prefer?"

I was, of course, stunned by this news—and I was in so much pain that I could not think clearly enough to make any decision at that point. *But never to lift Alexis again?* I thought to myself. *Impossible!* I went home and talked to Joe. "What does this mean for our family?" I asked him.

Somehow, we found the help I thought we would never find—and we got the extra funding from Handicapped Children's Services, as it was then called, to hire that help so Joe could at least keep working. Meanwhile, I was forced to just lie in bed trying to figure out an answer to this new dilemma.

After staying in bed for about three days the pain subsided and I was gradually able to think more clearly. I evaluated our situation, closely considering our assets. At that point Alexis was still in the GRIT program so we had help with her from 9 to 4 each weekday. And now, because of the crisis we found ourselves in, Handicapped Children's Services had agreed to pay for additional help with Alexis 8 hours a day on weekends as well as 4 hours for 3 evenings a week. It was up to Joe to do the rest for that first month until I could move around again. That included all the additional care for Alexis plus care for the other children, meal preparation and clean-up, and some minimal housework.

It was a very difficult month and it soon became apparent that even if I recovered somewhat there was no way he could leave me alone with the children during his sabbatical year. Sooner or later Alexis would have a bad seizure or choking spell that I just could not ignore, and I would instinctively pick her up. Yet the neurologist had warned me that if I did that, I could end up permanently paralyzed. Then what would we do? How could we cope?

Clearly the best solution was for the four of us to go to Toronto and leave Alexis behind for the year. That way I would not even be tempted to lift her, and my back could have the complete rest the neurologist had advised. But how on earth could I do that? What mother with any maternal sense and any sense of decency could abandon her six-year-old severely disabled daughter for a whole year?

I thought about what we had managed to accomplish for Alexis and who I knew who would remain in her corner if I were gone. Fortunately, Catherine, Alexis' GRIT assistant at that time, was a very compassionate, idealistic person who had experienced her own grief in life and was particularly sensitive to Alexis' vulnerabilities.

Catherine was getting married in two months to a young man who was working as a minister and both of them were heavily involved in his church. He also wanted to study law so he could work as a family lawyer helping people who really needed the help. Their alternative plan was to do a year's missionary work with the Inuit in the Northwest Territories.

An idea began forming in my mind. That evening I discussed it with Joe, and he agreed to it. The next day it was time to broach the subject with Catherine, which I did. I made her a proposition in words something like this: "Catherine, I admire how idealistic you are while at the same time you are so down to earth and do a wonderful job with Alexis. Not many people can combine those two qualities!" Predictably, she thanked me, seeming pleased that I valued her for who she was. But I had more to say.

"You tell me, Catherine, that you and Andy are seriously considering taking a year off next year to do missionary work up north because you both feel the need to contribute to people who really need some help in developing services." She nodded.

"But you also say that Andy wants to go back to university and study law so that in the end he can help more people in a more powerful way without buying into the usual lawyer games. He would be a different kind of lawyer, a lawyer who was there primarily to serve others, not himself."

"That's exactly right!" she said, obviously appreciating that I had understood his motivation so well.

"Well, I have a proposal for you," I went on ... "a way that you and Andy can do your missionary work while at the same time he can go back to university and work on getting his law degree. We really need help." And of course, Catherine was well aware of our situation since she worked in our home five days a week caring for Alexis.

I went on. "If you were to look after Alexis while the rest of our family went to Toronto, we would be able to stay in my father-in-law's home there rent-free.[14] That means we could leave you and Andy this home rent free and Andy could walk to the university from here. That would also save transportation and parking costs. Alexis will be going to school in the fall full time so all you would need to do is to care for her in the evenings and on weekends. She has a good relationship with you, and I would trust leaving her with you and Andy because I know you are good people and would never do anything to hurt her in any way."

Catherine, of course, was gobsmacked by this outrageous proposal but she was sharp, and I could sense her brain turning around. Of course, she needed to discuss the idea with Andy but within two days it was decided. The deal was done and the four of us started making our respective arrangements. Andy had already been making preliminary inquiries at the university. He immediately made an application to the Law program and was told informally that he would be accepted, although the formal acceptance letter only arrived much later. Catherine, too, made her plans.

In my impulsive way it had not even occurred to me that I needed to check with my Handicapped Children's Services worker before turning Alexis' world upside down like this, but now that it was all settled, I gave him a call. He seemed a bit perturbed not to have been let in on this earlier and arranged for an immediate visit.

Fortunately for us, our worker at that time was Bob Hoskins, also known as 'the six-million dollar man' because of his tendency to be generous in supporting his clients. Once he sat down with us and was brought up to date, his immediate question to Catherine was to ask her about relief care, a need that had never even occurred to me. She acknowledged that she would be newly married when this arrangement began, and she and her husband would like and need some time for themselves. Bob immediately offered her $400.00 a month to be used any way she saw fit so they could start out their marriage with a reasonable lifestyle not always stifled by Alexis' needs. I remember feeling almost annoyed by this, thinking that a rent-free house in our neighbourhood, furnished all the way down to towels, sheets and full kitchen equipment had to be adequate compensation for caring for one six-year-old.

I don't know now how I could have even thought that. I know that I always believed other people were better able to provide care for Alexis with far less energy expenditure than me because of their superior skills and inner sense of calm and intactness. In those days I still had a lot to learn about human nature and human limitations, and I had a long way to go yet in terms of finally getting myself in proper perspective.

There were various other wrinkles remaining to work out, like a monthly sum to provide for the special elements in Alexis' diet and any other expenses she might have, but finally all was in place and by mid-August we were ready to leave. The night before we left, I did not go to bed. All that day and all through the night I fanatically did housework to leave the place scrupulously clean and in order.

Logically, I should have been spending the day with Alexis but as often happened that took second place to my obsessions.

As arranged, Catherine and Andy arrived about ten in the morning and finally we were ready to walk out the door. We said our good-byes to Alexis and it suddenly hit me that not just in the last day, but in the entire last week, I had spent very little time with her since there were so many last-minute details to take care of. But it was too late now. The car was already loaded and running, Joe was behind the wheel and Janni and Juliana were settled in the back seat.

Joe came stomping back into the house to find out what the hold-up was. But I was in the middle of a long discussion with Alexis, apologizing, explaining and promising, trying my best to make up for past and future neglect in a few last hurried minutes. "I will see you at Christmas, Alexis. You will come out to Toronto and see Nonno, too! And Catherine and Andy are here and they won't let anything bad happen to you ... and you will probably have more fun with them than with us, anyway, because they aren't just going to sit around the house with you all the time like we mostly do!"

"Okay, enough!" Joe interjected. He said good-bye to Alexis and kissed her again! I could hear the rough note in his voice, and I knew he was suffering too. And what did Alexis do all this time? She just looked at us, although she cannot see we are told, and there was a sad, complaining note in her voice, or so I imagined. "She knows!" Joe said ... and I nodded my head, unable to speak because of the lump in my throat. He grabbed my hand and we left.

CHAPTER 24

A New Beginning

I **cried off** and on all the way to Winnipeg. *How could I have done such a terrible thing?* I asked myself. The children were very quiet in the back seat. They were feeling it too. And Joe was uncharacteristically patient with me, not his usual response to my tendency to second-guess myself. But I had been driven by a second motive as well.

Janni and Juliana had not been doing too well. It was bad enough that Alexis sucked up so much time and energy to their detriment. But they had just been through several months of dealing with my medical crisis that had taken even more away from them. They must have felt like orphans at that point. In the next few months I was to realize just how bad the situation had been and how dangerous for our family was the road we had been heading down.

We stopped for dinner at North Battleford, Saskatchewan, in a surprisingly sophisticated restaurant. At that moment I saw my children begin to emerge from the protective shell they had been hiding under for some time. They studied the menu curiously. Janni ordered Frog's Legs and Juliana ordered tripe. They both ate with gusto and I realized that that was at least one thing we had been able to do for them. We had introduced them to a lot of different foods and had little patience with the much discussed 'children's pickiness'. Thus, they had an appreciation of good and tasty food that many of their peers lacked.

By the end of that meal I realized that, whatever the cost, I had done the right thing for our family; even apart from my own serious back problems. And the tears that then sprang into my eyes were tears of relief and of an emerging sense of joy at the prospects that lay ahead. I only hoped that it was not too late to provide all the long overdue love and attention that they so obviously needed.

Joe was also aware of the need to spend more time and attention on Janni and Juliana, but he had an additional concern—me—and not just my medical issues but my languishing career. I had received my Ph. D. in 1980 and it was now 1984. All I had to show for those years in terms of career preparation was my volunteer work with GRIT and my edited book, *Different Hopes, Different Dreams*.

Once we settled into to his father's home in Toronto, Joe urged me to contact both Toronto school boards and inquire about a possible school psychology position. It was now mid-August and I told him that was a ridiculous idea. Surely, they had all their staff in place by now. But he scoured the papers and found that the Metro Separate School Board was looking for a one-year replacement psychologist. He handed me the phone and the phone number and just stood there waiting for me to call. It was a Friday morning.

When I reached the contact person and told her a little about myself, and explained that we were there just for the year of my husband's sabbatical I was asked to come in for an interview that very afternoon, as that was when they were interviewing the other candidates that had applied for the position.

"I can't," I said. "I'm sorry but I already have an appointment about another possible job opportunity." Joe was listening to me and shaking his head incredulously. The 'job opportunity' was actually an appointment with an employment counsellor to discuss how I could get a job in Toronto!

Fortunately for me and for us, Metro Separate did not find

anyone that sounded as appropriate as me for their temporary position, so later that afternoon when I had returned from my appointment, the same woman phoned me back and asked me to come in for an interview on Monday morning. This time I accepted gladly, and I was offered the position that very morning. Then I met with the human services consultant to determine where I fit on the wage scale.

I explained what I had been doing with my time since I graduated and what I had accomplished. I thought since it was all volunteer work, it would not count towards pay level, even though in my heart I knew I had made an important contribution. Apparently, this counsellor thought so too because it seemed like for every little contribution I thought I had made he notched me up a step on the pay grade.

Logically, this should have delighted me. Finally, all the hard work I had been doing over the past few years to get the book together and get GRIT going was being validated by a professional, something I had wanted to happen for a long time. But all I could feel at that moment was embarrassment and a sense of unworthiness, like I was really a fraud. In retrospect I guess I was suffering from imposter syndrome. Although the other GRIT parents I worked with had always appreciated my efforts on their behalf very much, some of the medical and academic professionals I had been involved with through the years had not, and I found it very hard to not believe that somehow they were right.

But now I had a job—in my field—a paid, professional job! And I would be going into work the very next day to get oriented before the school year started in a week. I went home and informed the family that I was taking them all out to dinner to celebrate and would pay the cost out of my first paycheque. I felt all kinds of feelings: pride, excitement, and an almost unbearable eagerness to just get started!

The next week was big. The children were going out the door to their new school and I was going out the door to my new job. Joe, too, was going to his assigned office at the University of Toronto as often as possible, but it had to take second place at the beginning to getting the rest of us settled in. Also, I was frequently on the phone with Catherine to see how Alexis was adjusting to her own new school situation. Fortunately, my father-in-law was retired and was manning the fort at home and preparing dinners!

CHAPTER 25

Emma, the School Psychologist!

I **felt positively** giddy to be starting this new school psychology position and once I was there, I pulled in all the new information avidly. As I did assessment work with the various children, I discovered that I really did have some talent in that area, and this was frequently confirmed for me by the feedback I received from my supervisor. I travelled all around the city in my father-in-law's car, providing psychological assessment and consultation services to students in seven different schools.

I met all kinds of interesting people, colleagues and clients alike. And I had the opportunity to participate in professional workshops including an intensive two-day workshop by Dr. Edith Kaplan on her specialized model of neuropsychological assessment, the Boston Process Approach.[15] Because of Alexis' problems this was my particular area of interest. I kept hoping that this deeper approach to analyzing brain functions would have some relevance for her.

As I worked with one student after another in various schools and with different principals and other school personnel, I came to realize something about myself. As much as I had wanted an academic career and had even continued to make half-hearted and unrealistic attempts to gain an academic position in the disabilities field, I really enjoyed working directly with people. I felt my strength and became aware of some inner skills I had not even known were there. It made me think of my father who had died when Juliana was born and I realized that I had learned something very important from him.

My father's story and my whole relationship with him became very poignant to me, and as my year in Toronto progressed, I thought more and more about this. As I dealt with children and parents from all kinds of circumstances, I found myself wondering what my father would do, and how he would perceive the situation. I considered what I knew about his early history that might have caused him to become the man he was. I wondered about certain personality qualities I might have inherited from him—because I knew from my studies that some of these qualities are innate: hard-wired.

I remembered particularly how nonjudgmental and respectful of others he was. An old Indigenous proverb that my father was fond of citing was "Never judge a man until you walk a mile in his moccasins." I was able to carry this tolerance and understanding into my work with students and later clients, but not always with others. My mother's influence had been too strong.

In the midst of all this joyful excitement of actually starting my professional career I did have one fear. The year was supposed to be for Janni and Juliana, for an opportunity to reconnect with them more closely and to get them on the right track. Increasingly I felt that they were turning to their friends for the support I should be offering them. Now they had been yanked out of their context and away from their friends and needed me more than ever—at the very time I was preoccupied with all the new learning and demands of my job.

But as it turned out my fears were unfounded. I was coming at this whole issue in the old way, from the point of view of joyless duty and obligation. Now I had something exciting to share with them. I had interesting work to do and interesting people to talk to every day and by the time I came home I was ready to relax and spend quality time with my children.

We did a lot of things that year that we had never had the time or opportunity to do before. Juliana and I joined a ballet class together. Janni found friends in a special giftedness group that had been set up by the separate school board. And both children enjoyed their time with Nonno and formed friendships in the Italian neighbourhood where he lived. With Italian culture at our doorstep, Joe had the opportunity to share more of his world with them. We cooked together, ate meals out together, went to movies and visited relatives together. Most importantly, we spent time together without one or another of Alexis' crises interfering, as had always seemed to be the case back in Edmonton.

CHAPTER 26

Further Reflections

One of the most wonderful things about our year in Toronto was that I finally had the time and space to think. The six years since Alexis had been born had been so chaotic and jam-packed with plans and duties and her medical concerns that I could barely move from one day to the next, much less reflect on what had happened the day or month or years before. But now, despite my busy schedule and the usual demands of a family, I had that time.

One thing I felt that I needed to do as I moved on in our life with Alexis was to better understand my strengths and my weaknesses, so I knew what I had to work with and what I needed to work around. It was actually quite a luxury to even have the time to think about such things and I did quite a lot of ruminating those first few months.

In particular, I slowly and persistently recalled fragments from my early life on the farm and the relationship I had formed with my mother. The yip of coyotes and the bay of timber wolves at night, the heat haze and buzz of flies over the wheat fields, the whine of mosquitos in the daytime: life on a northern Alberta dirt farm. The outhouse and the tall Jack Pine, the incredible pungency of tiny, wild strawberries, the sharp but comforting smell of kerosene lamps or the hiss of lanterns. The strange experience of standing in the road—no more than a trail really—and seeing at every turn the end of the world, the tall trees rising up to the sky and foreclosing all that lay beyond, if anything did. And a little person, such as I was then, could not be sure.

Riding to town, a six-house town only, by horse and wagon. The fascinating experience of watching the horse perform his horsely functions in front of us as he walked along in his harness: a black hole opening up bigger and bigger, impossibly big to the little eyes watching. When, years later, I learned about 'worm holes' in space, that sense of wondering what lay beyond, about an opening that had not been there and then suddenly was, came back to me.

I remember how peaceful that ride was—but it wasn't always that way within the drafty walls of our un-insulated farmhouse, built from the Jack Pine that surrounded us. In those very early years my mother seemed pleased with me, pleased by my funny questions and ability to quickly memorize the poems she read to me from *A Child's Garden of Verses*. But she was often irritable, unhappy and quick to anger. And soon she found reasons to be angry with me.

Some days I felt her anger through her hand and through her eyes. Yet other days were different. She read to me so musically, her love of language oozing through the words. She took joy in how I listened and remembered, telling the words back to her, keeping faithful to their rhythm.

My mother talked to me and told me things about the world at that time. But I don't remember them. I only remember her response one day when I must have said something particularly clever. "Someday, you will go to university and you will get a Ph. D." I spent too many years of my young adult life striving for that goal and when I finally succeeded, she was no longer there to see it.

In those early years on the farm my mother rode to the country schoolhouse about five miles away where she was the only teacher for students in all the grades. She did not travel in a car with a heater and windshield wipers and a roof. Rather, she went on horseback through the fall and the winter and the spring. Sometimes on the coldest days, she took the team and wagon and picked up school children along the way.

Mother was a committed teacher. She gave all she had, trying to impart to her students her own love of learning. She was encouraging, clear, logical, supportive and systematic. I know that because later, much later, I witnessed her in action when I was a student teacher myself. At that point, she was literally dying of cancer, but she was still an amazing teacher.

Another thing I remember about her and the comments she made through the years: she was always compassionate towards her students, always ready to help the weak one, the underdog. I have often wondered how she would have responded to Alexis if she had lived to meet her. I like to think that she would have believed in her, as did my mother-in-law; that she would have supported me in my efforts to help my daughter; and even that it would have helped to heal the huge breach that gradually grew up between us.

But when she came home from school my mother was a different person, often angry or crying or yelling at my father. I remember how frightened I always was, how I cowered. And to this day I believe I am fundamentally a coward, afraid of the world but just forcing myself, often at considerable cost, to face it anyway because bigger considerations are at stake.

When I was little, on those nights when my mother was particularly angry and upset, I would often wet the bed. If she heard my cries and got up, she would punish me. And then I hated myself because I knew I had done wrong. But mostly it was my father, the lighter sleeper, who heard me and who got up stealthily and comforted me and changed the sheets and my nightclothes. He told me years later that he would hide the wet clothes and wash and dry them by hand the next day when my mother was at school and then put them away so she wouldn't know. He told me not to tell.

So that was my early life and those were the peculiar family dynamics that formed me. At least, I think they were peculiar. But you never really know how other people live, or whether your own circumstances are really all that exceptional.

Fast-forward 34 years to the birth of Alexis. I relived this momentous event again and again in my mind. Alexis had arrived in this world all white and still, so different from the births of her brother and sister. I knew even then that there was something seriously wrong but later I seemed to forget. How could I forget something so important? I recalled how the nurse had taken her away before I even had a chance to see Alexis' face. Why did she do that? And then that moment when she brought her back all tightly swaddled up, so I could only touch my daughter's hand—her finger coiling weakly around mine. And then my promise to her that we would be partners. Would I have even said that if I had known how radically that rash promise would change all our lives?

Those early months after Alexis was born had passed hazily, as I now recalled. I think that I shut my mind down. I knew but I didn't know—and the doctors said nothing. I needed to buy a baby book. We already had "My little boy" and "My little girl." To buy a similarly titled book seemed to me redundant so, ironically, I bought one entitled "My baby's milestones." I did not complete very many entries in it.

As I have said, I thought a lot about my father that year, because he really did influence how I functioned as a psychologist and dealt with other people, both in good ways, as in my work with students and families, and in not so good ways, as in my difficulties in asserting myself sufficiently at times with others.

I did not inherit much of my father's musical talent, but I did have his sensitivity. The harsh treatment we both received as children stayed with us and helped to form who we became. Both of us shrank from conflict, lacked the ability to defend ourselves, and were slow to cast blame where it belonged.

My father crept around the edges of my mother's anger and put up with a lot of emotional abuse without responding in kind. When she directed her unreasonably fierce anger at me he would later tell me privately, "Don't mind your mother when she gets like this. She doesn't mean what she says to you. She is just high-strung, and she can't help herself. And there are things you don't know." Only years later, on the day my mother died, did he finally tell me the whole story about "the things I didn't know." Long before she met my father, my mother had a child, a son she had to give up. It tortured her all her life and profoundly affected her relationship with me, my brother, and my father.

CHAPTER 27

The Men I Married

I married Joe just a few months before my 30th birthday but he was not my first husband. Before him there was George Price, a philosophy professor at the University of Alberta. George died of kidney failure when I was 27. Of the 5½ years we had together he had been ill for 3 of them, and in critical condition in hospital for much of that time. It was hard to lose him—and very hard to believe I could ever trust another man that much again or feel as close as I had felt to George.

When I finished my undergraduate degree in philosophy and psychology at the University of Alberta, I chose to do a Masters' degree in philosophy largely because of how inspired I had been by George's undergraduate level Existentialism course. At the beginning I idolized him. I loved his beautiful mind, the lovely Welsh lilt in his voice, his deep understanding of the world, and his warm, charismatic personality. But as I got to know him better, I saw how he spent all his energy looking after others and neglecting himself. I saw how grey and thin and lost he looked some days and I worried about him.

Christmas was coming and I contemplated what I could do to ease his obvious loneliness. I thought I could buy him a small dog, a Chihuahua perhaps, that would provide some company for him during his long evenings alone. I, of course, wanted it to be a surprise so

I did not tell him my plan and was quite perplexed and disappointed when he seemed less than enthusiastic upon receiving my gift. It turned out that the apartment where he lived had a no pets rule and I was neither able to accommodate the dog in my own lodgings nor return it to the person who had sold it to me.

We conspired together on ways he could surreptitiously maintain the dog, and somewhere in that discussion something else happened. I had been marginally aware that he was beginning to see me as more than a student and a friend but had never acknowledged that idea to myself as it seemed too ridiculous due to the large age gap between us. But it happened anyway and the hero worship and the compassion I had initially felt for him turned into a deep and genuine love.

Soon the dog became an issue because of its annoying proclivity to bark for no good reason and a decision had to be made. In retrospect, taking it to the SPCA would have been an obvious solution. Another eager dog lover would most likely have snapped up a small, purebred dog like that very quickly. But either that thought did not occur to me or was not acceptable to me, and George and I began looking for a house to purchase where nobody could tell him whether or not he could have a dog.

We found the house and I spent as much time with him there as I could because I was finding every minute away from him increasingly painful. And as soon as it was possible to do so, George and I were married.

Living with George was like a soothing, healing balm after the emotionally charged family life I had known. Due to my mother's insistence, our family had moved to Calgary, shortly before my 13th birthday, a place my father never wanted to go. After that, he worked away from home most of the time, cooking in one construction camp or another. My mother was frustrated and unhappy much of the time and was often very critical. It seemed like she saw little of worth in me. But George did. He appreciated my mind and my personality and helped me to improve in both those areas. We spent hours every day talking together. From him I learned much I did not know about the history of the world and human affairs. Where my mother had been harsh, he was gentle, and where she had been punitive, he was supportive.

His illness, kidney replacement, and his slow, painful rehabilitation only to be followed by sudden relapse and death were very difficult times. I tried my best to give back to him at that time a small portion of what he had given to me. I wanted to give him all the love and care and nurturing he would need to either recuperate or to be gently eased out of this world.

When George died, I was halfway through writing my Masters' thesis in philosophy, an analysis of the ethical position laid out by the French Existentialist philosopher, Jean Paul Sartre. Although reeling from my loss, I knew that I could not use that as an excuse for not finishing my thesis. To not finish would have been to betray all that George had invested in me.

I finally finished the thesis a year later in the spring of 1972, around the same time that I met that irritating man, Joe Pivato. I would not have met him, and I most certainly would not have seen him a second time, but for my good friend, Edith Gruber. Like Joe, she was doing graduate work in Comparative Literature, but through that spring and the following fall and winter, she hosted several different parties. Joe and I were both invited to these events and she kept contriving to bring us together when we were there, always pointing out to each of us how much we ostensibly had in common with the other!

Years later, I asked Edith why she had been so persistent in her matchmaking efforts and she finally confessed. George had been an important source of support to her, academically and also personally when she was struggling to come to terms with the tragic death of her oldest son and trying to pull her life back together. Two years after that sad event, when George himself was dying, she had visited him in the hospital, and he had asked her to help me when he was gone and to make sure that if I remarried it was to the right kind of person. When I did finally begin seeing somebody on a casual basis,

Edith decided he was not someone George would approve of, and that this Joe person was—so she took action!

Joe, like Edith, was very persistent—and gradually I came to see his layers. Beneath his surface crustiness was a shy, naïve and idealistic person who, like me, loved knowledge for its own sake and wanted to contribute whatever it was he had to offer that would be of value to this world. But getting to know Joe Pivato at this level was neither an easy nor a straightforward process.

I tried to explain to him that I was not in the mental space where I either wanted or could handle another relationship. But he would not listen. His response was typically harsh: "Fine, just don't expect me to hang around waiting while you get yourself together." But I remained on my track and he remained on his and finally he decided to break off whatever relationship we had been in the process of developing.

Although I had been temporarily side-tracked into philosophy, my main academic interest had always been psychology and I looked at our split through a psychological lens. How did I feel? Now that he was gone, I realized that only yesterday the world had been in colour and today it was in black and white. That is the only way I can describe how I felt. Then two days later in the afternoon, I was walking towards my car in the parking stall at the university that Joe had been allotted because he was staying in a graduate student residence. He had passed it on to me since he had no need of it, and since I had loaned him my book of Aristotle's collected works for one of his seminars. I might add that these negotiations between us, as well as others, were all due to Edith's interference in our lives under the guise of being helpful!

Anyway, as I walked along, I saw something sticking out from under my windshield wiper, and when I got closer, I realized it was a red rose and a piece of paper. On the paper was written a love poem for me, and just like that my world turned back into colour!

Joe and I have been married now for almost 50 years, but I will never forget the feeling I had when I read that poem. I felt like my very self was coming back into myself, like I was a whole person again. Our relationship has never been peaceful and sedate. We rub each other the wrong way fairly constantly. But underneath that surface friction lies a deep mutual respect and appreciation that we each hold for the other. And with that came trust, and with trust came love: the love and trust I had thought I would never feel again!

CHAPTER 28

Alexis Alone

As I have said, I had a lot of time to think during our year in Toronto. I thought much about Alexis, and also about my mother. Despite her many challenges and limitations, Alexis has always had about her a kind of grace. And somehow that grace had brought to life in me the power to work harder and accomplish more for her that I had ever been able to do for myself.

In that sense we had become partners, as I so presciently told her when she was born. Through Alexis I had become a better and stronger person than I would have been otherwise. And through my efforts, Alexis was having a chance at a better and longer life than would otherwise have been the case.

I also thought a lot about the influence my mother had on me before her death on the day before my 23rd birthday. Her angry tirades and harsh criticisms when I was a child really did leave me with a lingering self-doubt that got in my way many times. But that was just one side of her, the part that I didn't understand, as my father used to say. Apart from that she was a good, and even an admirable, person: strong-minded, but also conscientious, hard-working, and idealistic. And I realized then that whatever strength and determination I had shown in my struggles to help Alexis were primarily the result of her influence—her influence and Alexis's grace.

At other times that year I reflected on my past readings on creativity theory, specifically on the descriptions by various creative individuals about the influence certain people had had on their lives, driving them along divergent tracks to search out new directions. I felt like something similar had happened to me, although at a more modest level. I always liked to carve out my own path and to find my own truth. I was not going to have a career researching creativity theory and the relationship between personality structure and divergent thinking, as I had once hoped. That was gone. But what I had gained in place of an academic life was the opportunity to live a creative life of my own because of the constant drive inside me to find a better way to help my daughter and the constant need to think outside the box in order to do so.

At Christmas time, as we had arranged, Alexis came to Toronto with one of her assistants and spent about ten days with us. She seemed happy to see us again, particularly her father, and we gradually fell back into our old rhythm. But all too soon it was time for her to leave. I called that evening after she returned to Edmonton to talk to her, to tell her I loved her, that I would see her again in a couple of months, and that I missed her very much. And I will never forget how she responded. It is burned into my brain. It won't sound like much on paper, but it meant everything to me.

"Aah, aaah, ah, ah, **ah**, ah!" Which immediately translated to me as: *Why did you leave me, again?* That was what I heard from her. And my brain and heart charged along two contradictory paths. *She knows me! She wants me! She is aware!* But at the same time, I felt a horrible, clanging guilt: *she feels abandoned!*

This was all too much to take in at once and it took me weeks to process it. But when I could more coolly reflect on our Toronto life, I still knew we had made the right choice, painful as it was for us and for Alexis. Our family had made a U-turn. We were happy and together once again—in a way that had not been possible since Alexis was born. In a family you sometimes must sacrifice for each other. Janni and Juliana had done their sacrificing. This year it was Alexis' turn.

Alexis' year with Catherine and Andy was not completely without complications. One spring-like day in late winter, when the ice and snow on the roads was starting to break up, Catherine took her out, fastened into her trunk support on the arctic sled. While crossing a road the sled hit a chunk of ice and flipped over. Alexis fell directly on her face against a hard chunk of rock and ice and chipped off a large corner of her permanent front tooth. Fortunately, it did not destroy the tooth but to this day, every time I look at it, I am reminded of the price Alexis paid for us to have that precious year in Toronto.

During Easter break I went back to Edmonton alone to see Alexis and also to meet with the GRIT parents whose children were now of school age and no longer eligible for the GRIT program. Over the previous two years in two separate research projects I had been drawing up plans for a grouping model that, if accepted by the public school board, would allow us to keep the GRIT program intact once the children were in the school system. But now I told the parents that in my opinion we should abandon all that and just push for straight integration (now called inclusion) in our respective neighbourhood schools with a fulltime assistant in attendance.

The parents quickly agreed with me, wanting to keep their children close to home. I returned to Toronto and they worked with the relevant school personnel to make it happen. As a result, our children were actually the first group of cognitively disabled children to be fully integrated into regular classrooms in Edmonton, well before their less-disabled peers.

This is not so surprising as it might sound. Because of their high level of need they had a correspondingly high level of funding support that made it financially possible to have individual assistants exclusively assigned to them. Thus, the assistant was able to maintain almost full responsibility for the child, with the teacher only needing to draw up the program plan in consultation with the school board's special needs experts and to provide the legal supervision required.

By the time our family returned to Edmonton that summer of

1985, the parents and Public-School consultants had everything in place to include our pilot group of GRIT children in regular classroom settings. The education specialist assigned to Alexis had approached the principal in the neighbourhood school that Janni and Juliana had been attending before our trip to Toronto and where Alexis had been integrated afternoons into the school daycare program for two years. However, the response was not what we had hoped for.

The principal decided against having Alexis as a student in the school. Apparently, a number of the parents had met with her and argued strongly against this idea. They saw Windsor Park as a superior school with a strong academic focus and they did not want to have someone like Alexis there taking up teacher time and energy that could better be spent on their children.

I felt so hurt and angry about the school's rejection of my daughter that I convinced my husband we should move to Aspen Gardens where Vernon Barford School was located. It was advertised as hosting an academic enrichment program for gifted children. My reasoning was that if one of my exceptional children could not be accommodated in our neighbourhood school, I could at least see to it that the other one was. Meanwhile, the school consultant assigned to Alexis' case found an integrated placement for Alexis at Allendale School.

Marcus, 11, and Alexis, 7, 1985, the summer we returned from Toronto

CHAPTER 29

Alexis and I both start school

That fall of 1985, after returning to Edmonton, I was able to attain a position as a part-time psychology instructor at what was then known as Concordia University College. I remained there for two years, during which time I was able to complete the provincial government research project I mentioned earlier. I also had the opportunity to teach a number of different psychology courses, as well as an education course that I found very interesting.

Meanwhile, Alexis was in her own school setting at Allendale. The school board educational consultant, Donna Barwick, had very carefully thought out her new placement. There was a strongly supportive principal at that school and an excellent teacher. I was still angry and resentful that it was not our home school and wasn't a school in the kind of neighbourhood I was used to living in. I also felt like we were dumping on them since Alexis was not a member of their community and that it was devaluing for both her and them. Furthermore, that school was already running a segregated program for autistic children, so they had a number of children who had unusual educational needs to begin with, and I didn't like that in terms of ratio.

As it turned out, however, the inclusive setting provided for Alexis during the two years she was at Allendale School proved to be the best supportive setting she ever had throughout her entire school career. This was despite the fact, as I found out later, that the school personnel did not initially believe it would work.

Apparently, after first meeting Alexis, the staff had resisted the idea of having her there in a regular classroom setting because of their fear that she would be too intrusive and would interfere with the other students' learning. But soon they could see from her increased alertness and happy sounds that she was enjoying being there. I guess Alexis gradually won them over with her own special charm that has worked on a lot of people throughout her life!

Alexis definitely recognizes and generally responds positively when she is going outside her regular routine. When she started at Allendale, she was 7½ years old. By the time she was 8, I had given up on the notion of fixing her. Instead, I had changed my goal to enhancing her quality of life as much as possible. So, from then on, I was looking very sensitively at her signs and at what made her happy, what motivated her and what engaged her with the world around her.

The inclusion process is very complex, and all key elements have to be in place for it to work effectively. The principal, the teacher, and the other children and their parents have to be onside. Most importantly of all, there has to be a happy and energetic assistant in place. We had the first four of these elements at Allendale at the beginning —but not the fifth. The assistant that the school board had hired for Alexis seemed depressed and lacking in energy, and Alexis responded accordingly, always being very sensitive to other people's moods.

What saved the situation for much of the first year, until the assistant finally left, was the teacher, Cathy Drew. She was absolutely wonderful with Alexis and knew instinctively how best to include her in the classroom without upsetting her or the other students—while still making sure the rest of the class had the best educational experience possible. I still remember one outstanding example of this natural ability Cathy had to go with the flow, to fit Alexis in wherever she could, and to minimize her differences from the other students.

In October of Alexis' first year at Allendale there was a Hallow-een Party for the children and their parents, so I was there. I was also there because the assistant had gone home sick at noon that day and I had been asked to come in and take her place with Alexis.

I have always noticed that Alexis has seizures when she is over-stimulated, and the loud party atmosphere presented just such a situation. This was still early in the year and it was the first time most of the parents had met or even seen Alexis, who was sitting in her wheelchair right in the middle of the classroom. She chose that moment to have one of her really bad blue lip seizures. It was so bad I could not get her to breathe independently, and for 15 ½ minutes I had to continuously do mouth-to-mouth respiration.

Every time I tried to stop the respiration Alexis would just turn blue again. This was not the intermittent cyanosis that can be ob-served with Alexis and others during Grand Mal (generalized) seiz-ures, which does not require intervention because it is fleeting. But the type of cyanosis where it seems like Alexis has literally forgotten how to breathe really does require outside assistance. So this was a serious medical matter that had to be dealt with. I was just very grateful I was there.

A few minutes into it I stopped the mouth-to-mouth long enough to hiss at the teacher "Should I carry her into another room?" I wanted to spare the parents, and especially the other children this drama. "Don't be ridiculous!" was her reply. "Just carry on!"

Cathy Drew continued to sit at her desk perusing a paper as if nothing unusual had happened. When worried parents came up to ask her "What's going on?" she responded, "Oh, she's having a seiz-ure and she's not getting quite enough oxygen. The mother prefers to do mouth-to-mouth when that happens. Otherwise, Alexis tends to sleep for a long time after and misses out on her school program."

Cathy's whole approach to this situation was a model of how to include children facing very different challenges than the average child. Of course it was easier for her that I was there—the mother who could assume ultimate legal responsibility and make that judgment call as to whether or not she needed to request medical help. But I think Cathy would have also trusted Alexis' assistant in my absence because I had come into the school at the beginning of the year and trained her as to what to watch out for and what to do if Alexis had one of her cyanotic attacks.

Quite apart from knowing that the assistant had trained as a nurse, the main reason she had been hired, the teacher recognized and respected the fact that she worked with Alexis every day and therefore knew Alexis and her seizure types far better than Cathy did. If it had really been necessary to call for an ambulance the assistant would have said so. Cathy was the kind of teacher who delegated where she safely could but quickly took charge whenever it was necessary. I think that the world would be a better place if all teachers had this quality.

But, as I said, it was clear to me—and probably to Cathy—that the assistant the school had hired for Alexis had her problems. When she suddenly resigned in February of that year, I thought immediately of the school's lunchroom monitor as a possible replacement for her. I had been at the school quite frequently at lunchtime during that year, as at that point I was only teaching part-time and had a flexible schedule. The lunchroom aide, a local parent named Norma Kloos, impressed me. She had good control over the students and was always friendly towards Alexis and seemed interested in her.

I took it upon myself (being the impulsive person that I am) to broach the subject to Norma and she immediately expressed a strong interest. A formal, fulltime position with the school board was definitely advantageous to her and not something she could normally aspire to since she did not have the usual educational qualifications required. But I was not interested in such qualifications for working with Alexis. I was interested in psychologically healthy, intelligent, pro-social and energetic people who saw working with my daughter as an interesting challenge, and who had a natural ability to get along with people. In other words: no hang-ups, no depression, and no big ego needs.

I explained my reasoning to Cathy who agreed with me and felt able to strongly recommend Norma for the position, having also observed her excellent interactions with Alexis in the lunchroom. The principal agreed to follow Cathy's recommendation, knowing that I, the parent, was comfortable with it, and Norma then took over as Alexis' assistant for the remainder of that school year.

The following year Norma also remained with Alexis, but Cathy was gone on a teaching exchange to New Zealand. Her replacement was very welcoming to Alexis but did not have the same level of classroom control as her predecessor. As a result, student acceptance and interaction with Alexis did not seem to be at the same natural and spontaneous level it had been under Cathy's supervision. Though, of course, this was a different group of students since Alexis had remained in the same grade three class two years in a row, so that could have been a factor.

I was only able to make these observations and draw these conclusions because I was allowed to sit in on the class whenever I wanted to. I think that free parental access to settings where our most vulnerable children are being cared for outside the home should always be allowed and it is one of the reasons I hold the Allendale School and its principal at the time, Ken Kellough, in high regard to this day.

One positive thing this new teacher did was to end each day by engaging the class in singing several bracing songs, often those she herself must have grown up with, like *Waltzing Matilda*. Alexis, of course, enjoyed this part of the day very much. Another great thing that teacher did was to plan out various field trips for the class, making sure the buses were accessible so Alexis could go along.

As a final end of year celebration, I invited the entire class to our home to have a picnic lunch and swim in our backyard pool. That turned out to be an exciting but chaotic occasion, and one that Alexis seemed to very much enjoy. However, the next day the pool colour turned from a peaceful blue to a rather ominous shade of green—and one can only speculate as to why. I am reasonably certain it was not Alexis' fault since I always took her to the bathroom before allowing her in any pool and it had never happened before!

In the fall of 1987, I was hired into a fulltime position as an assessment psychologist at the Edmonton Public School Board as part of a team providing specialized services to school children with multiple and severe disabilities throughout Edmonton and North-eastern Alberta. I can still hear, echoing in my ears, the round of enthusiastic clapping that greeted me when I walked into the Monday morning team meeting that first day.

I knew many of the various specialists sitting in the room through my advocacy work and they told me with seeming sincerity how pleased they were to have me as part of their team. I had been appreciated for my work in Toronto but to finally be recognized and valued as a fellow professional in the disabilities field in my own city was very special—all the more so because it had been a long time coming!

I found the three years that I spent in that position to be a very satisfying and enlightening experience. I learned much from the other members of this multi-disciplinary team and gained a new objectivity through working with children facing so many different challenges. I also found it to be a very nurturing experience as we worked together cooperatively and respectfully to find the best answers possible for our clients. And lastly, but perhaps most importantly of all, I was able to finally overcome the 'us vs. them' mentality that had gripped me so long as I worked from a parent perspective only to get Alexis and others like her what they needed from 'the system'.

CHAPTER 30

The Challenge of 'Academic Challenge'

During Alexis' second year at Allendale, and my second year of teaching at Concordia University, Janni was having his own school acceptance problems. He had always been too young, too small, too bright and too ready to provide the answers in class and not all of his fellow students had appreciated that. Now that he was in an 'Academic Challenge' setting I had been hoping that his eccentricities would be better tolerated. But that did not turn out to be the case.

As I worried over this problem, I went back in my mind to the beginning of our life with our son, remembering his early arrival before we were ready to receive him. Joe was in the middle of writing his Ph. D. Comprehensive Exams in Comparative Literature at that point, and he had two weeks to complete the process. I needed to get the final edit done for my first academic paper before the journal's publication cut-off date the following week. But then our son arrived, and these pressures and obligations were driven right out of our minds when we saw him for the first time. As for our deadlines, we were each given a week's extension and managed to muddle through.

I remembered my shock when I first saw our son's black hair and black eyes. I had somehow assumed that he would be blond. Yet his father had dark hair, so it was perfectly reasonable for Janni to have the same. Soon after, however, all his baby hair fell out and was replaced by blond hair that is blond to this day. And his eyes turned green. *Aha! I thought.* It confirmed for me what I had been feeling about him, that I had known things about him even before he was born and that there was a strange connection between us.

In those days, Edmonton babies were still kept away from their mothers in the hospital nursery between feedings, although the policy had changed by the time his sister, Juliana was born 15 months later. I remembered those first nights after his birth and the primitive survival urge that suffused me. *What should I do if there is a fire?* I had asked myself. *I will go to the nursery* (that I visited often during the day, staring at him longingly through the window) *and snatch him out of his little crib and run out of the building with him as fast as I can. I will grab all his blankets to keep him warm* (it was March in Alberta) *and I won't let anyone stop me. I will keep him safe, no matter what.*

The day after his birth, the paediatrician came in to check him over and told me that Janni was a normal, healthy baby. I was relieved to hear that and before the nurse could return to take him away, I thought I should change him. I laid him across the bed and turned around to get a fresh diaper. In those few seconds Janni rolled into the empty space at the end of the bed and landed on the cloth covered bed board that supported the mattress.

I was horrified. I rang for the nurse, explained what had happened and pleaded with her to page the doctor urgently. He came promptly and re-examined Janni who was not crying, just looking surprised. The doctor assured me that no damage had been done but gently admonished me to keep my eyes on him at all times because newborns were sometimes capable of rolling over. *Yes,* I thought to myself. *That is why I laid him down two feet from the end of the bed. But he must have rolled over twice!*

My main memory of Janni's first year is how he used to wake up in the middle of the night, never crying much but looking at me intently as I fed him and changed him. When he was 15½ months old his sister, Juliana arrived. After returning home from the hospital with her, I placed her in the middle of our huge kitchen table strapped into her carrycot with a bottle nearby that I had brought with me from the hospital since I would not have been able to take her out of the car seat to nurse her if she started to cry.

Immediately upon arriving home, we had a visitor and I took my friend, Pat, into the bedroom to show her the baby gifts that had arrived. Juliana started to cry so we returned to the kitchen to meet a startling scene. Janni had managed to crawl up on the kitchen table and had placed the bottle in Juliana's mouth. She was sucking away contentedly!

Our son always had a lot of imagination and could play happily by himself, and later with Juliana for hours at a time in his make-believe world. He also tried to include Alexis in his play since he was always hearing me talk about how Alexis needed stimulation and he tried to do his part.

For one of his imaginary games he would somehow manage to pick Alexis up and carry her into the closet in his bedroom, armed only with his 'light sabre'[16] Once inside with the door closed they would take off on a voyage to Andromeda, and he would carry on an animated conversation with Alexis in his gravelly little voice as they went. The light sabre would flash on and off as I could see in the space under the door and Alexis would respond excitedly. But when the two of them finally emerged she would almost invariably have a seizure because of the overstimulation. Still, I could never bring myself to discourage Janni from bringing Alexis along on his imaginary voyages!

Overall, though, it seemed to me that Janni gave too much for his age and asked for too little. He instinctively understood that I just did not have enough to go around and he did not ask for much attention. Janni tolerated his stints at play school and Montessori School but always preferred the freedom to structure his own activities at home. I wish now that I could have been more a part of them.

He did have some interesting experiences outside of home and structured settings in those early years, however. Almost every summer we spent a few days in the mountains hiking around with Alexis in her various carts. We also travelled to Toronto every Christmas to be with Joe's family and as mentioned previously, Joe's mother visited most summers for about a month. Janni had a very close relationship with his grandparents and his Zia Louise, Joe's sister, as well as Joe's other relatives in Toronto. He felt very loved and accepted by them all, his Nonno and Nonna in particular.

Finding the right school setting for Janni had been almost as big a problem as finding the right school setting for Alexis. Well before his fifth birthday, I could see that kindergarten was not going to work for him. He had already mastered the normal kindergarten activities and was beginning to find them boring.

A good mother would have sent such a son on to kindergarten anyway so he could use that opportunity to develop his social skills. She then would have provided him with the stimulating and novel learning opportunities outside of class that he needed so that he could continue to experience the joy of learning new things. But I could not be a good mother to him. I was too busy being a good mother to Alexis.

And that is why, as mentioned previously, he ended up in a school based on a British teaching model from another era where his boundless curiosity about the world around him and concomitant endless questions were promptly squelched along with his intense interest in science that was completely dismissed as simply being not part of the curriculum. Instead he was subjected to endless hours of mindless drills and an early introduction to cursive writing that to this day he has not mastered adequately. In addition, some of the students were bullies, perhaps reacting themselves to the overly strict regimen of the school. Janni, small, young and naïve, was the perfect target.

After spending his critical first two years of school in that very negative setting we moved Janni to our neighbourhood public school, Windsor Park, where he had an excellent teacher, Gail Cloutier, for his grade three year. She enjoyed his curiosity and his observations on various issues and worked with him patiently. But she could not entirely undo the damage that had been done. She tried, and we tried, to get back the happy little boy that had been, and bursts of the former Janni did return gradually. But he was never quite the same again after his private school experience.

One happy event I do remember during that first Windsor Park school year was a group series of evening astronomy talks and walks we participated in together. This was an adult event, but I managed to get him included because of his special interest in the subject. It was also a special interest of mine.

Our guide was a well-meaning volunteer, not a trained astronomer, and Janni often asked questions this person could not answer. But one evening another group member asked about Black Holes. The group leader could provide little information on the subject, but Janni could and did.

He explained their origin and mechanism very clearly to the lady who had inquired, going into considerable detail on the subject and she, as well as the rest of the group including the guide, appeared to thoroughly enjoy this impromptu lecture from a 7-year-old. It elicited the predictable gushing admiration from his audience that often occurred when Janni expounded on one of his subjects of interest to adults. It was only children who did not appreciate these monologues but, unfortunately, they were the ones whose respect and acceptance he really needed.

He needed our respect, too, but at home later Joe and I both took pains to explain to him that exceptional intellectual ability was not admirable in itself. It was a lucky gift and all that really mattered was what he did with it. We thought we had good reason for downplaying his mental abilities and emphasizing industry and character development. We had seen other bright children who either became alienated because of being bored, as had happened to my brother, or developed a repulsive sense of specialness. In both cases, they usually do not do as well in their adult life as they should, given their abilities. We did not want our son to go down either one of those paths.

There were some happy experiences during his three Windsor

Park years, and they passed reasonably well. But he was still out of step academically with his class and after a psychological assessment in grade five it was determined that he would be better off just skipping grade six.

It was at that point that we moved to Toronto and we enrolled him in a grade seven class in St. Raphael's, the neighbourhood separate school where Joe's father lived. Janni's penmanship was, and is, terrible and it was clearly interfering with his capacity to get his thoughts across in written form to the best advantage. To help him deal with this problem, we bought him a second-hand IBM electric typewriter and enrolled our then 10-year-old son in an evening typing course for adults at a nearby public school. He coped with that situation quite well and enjoyed the interactions he had with his fellow students there.

Learning how to type and having ready access to a typewriter made it possible for Janni to produce his school assignments more neatly and easily than previously and in a form that could be read and properly evaluated by his teachers. Computers were on the horizon then and a few years later we purchased a Commodore 128, which opened up a whole new world for him!

Another positive thing happened during his grade seven year in Toronto. Every Wednesday afternoon he and other children throughout the Metro separate school system identified as gifted were bussed off to participate in a special program together in one of their new schools. He enjoyed the activities and the chance to interact with students who shared his eccentric interests.

The following year, back in Edmonton, Janni entered grade eight in the 'Academic Challenge' program at Vernon Barford School, just a few blocks from our new house. Before starting there, he quietly informed us that he was no longer to be known as Janni but would now go by his first name, Marcus. He had been named after Joe's uncle, a priest and monsignor in Italy for whom Joe held a particular affection and respect. Like many parents before us we did not think through the repercussions of saddling a child with an unusual name.

Marcus, formerly Janni, was 11 when he started at Vernon Barford and later that fall I was asked to give permission for an intellectual assessment for him. I agreed but wondered why since he had already been identified through testing as 'gifted' in his two previous schools. Two weeks later I was called in to talk to the counsellor about the results. I thought that he might suggest that Marcus be put back a grade because he was so young. Instead, what he had to say was quite the opposite.

The counsellor indicated that the 'Academic Challenge' setting still might not be meeting all Marcus' intellectual and social needs and suggested that he and I join a special citywide support group set up for gifted children and their parents. This group engaged in various activities together and formed friendships. I am ashamed to say that I did not follow up on this suggestion because that is where our son would most likely have found others like himself who would relate to him positively. I was so immersed in the various advocacy and support groups I was involved with for Alexis' sake that I just did not have the energy.

In November of his grade eight year, Marcus informed us that he had met another student in his school that he would like to get to know better and he asked me if he could invite David over. I agreed. The following Saturday at 7:30 in the morning, still garbed in my pyjamas and dressing gown, I was staggering down the upstairs hall of our home where our bedrooms are located, when I almost ran into a total stranger! David introduced himself as Marcus' friend and apologized for "the intrusion at such an early hour." "It's Murphy's law," he explained sagely. "The bus never comes when it is supposed to except when you don't want it to! I did not want to ring the bell and disturb you, so I just came in quietly and was searching for Marcus' room."

"Oh, I see" I gasped. I pointed out the closed door to my son's room at the head of the stairs and then quickly retreated back down the hall to our bedroom. As I reviewed this strange conversation with Joe, who had been awakened by the sound of voices, I suddenly

realized why it sounded so eerily familiar. It held that same combination of sagacity and naiveté that our son's iterations often did. I
felt a simultaneous sense of horror and glee: horror at the thought of
having to interact with another such complicated mind and glee at
the prospect of Marcus finally having someone he could relate to at
his own level who could give as well as he got!

The rest of that year passed unremarkably although I was aware
that our son had not exactly endeared himself to many of his classmates. I speculated that when Marcus was parachuted into that already established clique it disturbed the existing pecking order and
undermined their collective sense of specialness. I knew that to some
extent Marcus was responsible for this. He lacked the emotional intelligence to know when to shut up and he was not good at reading
other people. His new friend, David, was also an outsider and young
for his grade level. He, too, had entered the program late and not
been fully accepted by the others. But together they seemed to be
weathering it.

In grade nine, however, the situation deteriorated. David was
moved to another school and the simmering resentment that the rest
of his classmates had held for Marcus turned into active bullying.
The result was that he was coming home from school very unhappy,
retreating more and more into his computer fantasy world and having
difficulty sleeping at night. Then something happened that demanded
action on my part.

The chief bully in the group bumped him all the way across the
gym floor on his head and Marcus came home complaining of a head-
ache. At that point I felt a raging sense of anger. I had already been
to the school on a couple of occasions to discuss this bullying issue
and the principal had simply responded with a laissez-faire attitude:
"boys will be boys; let them work it out among themselves." But this
issue was beyond what I could allow our son to tolerate. We already
had one child with a brain injury; we were not going to have two!

Joe was away at that point. With my urging and assurance that
I could handle the home situation on my own, he had accepted a

half-year visiting professorship at an Australian university. So, I was left alone to puzzle out how to help Marcus with this situation. I mulled over what we might have done in raising him to make him so vulnerable to this kind of treatment—where we might have gone wrong.

With Joe gone, I turned to my friends and university contacts for support and answers to this problem. One of those people was my former educational psychology professor, Dr. J.P. Das. He later received the Order of Canada for developing a new type of intellectual assessment scale that takes into account various thinking styles and I had allowed him to use this instrument to do some specialized assessment work with Marcus. From the results he obtained, Das had developed a rather lofty opinion of his intellectual abilities and his suggestion was to circumvent the school system entirely and send Marcus to an American university that catered to bright teenagers who had mentally aged out of the system. Scholarships were available and Marcus would be turning 13 in a few months. Das, as he liked to be called, assured me that, through his connections and the weight of his recommendation, he could make this happen.

I did not doubt that Das could succeed in this venture and Joe and I did consider his idea briefly—by long distance over the phone that in those days was still quite expensive. We felt fairly certain that Marcus could meet and even enjoy the steeper academic challenges, but the social challenges would present a far more daunting issue. And I also knew that his ineptitude in this area was in good part our fault.

There was so much we could and should have done to help him develop his personality and emotional intelligence, and to foster the physicality and sense of play so evident in him when he was younger. But life had just been too packed and too grim. We had been exhausted and preoccupied by all our struggles with Alexis' ongoing health and placement issues, and, as a result, had been unable to provide our son with all that he needed from us.

Joe and I decided that the best we could do at this point was to keep him close to us, and to help Marcus in whatever ways we could to learn more effective techniques for negotiating his world. His father's advice: "Keep your head down; don't say everything you are thinking; play dumb." My advice: "Look to the future; these people who are bothering you will be gone from your life soon enough; seek out others who think like you." But one thing I knew. He was not staying in his present setting with those bullies a day longer than it took me to find a suitable alternative!

Once I had calmed down, I made an appointment with the school counsellor. I expressed my concerns to him in the strongest terms and stated bluntly that I wanted to withdraw Marcus from the school. What alternatives did he think might be appropriate for him? He suggested that we enrol him directly in the second semester of grade ten at Harry Ainley, the local public high school a few blocks away. "Marcus is working well ahead of grade level so there is really no need for him to complete his grade nine year," I remember him saying.

Perhaps this would have been the better alternative, but I suspected that the same problems would occur in that setting and perhaps even more so. I asked the counsellor if there was another setting in the area catering to bright students and he recommended a school not too far away with a strong reputation for academic excellence. We placed Marcus at Grandview School and he made it through the rest of his grade nine year without any further incidents of great concern. He even has some happy memories of the brief time he spent there.

The following year, and with his agreement, we did not enrol our son in the mega public high school the counsellor had previously suggested, even though it boasted the International Baccalaureate Program which would have been such an obvious fit for him. Instead he went to Louis St. Laurent, the neighbouring Separate (Catholic) high school that had an Advanced Placement Program. And it turned out to be a good answer for him.

Finally, Marcus was in a setting where he could be comfortable and where he could proceed with his studies at his own rate. He found other students there who shared his passions for math, physics, computers, and 'Dungeons and Dragons', and he formed friendships that have lasted to this day.

During his undergraduate university years, while pursuing a degree in Honours Math, Marcus worked with one of these friends to develop and refine an online bulletin board where people could pay to join up and then share their ideas and experiences in that forum. This was still in the pre-internet days. On his way through high school and university he had won various scholarships and he spent the money on hard drives and other computer equipment to advance the system. Of course, it was immediately outmoded when the internet finally became available to the general public, but it was a rewarding exercise and something that helped him to further develop his social skills in the process.

Today he is happily married to Dr. Reem Yassawi, also a mathematician and university professor, and they have two teenage daughters. He teaches at a French university where he has a congenial group of colleagues and he also has various research collaborators in Europe, Britain, the United States and Chile. He is focusing on mathematical modelling for social justice issues and voting theory. We are proud of our son and who he has become—but I would not like to live through those years of raising him again!

Alexis, 9 and Marcus, 13, rolling around on the floor

Juliana and Alexis in Mexico, February, 2000—a tickling match!

CHAPTER 31

Juliana in the Middle

Juliana was a middle child with a vengeance. When she was young, she often seemed to be off-balance, on the defensive, even a little bit sad. Many times, I have asked myself why ... and I am still asking that question.

She was born on the day of my father's funeral. I had known he was dying—in the small-town hospital where I was born—150 miles away. But I could not go to him because I was already overdue—because Juliana's birth was imminent—because it wasn't safe. Or so I was told.

Joe took me to the hospital that day and then left immediately in order to arrive in Elk Point in time for my father's funeral. I wanted it that way. I needed to have him there ... more than I needed him to be at the birth of his second child.

I had been grieving heavily and continued to grieve throughout Juliana's birth—not an auspicious beginning. I felt her leave my body, this person who had kept me away from my father. And then I felt empty.

Soon the nurse gave her to me to hold and I remember my surprise. She was big and pink and bald and kind of ugly with her squashed in nose. Not at all like her brother had been and nothing like the pretty girl and beautiful woman she was later to become.

I don't remember much of that first year of Juliana's life. Such intense grieving can affect memory. It can affect an unborn child. It can affect the delicate bonding process that happens between a mother and child in the first year of life. What I do remember is that Juliana generally seemed less happy than her brother.

By the time she was 9 months old, she was taller than Marcus who was 15 months her senior. And she is taller to this day. In those early years she wanted dresses and pretty things, but I usually kept her in pants—just easier. She wanted long hair but screamed impossibly whenever I tried to comb it—so I kept it short. And yet there was always about her a certain sweetness.

Throughout my pregnancy with Alexis, I was strangely exhausted. I think now that it was a portent of what was to come. Marcus and Juliana attended Montessori School in the afternoons so I could work on my thesis. In the mornings I performed the necessary maintenance tasks and then brought them downstairs to watch *Mr. Dress-up* and *Sesame Street* from 10:30 to 12—on the second-hand, black and white portable TV my father had purchased for us. That area was completely childproofed for their safety.

After they were settled, I would go back to bed and sleep. I remember being so exhausted that I could hardly wait to get there. At 12 o'clock when the two shows were finished, two-year-old Juliana would trot into the bedroom and say to me in her sweet little voice, 'Wunch time, mommy. Did you have a good nap, mommy?"

Despite her strong contrarian tendencies, she always had another side to her personality, and from early on Juliana was very protective of me, and later of her sister. But her rebellious streak remained. I remember a particularly frightening incident that occurred when I was about eight months pregnant with Alexis and decided one morning that the three of us would visit the Teachers' Store.

This store was the one place in Edmonton at the time to buy open-ended teaching tools and toys for preschoolers, items I considered important for optimal child development. I managed to find the store and made the desired purchases. When we emerged, I spotted another interesting store and headed in that direction with one child holding securely onto each of my hands.

As we approached the store, Juliana suddenly spied something that interested her on the other side of the avenue. She jerked her hand free and headed for it, directly in front of an oncoming car. Time seemed to stand still. If I dropped Marcus' hand, could I trust him to stay on the sidewalk? I dropped it and snarled at him in my meanest voice: "Don't move!" Then I jumped awkwardly into the road and snatched Juliana from in front of the wheels of the oncoming car, just a foot away from her at that point, despite the sound of screaming brakes.

Once safely back on the sidewalk, I grabbed both children's hands firmly, but my legs were trembling so hard that it was all I could do not to collapse, and the baby lurched mightily inside me. I turned around, all thoughts of further shopping forgotten, and ushered them into the safety of a nearby restaurant where we could sit down and recover. As I sat there, Technicolor images flashed through my mind and I realized what a precious gift I had in Juliana and how quickly and easily I could have lost her.

Juliana continued to grow—and grow and grow. By the time she was five she was taller than most eight-year-olds, and as an adult she grew to be over six feet. She should have gone to kindergarten, to have had the advantage of the French Immersion program, to have been given more time to play. But, in the midst of all my grieving over the loss of my father and then my preoccupation with trying to fix Alexis, I had no time or strength or heart to deal with those other gushing mothers, or to be a proper kindergarten parent.

Juliana was born on July 9th, the ideal birthdate to start kindergarten in September when she turned five. But I rationalized that she was too tall to fit in with her peer group and I had her tested at the private school her brother was attending. She passed and started grade one that year instead.

Juliana needed a lot of cuddling when she was young, and I can remember times I saw her looking at my lap—but it was usually occupied by her sister. Alexis was so floppy that for those first few years of her life the only way I could feed her safely was to hold her with one arm securely around her for support while I used my other hand to feed her. In that way, when she started to choke I could quickly move her whole upper body forward to prevent her from aspirating, i.e. inhaling food or liquid into her lungs. And feeding Alexis was a long, slow and difficult process. At one level Juliana understood this, but I saw how she needed me all to herself at times and it tore away at my heart.

Life was not all bad for her, however. Joe's mother, Mary, visited every summer and was there each time one of our children was born. Mary was not very mobile at that point and spent a lot of time sitting in an armchair in the living room holding the current baby, or reading to the children, or folding laundry while she visited with them. In the meantime, I was rustling around cooking or doing laundry or cleaning up. Juliana remembers her times with her Nonna very fondly.

The other big positive factor in Juliana's life was her father. The two of them always seemed to have a special bond that persists to this day. They share a number of common talents and interests and he was better able to tolerate her various eccentricities than I was. She was, and remains, very close to him.

I noticed early on that, when she was in a good space, Juliana was very sensitive and empathetic to others. I remember an early incident when she would have been about 4 years old. Through an advertisement in the paper we had hired someone to spend a few evening hours with Alexis a couple of times a week, so we could have a break. This woman worked with Alexis downstairs in the children's playroom and Janni and Juliana were often around. She had not been there many times when Juliana came upstairs to talk to me one evening.

"Mommy ... that lady is not being very nice to Alexis," I remember her saying. I went to the head of the stairs and listened. It was true and I was horrified. I called the woman up and confronted her while Joe went downstairs to be with Alexis. She confessed that she had a drug problem and said that she needed the job and would do better. I replied that I was sorry for her troubles, but I had to put Alexis first and I ushered her out the door.

As a young child Juliana showed a special interest in music. In 1981, when she was six, the Gateway Association for the Mentally Handicapped, as it was then called, organized an integrated fashion show in which some of the ambulatory children with disabilities from our group would participate, along with their siblings. Sears provided the outfits and Janni and Juliana were asked to take part, dressed in matching camouflage shirts and pants, a fashion style for young children in vogue at that time. But there was no obvious way for Alexis to participate and that upset me.

We had purchased an organ after my father's death and I sometimes sat there playing little tunes and encouraging the children to sing. I still hoped to somehow keep his love of music alive in my family. As the fashion show neared, a series of minor notes began tripping daintily through my brain, akin to the Norwegian folk songs Dad used to sing. I thought of words to go along with the tune and a song for Alexis gradually emerged. I picked it out on the organ and played it off and on throughout the day, gradually refining the lyrics as I went along. I thought maybe I could perform it at the fashion show and have Alexis with me on the stage so that she could be part of the fashion show too.

That night I went to bed happy for the first time in a long time. But the next morning when I awoke and tried to sing my song it was completely gone! All the old sense of loss and hurt came roaring back inside me along with anger. *Why had I not written the notes down?*

"It's gone, all gone," I muttered to myself sorrowfully as I prepared breakfast in the kitchen. Suddenly Juliana spoke and I still remember her exact words.

"Do you mean this, mommy?" she asked. And then she began to sing my song, beautifully, in her clear child's voice. I remember my feeling at that moment: a wondrous sense of awe and gratitude. I had my song back—and my daughter was musical like my father had been. All that music had not gone from my life with his passing as I had thought. But despite the power of that moment, the memory of it was soon submerged in the rushing events of daily life and I forgot how remarkable it had been.

Until she reached high school, Juliana was an indifferent student. It seemed to me like she did not even try, like she deliberately misunderstood simple, straightforward material and then blocked out all efforts made to help her. She almost failed grade nine English and the teacher suggested that it might be necessary for her to take the remedial English course in grade ten. This daughter of at least average intelligence, this daughter of an English professor!

But something else happened towards the end of Juliana's grade nine year that seemed to change everything. A talent show was planned at her school and she decided to participate. She must have practiced beforehand, but we never heard her. It was just one of the many things she did not share with us or ask for help with at the time.

Joe and I managed to arrange assistance for Alexis that evening so both of us could attend the talent show. The school auditorium where it took place was packed and there was the usual undercurrent of whispered conversations between and even during pieces. But three bars into Juliana's rendition of 'The Rose' the room became almost eerily quiet. I felt chills radiating up and down my spine and my throat filled with a silent gasp. The power and poignancy with which she delivered that song, and the purity of each note utterly overwhelmed me. I felt like she had been born again. I felt like my father's music had come back to life. In fact, I felt so many conflicting and overpowering emotions that I could barely contain them.

Where had that discipline, that commitment, come from? I asked myself: How had I missed seeing that amazing talent and drive right under my nose? In short, that performance was a life-altering event for me in terms of my relationship with Juliana. And apparently it had a similar effect on her because after that she became for the first time a serious student.

Juliana's English grades improved, and she made it into grade ten without qualification. In high school her innate intelligence seemed to emerge from wherever it had been hiding all those years. She finally started getting good marks and even qualified for provincial scholarships in grade eleven and twelve to help pay for her university education.

But all through those rough Junior and Senior High years when Juliana and I were frequently at loggerheads, she remained protective of me whenever she perceived that I was in a vulnerable situation. I remember one evening when I was preparing for a dinner party the next night with her assistance. I was making a new kind of light lemon cheesecake and I needed to make two to accommodate both our guests and family members. The process was complicated and time consuming. It was already late, and I had to be at work early the next morning. Finally, it was done, and I lifted one cake carefully onto the counter and then the other. But I was very tired at that point and dropped the second one. The glass plate broke and the contents scattered all over the kitchen floor. I just stared at them in horror, wondering how I could ever muster up the energy to clean up the mess and make another cake.

But Juliana interrupted my sad thoughts. "Don't worry, mommy," she said. "You go to bed and I will clean it up. And tomorrow night I won't eat any dessert and then one cake will be enough." I just looked at her in wonder, at this daughter of mine who always craved sweets. The pride and satisfaction I felt for her at that moment more than offset the loss of the cake!

Unfortunately, my epiphany with regard to Juliana and my new accord with her was a little late in coming. After high school she began a Bachelor of Fine Arts Program at the University of Alberta, and a year later she was admitted to The National Theatre School. Shortly after her 18th birthday she left for Montreal and never lived at home again.

Following a stint at Theatre School, Juliana completed an undergraduate degree in Music at McGill, majoring in Voice, and then did a second undergraduate degree in Fine Arts at Concordia University. Her marks were impressive, and she was offered a scholarship to attend The School of the Art Institute of Chicago (SAIC) where she subsequently attained a Master of Fine Arts Degree in Sculpture.

Since finishing her formal education, Juliana has combined her interest and talents in art and music to produce a number of mixed genre art works and had two solo exhibitions shortly after graduating from SAIC. She now teaches Art part-time at the University of Toronto and is happily married to her husband, Marc Couroux, a fellow artist and musician and a professor at York University. They have two children, a boy and a girl. Juliana recently completed her first book project, an edited work on the late artist/writer, Roy Kiyooka, who deserves greater recognition than he has received.

In her spare time, Juliana has read and made useful comments on every single one of my Claire Burke Mystery books before they have gone to press, and I have come to admire and depend upon the fine, analytic mind that I never knew she had!

When I think back to those early years, I wonder how Juliana managed to hide her light under a bushel for so long—and why? Naturally, I have contemplated this enigma through a psychologist's lens. What I have concluded is that there was no clear space for her in our highly polarized family, with special needs children at both ends of the spectrum. The only way she could make room for herself, draw attention to herself and get at least some of her own emotional needs met, was to make an art out of being less than adequate. The only zone in which she could safely explore and develop her talents was outside the educational arena.

Whatever the real explanation is, assuming there is one, Juliana derived enough nurturing from her family, even in such challenging circumstances, to develop into a reasonably happy, mature and effective adult. So I guess we must have done a few things right along the way.

Following is Juliana's response to what I have written here:

My Mother

My mother
A density of contradictions
hurling herself through gale force resistance
to meet near void on the other side

in my child's mind,
my sister and my mother are one:
needs met, calls answered,
faith understood.

She speaks, if you can find a way to listen
She points, if you can tune to her frequency of motion.
She loves you
from within her storm

When is it clearest?
At night, in the dark,
when she calls you to her room
craving a few more words, relief.

I walk her patterns
her thousand tiny details
the time and the tenderness
the litany of regulations.

I imitate her calls, her tics,
her twists of presence and absence
the pulse of urgency
held in place by ritual and care.

No longer a baby, I stood looming over my mother's lap
I am told
a moment burned into her heart
I am told

CAPTION: Alexis enjoying a visit with her sister, 2013

Alexis, age 11—School picture from St. Boniface

CHAPTER 32

After two years Alexis moves on

It was during Alexis' second year at Allendale that the financial implications of accommodating children with such a high level of special needs hit home to the Public School system board and there were frightening rumblings in the air about a change to school admission policy. Also, the provincial government was talking about cutbacks to education funding for the coming year. By December, the writing was on the wall, although the official announcement did not come out until May. For the upcoming school year all parents of high needs children who were registered supporters of the separate school system would have to send their severely disabled children to separate schools. Since Debbie and I were both Separate School supporters it meant that neither Kent nor Alexis could remain in their public school settings after that year.

A short while after we moved to Aspen Gardens, I had observed that there was a Catholic elementary school, St Boniface, just four blocks east of our home. As soon as I found out about the necessity to transfer Alexis to the Separate system for the upcoming year, I made an afterschool appointment with the principal there to talk about enrolling Alexis in grade five for the coming year.

When I made the phone call to set up the appointment, I did not mention that Alexis had a disability. My normal inclination is to be up front in all my business dealings but I was feeling stung and a little bitter about Alexis being dumped by the public board. I was also fearful of not being able to attain the same type of inclusive educational setting at St. Boniface that she had been enjoying at Allendale.

On the day of the appointment I took both Juliana and Alexis to the school to meet with the principal. "I would like you to meet my daughters," I said when we were introducing ourselves. "This is Juliana and this is Alexis"—and he got this vague smirk on his face when he saw Alexis in her wheelchair and my tall, beautiful older daughter standing beside her. That smirk is an endearing memory I carry with me, and not all my memories of that school are as positive.

After I stated again that I wanted to enrol Alexis in grade five for the following year he talked about how the parents had made a big uproar the year before because somebody who was visually impaired and also had some kind of learning disability had been enrolled. They didn't want him there. His cognitive limitations were relatively minor, and now here we were with Alexis. How could he hope to convince the parents and teachers to accept her?

"Well, this is what we want," I said. "This is her neighbourhood school and we want her here." That meeting occurred before I put forward the proposal that Debbie and I had been in the process of developing to the Separate school board, but we had already worked out most of it and I discussed our ideas for how it could work with him.

"In any case," he replied, "the Separate School System runs on a centre-based model and principals really don't have the authority to make a decision like this. It has to go through the Board." We went home and I continued refining the new model.

Given the cost constraints that both boards were facing with the looming funding cutbacks, and because the Separate board, due to its lower student numbers, had less funding available to serve high needs students than the Public board, Debbie and I knew that we would have to present a very cost-efficient solution if we were to convince the board to allow an inclusionary option for Kent and Alexis.

What we were proposing was that they be paired together with one assistant in an elementary classroom and that this be done on a pilot basis. We already had Norma's agreement to take this on if the Board accepted our proposal and we stressed her competence and her experience working with Alexis. We also provided contact information for Alexis' Allendale principal and teacher so they could check on Norma's performance and how well Alexis had functioned in the class. We provided the same contact information for Kent's assistant, teacher and principal at the neighbourhood public school he had been attending in Debbie's area of the city.

In the proposal I also mentioned some of the methods Allendale had employed to make the inclusion of Alexis feasible. For example, they had developed a roster of student volunteers to wheel Alexis around the school yard at lunch and recess so Norma could have a break. And I suggested that if they had a lunchroom assistant in St. Boniface, the school we were targeting, they might like to make some financial arrangement with him or her so that she could help out at lunchtime when necessary.

I also pointed out that I lived only four blocks from St. Boniface School and had a flexible schedule so I could be there to help out or in a crisis if I was not at work. And Debbie was prepared to sign a document giving me full responsibility for Kent if a situation arose making it necessary to act quickly. Finally, this could all be done on a pilot basis and they could do an official review near the end of the following school year. If it was not working to their satisfaction, they could consider ways to either fix it or cancel it at that time.

In other words, the Separate school system in Edmonton had nothing to lose by adopting our proposal and everything to gain. They could look progressive and inclusionary with no more expenditure of funds than would occur if Kent and Alexis were sent to St. Gabriel's, their school with the separate class setting for "dependently handicapped children," as they were then called. Also, they would have a proven, experienced assistant to take the bulk of the responsibility, and they would be working with two sets of parents fully prepared to cooperate and support them.

At that time, Kent was still able to walk as long as he had something firm to hang onto and to roll along in front of him. Alexis' wheelchair could serve that function. In this way one assistant could navigate both children from one place to another. There was one problem with this idea, though: Kent's sudden, violent bouts of head-banging in which he seemed to deliberately aim for any hard object that could hurt him. Alexis had a head support on her chair and the adjustment rod stuck out from the back about three inches. If Kent ever connected with that rod the resulting damage could be catastrophic. But, with Norma's help, we found a solution. We pierced the rod with a dense rubber ball of a large enough dimension to provide sufficient cushioning against Kent's head-banging attempts. We then practiced walking the two of them in this way to make sure it worked and that the ball would remain securely in place.

When the document was refined to our satisfaction, I contacted the Separate School Board superintendent and arranged a meeting with him. We had met previously on several occasions because of my involvement in advocacy work so he knew who I was, and we had an amicable relationship. I presented him with the document we had prepared and then went through it with him, elaborating where necessary. He seemed reasonably impressed by it and said he would take it through the necessary channels and get back to me. I went home and waited but nothing happened.

On the very last day of June, which in my mind is unconscionable if you want to talk about timing (we had started this process in late February) we finally got the go ahead from the Separate School Board, and Alexis and Kent were to start in the grade five classroom at St. Boniface the following September.

CHAPTER 33

The Formation of Integration —Action Alberta

Once Debbie and I had been assured that we had a secure school placement for our children in the fall, we were able to turn our minds to the larger issues around school inclusion in Alberta at that time. We were still incensed by the Public School Board's decision to exclude our children, but at the same time we realized that they had had little choice due to provincial cutbacks.

And the looming threat of the new School Act, 1987, Bill 59 that had just been drafted by our provincial government convinced us that more radical action on our part was required. Under the new Act the proposed legislation provided a definition of "non-educable" persons that could enable Boards to exclude individuals falling within that definition for administrative reasons without running afoul of the provincial policy of education for all.

When I was in Toronto during the 1984–85 school year, I had involved myself in some of the advocacy activity there in the area of developmental disability and I had made several valuable contacts in the process. I was well aware of their Integration Action movement to include all children with disabilities in regular classrooms and decided that we needed to organize a parallel group in Alberta in order to put some pressure on the boards and provincial government to make that option broadly available in our province. And at the same time, we wanted to make sure that no child was excluded regardless

187

of the severity of their disability and the seeming pointlessness of providing a conventional educational setting for them. I should mention here that education is under provincial control in Canada.

I knew this was not something that Debbie and I could pull off on our own. We needed some strong allies, and to find them we might have to look in unlikely places. During the two years that Alexis was at Allendale I had made various contacts and one of them was Heather Raymond. Heather was the teacher in charge of the autism program housed at Allendale and I knew that her work with her students was highly regarded by parents and administration alike. Although committed to an Applied Behavioural Analysis approach to dealing with students with autism, Heather had already done some integration of selected students into specific subject classes. However, she firmly believed that a centre-based program where a rich pool of expertise could be assembled to help students facing these challenges was necessary. In other words, she was in favour of partial inclusion but not full inclusion. This ran counter to the new ideas on full inclusion then wafting across the country from Marsha Forrest, Judith Snow, and others in Ontario.

I arranged to meet with Heather at West Edmonton Mall and we engaged in a very intense discussion, each of us putting forth our own point of view. At the end of it she could see where I was coming from and agreed to work with me on this new cause and to pull in whoever she could who would be helpful in promoting it.

I will quote here from the first newsletter (Summer, 1987) that I prepared for what was to officially to become *Integration Action Association for Education—Alberta*.

"May 28, 1987—first meeting of IA-A. 35 Edmonton parents and professionals were in attendance. News coverage by CBC-TV. Letter of support for our endeavours from Nick Taylor, leader of Alberta Liberal Party; telegrams of support from Integration Action, Ontario's Marsha Forrest and Judith Snow: a letter from Stan Woronko, outgoing president of Integration Action-Ontario, explaining how they had formed, fund-raised and were dealing with legal issues and government lobbying. At this meeting there was unanimous agreement on the need to proceed with the formation of a legally constituted provincial association to deal specifically with issues pertaining to integrated education. A steering committee was struck, and specific tasks assigned to individuals to be completed before our next meeting. Bruce Uditsky[17] spoke about the possibilities of legal action (*if necessary*).

"(IA-A newsletter, Summer, 1987)"

On June 20th, the second meeting of Integration Action Alberta took place in our back yard with 30 people in attendance including people from other parts of the province. Marsha Forrest had suggested we float a helium balloon over our house in order to orient the new people and offered to pay the cost, so we made the arrangements. But Joe was away, and Debbie and I had a lot of trouble filling the balloon without allowing it to float away in the process. We were wrestling with it rather desperately when our neighbour came to the rescue, and between the three of us, we finally succeeded. I then wrote "Integration Action" on its smooth white surface with black felt pen.

After we launched the balloon, I jumped in my car to pick up something else from the store that we needed for the evening. From the road I glanced up—it looked very impressive and professional—and then it burst into a million pieces right before my eyes! Apparently, the alcohol in felt pens dissolves rubber!

Somehow most people managed to find us anyway and among them were Reg Peters, the Executive Director of Alberta Association for Community Living, Alex McEachern, the government MLA from Edmonton Kingsway, and reporters from both CBC-TV and the Edmonton Journal. Debbie's job had been to organize as much media coverage as possible and she did her job well!

The meeting was interrupted first by a noisy lawn mower next door until Tammy Springer, in her impulsive way, leapt over the fence and ordered the perpetrator to stop. Then, halfway through the meeting, a fierce rainstorm began, and we all had to make a rapid retreat inside, including the seeing-eye dog of one of the people attending. Despite these distractions much was accomplished. Margaret Laird, a teacher from the small town of Hinton, near Jasper, Alberta, spoke about the successful inclusion of a child with cognitive disabilities in her classroom, and Bev Ray (parent of a child with Down Syndrome) discussed her progress with Consumer and Corporate Affairs in drawing up an acceptable set of by-laws and a constitution for our new association. Heather Raymond went through the list of fund-raising options she had been exploring and Francis Macri, a lawyer friend of ours, reviewed the implications of the new school act.

On July 9th, 1987, Francis and I met with the Minister of Education, Nancy Betkowski, to express our concerns about the proposed new school act. By that time, we were officially incorporated as a provincial organization, thanks to Bev's persistence and hard work, and thus in a position to be taken seriously. We acknowledged that there was much in the new bill that was positive from our perspective, specifically legal provision for the education of all students, including those with disabilities. But our concern was with the introduction of the term, "non-educable persons" which presumably could exclude some from the category of 'student' and therefore from the right to a public education.

We were assured that this was not the intention, but Francis and I felt that the term, 'non-educable', was "soft" enough to create a loophole that some boards might take advantage of to avoid funding high needs students such as Kent and Alexis. We were assured that an appeal to the courts would always be an option and that the new bill was written in such a way that, if necessary, a ruling from the Education Ministry could supersede the ruling of any individual Education Board. We countered with a concern as to what would happen then to the many severely disabled children who were wards of the state and had no one to advocate for them in such situations.

After hearing us, our concerns over the introduction of the term, 'non-educable' into the new bill were acknowledged as potentially problematic and Francis was invited to make submissions on this subject directly to the legislative drafter, and to join a committee dealing with drafting concerns. Subsequently, the term, 'non-educable' was removed from the act. What part we played in this I do not know. I am sure others must have voiced their concerns as well.

CHAPTER 34

The Dark Side of
Pressured Inclusion

T he fall of 1987 arrived, and Joe was gone for the entire year to occupy a visiting chair in Italian-Canadian Studies at York University in Toronto. I was on my own with the family. This time there had been no possibility of the rest of us, or some of the rest of us, going with him. He would have given up this opportunity if I had asked him to, but I could not do that. All I could do was to assure him that we could manage. Just as Alexis was starting in a new school in a new school system!

Alexis' new teacher was older and well-meaning but on the rigid side. She seemed to care about Alexis but in a pitying kind of a way. I would rather people respect Alexis for how hard she tries than love her for being pathetic.

As I recall, this teacher's attitude towards me was also very different from what I had experienced with both Alexis' teachers at Allendale. There, my input about what would work best for Alexis had been valued and even sought after. Even when my ideas were not so great, those teachers at least respected me enough to mull them over for a couple of minutes before dismissing them. Not so much in this case!

Norma remained with Alexis and Kent for that first year at St. Boniface. The other students in the class seemed to accept the two new students and rolled them around the playground at recess time in their chairs. Norma managed the situation, but it was difficult.

The school board's educational consultants came out regularly to consult with the teacher about the programs that had been designed for our children. The teacher was then directed as to what she should be doing with them, and she in turn passed this information onto Norma, whom she saw as her assistant. This top-down approach makes sense when dealing with children with learning disabilities where the teacher would likely have a larger body of relevant knowledge than the assistant. Unfortunately, it did not make sense in this situation where they were all in uncharted territory. The only person with any real competence in terms of meeting the physical and educational needs of Kent and Alexis was Norma, who had learned by experience, and through the careful coaching by Debbie and me as to what worked and what did not work with them.

Even if the consultants had received specific training in dealing with individuals with multiple and severe disabilities, they would have had a limited amount to offer since the strengths and challenges within this category vary widely. You can only really learn what works and what does not work with people facing such severe challenges through extensive and intensive interaction, the kind that only an assistant who works with them daily is likely to acquire.

Because Norma was competent, hard-working and diplomatic, and because the principal was supportive and genuinely wanted to see this experiment work, and because the teachers and students were willing to go along with him and try, Kent and Alexis made it through the year happy and apparently well served. However, Debbie and I both knew that caring for two children with such a high and complex level of needs was too much to ask of anyone, although Norma rarely complained. And long before the end of the year Debbie was already exploring the possibility of placing Kent in her neighbourhood separate school for the following year with his own personal assistant.

CHAPTER 35

Crisis and Rejection

Overall, things went fairly smoothly that first year in the separate system, 1987-88. Everyone seemed to be trying hard to make this very unusual situation work and I was beginning to relax. When Joe announced that he was going to Sicily in May to present a paper at a conference and asked me to see if I could arrange things so I could go with him, I thought maybe I could work it out.

It had been a very long time since the two of us had been away together alone, so I worked hard to make it happen. I arranged for Juliana to stay with the family of a schoolmate and close friend who lived nearby. Antonella Ciancibello, a friend of ours who was still single at that time, offered to stay in the house with Marcus to keep him on track and keep the house in one piece.

Last, but hardly least, I arranged for Alexis to go to a relief home and for bussing to take her back and forth to her school during the week. Since I had plenty of advance notice of this conference, I went out with her to that home three separate times to orient her to it and the staff to her. I made elaborate lists of how to feed her and what her various communicative signs were and any other information I considered vital. And most importantly, I informed the relief home staff about her seizure pattern, what to watch out for and what to do.

Joe and I remained in Italy almost two weeks visiting the various relatives across the north and then travelling South and over to Sicily for the conference for the last few days of our stay. Finally, our time neared its end. We were leaving Sicily the next day, crossing back on the ferry over to Calabria and then driving north to Milan where we would catch our plane.

I don't normally have nightmares but in the middle of that last night I awoke screaming and terrified. Joe asked me what was wrong, and I told him something had happened to Alexis and it seemed like Marcus was involved somehow. I wanted to phone home right away, but we had no phone and in 1988 overseas communication was not as easy as it is today. Also, there were general strikes going on in Italy at that time which further complicated things.

I could see that Joe had a hard time taking this dream of mine seriously. His response was that if something really had happened there was nothing we could do about it anyway and we were literally on our way home so we might as well wait until we got there to find out.

We had a layover in Toronto before going on to Edmonton and after we landed there, I found a pay phone and called home. I was still as concerned as I had been when I awoke from my dream. I talked to Antonella, the friend staying at our home, and found out something had indeed happened, and the timeline more or less matched the time of my dream. Alexis had gone into Status Epilepticus, was still in the hospital and appeared to be less responsive than she had been before this event happened. In other words, it was likely that she had experienced more brain damage!

Apparently, a new overnight person had been on duty at the relief home the night it happened and did not realize that Alexis' constant head bobbing was a form of cluster seizure activity and Alexis was put to bed in that state. By the next morning the constant head bobbing was still happening, and she was sent off on her long bus ride to school in that condition. As soon as Norma saw Alexis, she realized there was a serious problem and called the ambulance.

As it happened, Marcus was walking by on his way to school when the ambulance arrived and when he found out it was Alexis who was having the problem, he went with her to the hospital and was able to provide the necessary information. Norma, of course, could not accompany her because she had Kent to care for, but after 10 years of living with Alexis, Marcus knew exactly what to tell them about her condition.

Alexis did appear to lose ground after this incident and of course I was very upset and angry that it even happened after all the elaborate precautions I had taken to orient staff. Furthermore, it is not the only unfortunate thing that has happened to Alexis in her life. When people have no protective reflexes and no way to communicate directly, things happen. But after that I never fully trusted staff again. On the other side of the coin, I learned to trust my gut.

A study was done at the end of that first school year at St. Boniface to assess whether or not there had been any gains for Kent and Alexis sufficient to justify keeping them in an inclusive setting. I was not given the written results of that study but, in terms of maintaining them at that school for the second year, the feedback I received from the teacher and principal was that parents of the other students did not want their teacher to be preoccupied with accommodating handicapped children in their classroom. They wanted the focus to be on computer programs and other enrichment activities that would directly benefit their own children.

By this point in time, the integration movement had spread in small pockets across the country including Edmonton. I argued that the inclusion of children with special needs in regular classroom settings was advantageous not only to those students but also to the other students in the class. By providing non-disabled students with the opportunity to socialize with children facing such difficult challenges, and role modelling how to communicate with and respect them, we hoped to inspire this new generation to be more compassionate and responsible citizens in their adult lives.

Unfortunately, in an upper middleclass area like Aspen Gardens, the majority of the students came from rather privileged family back-grounds, many with aggressive, upwardly mobile parents whose idea of enrichment was not human capital. It was money and the things that money can buy including status, position, power, and prestige. They had their own ideas of what enrichment was, and that did not include learning sign language or pushing somebody around the playground in a wheelchair at recess time. Despite parent resistance, however, Alexis remained at St. Boniface for a second year with Norma. Kent was transferred to his own neighbourhood school with his own assistant. We took this to mean that the Separate School Board was now recognizing that inclusion of this population in regular classrooms was feasible and inevitable and that other children in the system facing similar challenges would have this type of opportunity in the future. But that is not what happened.

During the second year it became increasingly apparent that the other teachers and assistants at St. Boniface were no longer buying into the idea of having someone with such severe disabilities enrolled as a student, and Alexis and Norma became an ever more isolated pod in that school. Nobody offered to relieve Norma at lunch by staying with Alexis for a half hour, for example. And towards the end of that year I was informed that an expert from the Department of Education at the University of Alberta would conduct an evaluation of this 'pilot model'. The same process was happening in Kent's new school.

In due course I heard that the report had been completed and the conclusion was that both Kent and Alexis could be better served at St. Gabriel's School, the specialized program for children with multiple and severe disabilities to which they had initially been referred. I was told that they were actually using the model I had proposed for GRIT 2 and had shared with the separate board some years previously. This was the pod system with a small number of high challenge children in one homeroom but integrated into regular classes on an individual basis wherever possible. However, I had long since given up on this model, seeing it as inadequate.

In short, the pilot project was over, and we were back to square one. But early on in my adventures with Alexis and the system I had learned to take nothing for granted, and in my head I had already been mulling over a contingency plan if this should be the outcome of the review.

CHAPTER 36

Alexis and Lydia at
St. Gabriel's School

T hat was the end of June 1989 and Alexis was 11½ years old. In those days we received some limited financial support from the government department then referred to as *Handicapped Children's Services,* and every year that Alexis grew older it seemed that we were entitled to a little more support for a number of hours after school and on weekends. We had come to rely on the hours of freedom this gave us, and that spring we had hired a wonderful assistant to work with Alexis during those hours. As with all the assistants we were able to access in those years, I had trained her carefully to carry out the range of motion program and to use the other therapy equipment and program ideas we had devised for Alexis.

I was not at all comfortable sending Alexis alone in a handicap bus across the city to St. Gabriel's and stated that I could not do it unless our own assistant went with her. I stressed Alexis' very real health concern, i.e. the seizures where she sometimes stopped breathing, and I think the separate school board was probably more than happy that I had someone I trusted who could take the bulk of the responsibility for Alexis while she was away at school.

Lydia had come to work with our daughter after growing up in a Hutterite colony in northern Alberta. She had been obliged to leave school when she was 14 in order to assume her share of the communal responsibility by taking full charge of their huge flock of ducks. By the time she was 17 she had decided that this was not the life for her and had left the colony.

At that same time, I had been advertising for part-time help with Alexis and had received several applications. One of them was particularly strong in terms of qualifications and I interviewed and hired that person. However, I had a funny feeling in my gut when I did this, but in those days I did not pay enough attention to my inner signals. This girl trained with our outgoing assistant and picked up on Alexis' program very quickly and competently. But the night before she was to start I received a phone call with some excuse, I can't remember what now. It is lost in the sea of excuses I have received since that time. Anyway, she was not going to be able to accept the job after all.

At that point I had cancelled the ad and turned away all subsequent inquiries. In those days—that would have been the spring of 1989—home internet access was not yet available, and I did all my job hiring negotiations over the telephone and by advertising in the Edmonton Journal. Mercifully, one last person had phoned me for a job a couple of days previously and I had kept her number and set up an interview.

I had heard Lydia's story over the phone when she called, and I knew she had no relevant qualifications and far less education that I had come to expect in Alexis' assistants, so I did not even interview her before hiring the other person. However, I still felt I needed to help her in some way. Maybe just providing her with an interview experience and then giving her useful feedback would help her in her efforts to find employment, I thought. I don't know if my decision was 100% altruistic or if it was in some sense a response to what my gut was telling me: i.e. I needed a back-up plan.

In any case Lydia came for the interview. I can see her now, where she sat in our big garden room answering our questions but with minimum words. My husband, who always assisted me during interviews in those days, asked his usual questions: How tall are you? Have you ever had any back problems? What languages do you speak besides English? None of these questions would be considered politically correct today—although we do need assistants of a certain size and with healthy backs to be able to safely deal with Alexis. But second language ability is definitely not a requirement, particularly for Alexis who is non-verbal! Joe, however, has his own professional interest in that area so that is what he asked about.

I jumped in at that point to explain the lifting requirements for Alexis. The reply was "I can throw 120-pound hay bales around. I guess I can lift *her*."

I was hoping she would forget about the inappropriate language question, but Joe asked again! "I speak three languages," she said. "High German, Low German and English."

Joe seemed satisfied with this level of language acquisition, and in the end I was satisfied that Lydia would not treat Alexis like another one of her ducks, or throw her around like a hay bale. Also, I did not feel we had much choice at that point. Joe and I were both working, and we absolutely had to have help during the days.

As it turned out, hiring Lydia was one of the best decisions we ever made. She was wonderful with Alexis and Alexis loved her. And that is how it happened that Lydia, after working with Alexis in our home through that spring and summer, was hired by the principal of St. Gabriel Elementary School as Alexis' assistant!

Once again at St. Gabriel's, Alexis had a teacher who thought she knew best about what to do for her. She may have been excellent working with ambulatory children, children with Down syndrome or Autism, but she knew little of relevance about working with a child who was blind, had a severe seizure disorder, multiple food allergies, no upper trunk control or functional use of any of her limbs, no formal communication system, and no ability to filter out extraneous stimuli so that she easily became overwhelmed by excess noises and verbiage she did not understand. In short, she was not Colleen.

Despite this, the teacher felt it was her responsibility to design the program for Alexis, aspects of which were so unsuited to her needs and capabilities that forcing them upon her just made Alexis cry, and that made me very frustrated when I heard about it. But, after working with my daughter for six months in our home, Lydia knew what Alexis needed and what she could and could not do so she just went ahead and skilfully modified the program to what she felt was appropriate.

One amusing example was the program to train Alexis to bring food to her mouth. As stated previously, Alexis has minimal arm strength and she cannot see. Also, she has poor mouth control and chokes easily. It is dangerous to divide her attention in any way when she is eating. She needs to be peaceful and relaxed and able to focus exclusively on manipulating the food in her mouth and swallowing. I explained all this to the teacher, but she was unwilling to change the requirement.

Lydia came up with a solution, however. She understood, without having any specialized training I might add, that for Alexis to accomplish this task she must be motivated. Alexis likes bananas and at that time was able to safely eat them whole by gumming off little bites at a time. And although she is cortically blind, she is aware of light and possibly colour. Lydia found a fat, yellow crayon and wrapped Alexis' hand around it. Then she gently guided her hand to her mouth, saying as they went "Banana, Alexis! Eat some banana." At the last moment, just as Alexis opened her mouth to receive the banana, Lydia quickly switched the yellow crayon for the real thing.

In today's litigious and politically correct world I don't know if some expert would find an ethical problem with this, but I do know that Alexis would never have been able to hold onto and lift a real banana because of its relative weight and bulk, even with assistance. The smaller, lighter crayon was a more reasonable challenge for her.

What of the "specialized expertise" we were promised when we agreed to the St. Gabriel's setting? All I can tell you is that on the occasions when Alexis did have a run of really bad seizures, all her teacher did was call an ambulance to take Alexis to the hospital. This was both unnecessary and highly traumatic and disruptive to Alexis since she ended up each time with a Valium injection to stop the seizure run and was then unable to resume her normal sleep-wake schedule for days. The different setting, loud noises, strange smells, and general air of crisis present in an emergency room also frightened her. We coped with far worse seizures at home without calling an ambulance and they did the same at Allendale and St. Boniface.

So, the year passed, but every time I walked by St. Boniface School and saw the ramp that had originally been installed to accommodate Alexis, I felt sad. One day when I passed, I saw a child in a wheelchair being wheeled up the ramp. Naturally I had to find out who the child was, and I used my contacts to gain this information. It turned out that it was the son of the expert who had written the report advising that Alexis be removed from St. Boniface. I did not know how I felt about that. On the one hand I guess I was happy that another disabled child would have the opportunity to be included in that school. On the other hand, it felt to me like perhaps Alexis might not have been ousted if that other child had had a different set of parents.

CHAPTER 37

Alexis goes to high school

As the year at St. Gabriel's wore on and Alexis' 12th birthday passed I knew that I could not tolerate having her there for more than the current year. She was no longer welcome at St. Boniface, but about 12 blocks from our home there was a junior-senior high school complex belonging to the Separate board.

Our older children were currently attending the senior high part there at Louis St. Laurent, so that seemed the logical place for Alexis to go. Yes, she was still young for high school, but her brother and sister had also been young, so I rationalized to myself that it kind of fit in with our family model. And to put out all the energy needed to convince the Junior High principal to take her only to have her aged out in a year or two was more energy than I had at that point.

I made an arrangement to speak to the high school principal and explained my wish to place Alexis there and my concerns about maintaining her at St. Gabriel. John St. Arnault was quite senior in the Separate School system at that time and, in fact, some years later was to become their superintendent. Even then he seemed far surer of himself and of what he could and could not do than the principal at St. Boniface had been. He also struck me as very compassionate and as someone who had a larger world vision than many. I explained to him the program we had worked out for Alexis, the availability of a well-trained assistant, the severity of Alexis' seizure disorder, and our desire to have her close to home so her father and I could get to her quickly if something serious happened. He listened carefully; asking questions from time to time and then, quite miraculously I thought, accepted her for the fall term with Lydia to be transferred over from St. Gabriel's to be her educational assistant.

As it turned out, he was the principal for both the junior and senior high sections of that school complex and Alexis was assigned to a grade eight class for that first year. He explained that she would be moved on according to the most suitable class setting for her and the most suitable and willing teacher. One happy thing I remember from that year is that the Home Economics teacher noted the bibs that Alexis wore because of her constant drooling and chose as a class sewing project the making of Western neckerchief style bibs for her if I would agree to pay for the materials. I happily agreed and the teacher then purchased a large number of western style neckerchiefs. The students each chose one and then folded it in half diagonally and lined it with a piece of towelling. The edges were then sewn together with ties, a button, or a snap fastener sewn on so the neckerchief could be secured around Alexis' neck.

The teacher first did this with one of her classes but then another class wanted to participate so Alexis ended up with about 35 neckerchiefs, few of which were perfect in their construction. She wore those for years with their various tucks and crooked sewing lines, and every time I looked at them I got a warm feeling inside. They represented to me the very essence of inclusion. The neckerchiefs provided the students with a relatively easy sewing project at no additional cost to their families. Alexis then had a varied and plentiful supply of them to wear and the students saw on a daily basis that their sewing efforts had produced a worthwhile and useful result!

At the end of Alexis' first year at Louis St. Laurent, the principle arranged a meeting with me to discuss Alexis' educational placement for the following year. By this time, I had nothing but suspicion with regard to these meetings. Therefore, I asked the directors of both the provincial and city advocacy groups for individuals with developmental disabilities to attend that meeting to help me argue my position for continued full inclusion of Alexis in the school system. Francis Macri, our lawyer friend, also agreed to attend.

I spent many hours researching the limited information available on outcome measures for children as heavily challenged as Alexis and carefully prepared my case for why Alexis should remain at Louis St. Laurent. This was an arduous, complicated process and I arrived at the meeting tired and bitter. But, before I could even make my case, Principal St. Arnault informed me that Alexis was welcome to remain at the school until she reached the mandatory school leaving age of 21. What he really wanted to discuss at the meeting was how to provide the most effective ongoing educational program for her!

I hardly knew what to say or do. By that point I was so used to fighting every single year for my daughter's placement that I could not even feel happy. Instead, I just felt guilty about the kind people who had taken the time and trouble to come out to support us at this meeting, when apparently it had not been necessary. The meeting carried on then, but it is a blank in my mind. Afterwards I felt nothing, not joy, not excitement, just a monumental fatigue. I had been fighting and strategizing for so long that I hardly knew what to do with myself. I was simply unable to grasp what a victory and a blessing this was.

It took me a couple of weeks to lay this heavy burden down that I had been carrying for so long—ensuring Alexis' proper place in the world. At least for the remainder of her student life she was now secure. My thoughts then moved to the suggestions for Alexis' school program for the upcoming year. Were they okay? Were they the most appropriate, and the best that we could offer her?

1995, Alexis' high school graduation, age 17

Leaving School Behind

Alexis' years at Louis St. Laurent High School were relatively uneventful. Lydia remained with her and, with a strong principal at the helm, everything rolled along smoothly. On the few occasions where a problem arose, I was informed about it immediately and the school made the necessary changes to her program or setting.

Because she had started grade eight there at age 12 and had been moved along with her cohort, Alexis was in the grade twelve graduating class when she was 17. The principal explained that she would not be graduating because she would be returning to school in the fall attached to a different class, possibly a grade ten class, so she could go through her high school years a second time with the same group. But I had a different idea. I wanted her to graduate.

I explained my thinking to the principal, and he suggested that I talk to the board superintendent. At my request, the superintendent notified the appropriate government officials that the separate school system could no longer provide an appropriate educational setting for Alexis. As a result, she was released from school life at the end of that year and granted funding for a day program.

Although I felt only gratitude for all the professionals who had done whatever they could to include Alexis and make her feel part of what was happening at Louis St. Laurent, I knew in my heart that it was not working the way I had hoped. There was no real place for her there, just a made-up, patched together place—and it was nobody's fault. They did their best and certainly it was the best option available to us at the time. The problem was the thinking behind inclusion for somebody as multiply disabled as Alexis.

Blind and unable to use her hands to sign or her mouth to speak, Alexis could not communicate directly with her fellow students. The students, meanwhile, were at a particularly vulnerable stage in their lives, trying to negotiate their teenage years while at the same time meeting certain academic standards that would allow them to move on to successful adult lives. With all these preoccupations, they had little time or energy left over to work at building a relationship with someone as disabled as Alexis.

Our whole family, along with some friends, attended Alexis' grade 12 graduation ceremony, and waited to see what would happen when she was wheeled up on the stage. Would they acknowledge the hard work of Alexis, her family, Lydia and the school system to get her this far? But nothing of that kind happened. Her name was announced, and she was handed her certificate of attendance. Some perfunctory clapping followed by the audience, but it was less than I had heard for the other students, and I knew at that moment that my choice for her to graduate and leave school after that year had been the correct one.

The ceremony left me with a hollow feeling in my stomach and a determination to carve out an adult life for my daughter with more meaning and dignity attached to it than what she had experienced up to that point. Earlier that spring I had applied for and received a step-grant to employ a university student and had tasked her with developing a day program for Alexis. This person had already worked part-time with Alexis, and therefore had a good idea of what she could do and what she might find interesting to do. She searched out various venues in the city that could possibly accommodate Alexis and be of some meaning and value to her.

At my request, she also explored the possibility of Alexis attending some university courses as an auditor. The coordinator of the On-Campus program, established to include a small number of students with disabilities at the university, very kindly met with her and gave her some pointers and connections to pursue. As a result, Alexis was allowed to audit two university courses in each of the fall and winter terms.

The following year was a busy one for Alexis. Apart from her university classes three days a week, she spent time at the museum, art gallery, space sciences centre and in the evenings or on weekends she attended various plays, festivals and musical events either geared to children or designated as family friendly.

I arranged my own annual program review for Alexis after the second term of the university year had completed, modelled on what Louis St. Laurent school had done each year she was there. The student and I, along with another part-time staff member, carefully reviewed her year's activities in an effort to determine which had been worthwhile for her and which had not. We concluded that the university courses had been the least satisfactory part of them despite various professor and student efforts to make Alexis welcome. It was painfully obvious that her only role there was to remain quiet, listening to material that had no meaning for her. This was, in my opinion, just an exercise in pretend normalization and validation and I wanted more significance than that in Alexis' life.

Why had I pursued a university placement in the first place? I asked myself. This was exactly what I had always thought about such a placement, especially for someone as disabled as Alexis. I had done so because of my tendency to second-guess myself, to believe that others know better, to fear that my biases would limit Alexis' opportunities in life. But, on the positive side, I had been trying to push the boundaries, to open up as much of the world as possible to my daughter. Well, now I knew!

The year after that, Alexis continued attending various venues but no longer took part in the university scene. Thus, her schedule was more relaxed, and we could easily accommodate her bad days or serious seizures by keeping her at home without feeling that she was missing out on anything. It also meant that she could get a later start in the morning and we could attend properly to all her personal care and exercise needs before she went forth into the world.

CHAPTER 39

Community living at home

About this time, we started a different venture for Alexis. She was approaching her 18th birthday and needed to begin the transition into adult living. I had been thinking for a long time about future placement opportunities for her, something we were being encouraged to do by our Handicapped Children's service worker. The usual choice was simply between different agencies who ran different group homes, but I did not feel comfortable with this option. I wanted to keep Alexis at home and to maintain some measure of control over her diet, exercise program and various activities. But I did not want to continue with the tedious, everyday administrative and hands-on work that living with Alexis entailed.

One day I broached my idea of how I could make this happen to Joe. If we wanted to maintain Alexis at home and at the same time have full or nearly full staff coverage, we would have to bring two other individuals with similar levels of disabilities into our home so that staffing costs could be shared by the three of them through their funding allotments.

Joe strongly resisted this idea because of the invasion of privacy it would entail. He was, and is, a very private person. We argued back and forth and even involved professionals to mediate on a couple of occasions because neither of us seemed willing or able to give up our position. I continued to explore all the options available to Alexis for adult living and shared this information with Joe. Like me, he wanted to keep Alexis at home and finally he saw that if we wanted to have a more flexible and less onerous lifestyle than what we currently had, we would have to compromise and invite other children into our home.

I knew of two other teenagers whose parents were also open to a change in lifestyle for their children and together we approached PDD about setting up a unique model that would allow them to live together on the main floor of our home but with full staffing support in place managed by an agency that would take charge of all admin-istrative details.

Early in 1995, shortly after Alexis' 17th birthday, these two young people, aged 15 and 16, moved in with us. People who were much richer than us had overbuilt our home and then the Alberta economy had taken a severe downturn and house prices had crashed. The previous owner, a banker, had invested in a lot of improvements but was then transferred to another city. The trust company that employed him paid him out for the house and it was placed on the market.

When the real estate agent took us to see it, I realized that with its high ceilings, wrap-around windows and skylights it would be perfect for Alexis in our long, dark Edmonton winters and strongly urged Joe that we should buy it. But it was out of our financial range. Finally, he agreed that if they would accept the very low price that was all we could offer then we could have it. Miraculously, they did, and that is why we then had that wonderful facility to share with others.

The main floor has a living room and two dining rooms, all about the same size. Once we had ceiling tracks installed in them to accommodate lifts, they served admirably as bedrooms for the three teenagers. That floor also has a 1000 square foot garden room over-looked by a separate dining area adjacent to the kitchen. It has two glass walls opening onto a patio through two sets of sliding glass patio doors. It is finished in cedar with a very high cedar ceiling and multiple skylights. There is a huge fireplace in the middle of one glass wall and a little pond, complete with three small fountains, runs through part of the room. This beautiful and spacious area is perfect for allowing wheelchairs to move about freely. We were all somewhat overwhelmed by it when we moved there in 1985—except for Alexis who settled right in!

Ten years later, when the other teenagers moved in, Joe and their fathers made some changes to the garden room and nearby bathroom and laundry areas to make them more wheelchair accessible, but once that was done the area provided a pleasant, relaxing space that readily accommodated them all. Meanwhile, we installed a modest second kitchen in the basement in what had previously been set up as a bar area. Between that and our separate bedroom and study areas upstairs, we retained sufficient private space for our own purposes.

It was a big and exciting change to have the other two teenagers, Brandi and Rajan, in residence. We had our mealtime routine for Alexis, as I have described elsewhere, and we expanded that to include the others. Hence, we were now preparing 21 dinners in advance per week. It was quite the factory operation! Other daily living issues had to be coordinated as well and the formerly sedate atmosphere of the house was transformed, giving our home more life than it had ever known under our occupancy alone.

Marty and Richard Cender visited their daughter, Brandi, every night after work and it was soon evident that they were having a great deal of difficulty letting her go. Yet they had been the most enthusiastic about this new living arrangement and had done much to help get the house ready for the move. After five months of this, seeing the sad looks on their faces every time they said goodbye to their daughter, I talked to Marty one day.

"If you don't want to do this anymore, Marty, and you want to take Brandi home, I understand."

She looked at me sorrowfully. "We would never do that, Emma. It would destroy your model. The funding is based on having three clients here, not two."

"But if you could, you would, right?"

"Yes, but we would do the same thing as you have done. We would copy your model and find two other individuals to share our home with Brandi."

"If Joe and I cover the nights then we could maybe make it work," I mused.

At about that time, our arrangement with the agency was breaking down and it was a good time to make a change. Rajan's mother, Kathy worked with me to incorporate us as a separate entity and become a new agency under PDD. In that way we would have control over the staff we hired and the shift hours so our children could go to afternoon activities for a longer time. The seven to three nursing shift hours that the agency employed had been a chronic irritant for us.

I explained to the PDD worker in charge of overseeing our current operation how we could still meet the necessary budget restrictions while operating as an independent agency and serving only two children instead of three. Joe and I would cover the nights as volunteers, and I would do the program administration and supervision at no cost—which would leave us enough money to afford a one-to-one staffing ratio. It was soon agreed and within a short time we were incorporated as the Home-Within-A-Home Society, an official PDD agency with a board, by-laws and bank account to which the funding dollars for staffing could be legally released.

Meanwhile, Marty and Richard took Brandi home and they did indeed find two other girls with similar needs and set up a version of our model. I am happy to say it is still working very well twenty some years down the road. Sadly, Richard passed away a few years ago but Marty has bravely carried on.

A Critical Event

Life went on and it was obvious to us that Rajan and Alexis were as well matched, both psychologically and in terms of their physical needs and sensory impairments, as we were ever going to find. He seemed to feel happy and secure with us and comfortable with Alexis and we came to feel very close to him. However, I now had all the administrative work to deal with that the agency had previously handled and there was extra work for Joe as well in terms of fixing their equipment when it broke down and sharing the job of getting up with one or the other of them at night when needed. We were also stressed because of the increasing difficulty Rajan was having with swallowing and the constant fear that he would aspirate. I tried to convince Kathy that Rajan really needed a stomach tube but without success. Finally, something happened that brought the situation to a head.

On a Sunday afternoon as her shift was finishing, Marie, our most trusted assistant at that time, informed us that we needed to fix the ball tap in the bathtub. The inner workings had become loose, resulting in sudden, erratic changes in water temperature. She urged Joe to change it immediately before something happened and he said he would get to it.

When things go wrong, Joe is the kind of person who attends to them promptly. But a lot of things had recently needed fixing at that point, and he was tired of it all and a little resentful. Also, Marie could be a little pushy at times and this tends to create resistance in people. He said he would fix it later in the week—but three days later something terrible happened.

Joe and I were both away that day, a rare occurrence. One or the other of us always ran to help out when an incident occurred in the house and the assistants were (and still are) used to having this level of support from us. But that day we were not able to provide it because we both needed to be elsewhere. Two assistants were present in the home to care for Rajan and Alexis but one was new and still in training.

It was mid-morning and Rajan was on his commode in his bathroom area and Alexis was on her commode in the laundry area where the raised bathtub was located. She had just finished being bathed and dressed, but as she sat there, she suddenly started throwing up. Then, she panicked, spreading the resulting mess all over, including in her hair—and that is when a fateful decision was made.

"Let's get her back in the tub. Get her clothes off," the senior staff advised the trainee. But Alexis was thrashing so much it was almost impossible, and the mess was everywhere! Finally, they succeeded and the senior staff turned the water on, the tap being positioned in exactly the same place as it had been during her recent bath. Alexis started screaming and thrashing but it looked just like a grand mal seizure, so the assistants were focusing on keeping her from hurting herself by flailing against the sides of the tub. In those few seconds before they properly comprehended what was really happening—that it was actually scalding water that was pouring out of the bathroom tap—Alexis sustained second and third degree burns to both of her feet, her left foot being particularly affected. That was 25 years ago, but to this day we can see how damaged the skin is and we have to be very careful to protect her feet with sunscreen any time she is exposed to the sun.

Our senior staff member was allowed to drive our wheelchair van and she took Alexis to the Medi-Centre where our family doctor worked. He provided immediate and excellent treatment for he was a highly skilled and experienced physician. But he was very upset. Joe returned home that day before me and the doctor phoned to chastise him severely for having the water temperature set high enough to cause such extreme burns.

For six weeks we took Alexis back and forth to the hospital to get the dead and damaged tissue debrided. This caused her considerable pain and I was anguished for her—anguished and angry. I was angry at my husband for not fixing the tap right away, at the experienced assistant for not checking the water temperature, and at myself for not realizing that it should have been turned down in the first place. And, most of all, I kept thinking about how much worse it could have been if it had been Rajan in the tub instead of Alexis.

Rajan was not as strong as Alexis. Also, he was much stiffer, his reflexes seemed less responsive and he was far slower to complain. Would he have been able to jerk his feet away as quickly as Alexis had done? Would he have had the muscle strength and coordination to do that even if he had been in sudden agonizing pain, as Alexis must have been? I did not know. It could have happened. And I asked myself if I was even fit to run this operation.

Joe and I were tired. We were stressed. And this horrible thing had happened. I asked myself what to do and I concluded that the only solution was to simplify the situation in order to make it manageable. I could not let Alexis go but I could let Rajan go, though I did not want to. As I have said, he and Alexis were a nearly perfect match and both Joe and I had grown to care about him. But if we could not serve him well, and at the same time could not serve our own daughter well, what was the point?

I ran my idea by Joe and was surprised to encounter stiff resistance on his part. He wanted Rajan to stay. Yet this was the man who had never wanted this group project in the first place! Joe had grown attached to Rajan and saw how Rajan and Alexis seemed to get along and be in sync with each other in their own way. But I was adamant.

And so we parted and within days of Rajan going to his new

home Kathy was told that he needed a stomach tube or they could not continue caring for him. He got one and has maintained a healthy weight ever since. I sometimes wonder if I had been as insistent as the new agency about the need for a stomach tube, could I have changed Kathy's mind? Could the move have been avoided then? But that is something I will never know, and neither will Kathy. We are both different people now than we were 20 years ago.

For several years, before the pandemic emerged in 2020 and made it impossible, Rajan was visiting Alexis twice a week for several hours each day. We tried to make it a positive experience for him. When we bought the hammock I mention elsewhere, I had Rajan in mind as much as Alexis—and he enjoyed it very much, so much that he now has one the same in his own home! He liked to be outside with Alexis in her gazebos when she was eating, but when she ate inside Joe stopped the staff from placing him close to her. He worried that Rajan would smell the food and feel sad because he could not have any. Rajan enjoyed doing his exercises on Alexis' exercise table while she was on her electric foot bicycle or some other device and he liked going for walks with her when he could. We had to be sensitive to him not sitting in one position for too long, though, because it is bad for his skin.

CHAPTER 41

My Daughter's Work

We have always had certain expectations of ourselves with regards to doing whatever is possible to foster Alexis' wellbeing. But we have also had expectations of her. She is able to use a commode successfully at least some of the time and we expect her to do so whenever possible, while making allowances for the inevitable brain scrambling that occurs during seizure activity or feedback confusion when her body is in an out of a balanced physiological state such as during menstruation.

Alexis has always been treated well and her needs have been attended to promptly and sensitively. Therefore, we expect the same kind of social consideration back from her. We don't expect her to complain loudly for no good reason or to vocalize in settings where it is inappropriate to do so. As a result, we can comfortably take her to restaurants, church and movies or Imax shows. And if she has a spell or seizure that is beyond her control then we remove her from the setting. Somehow, she understands what we expect of her in these situations!

Alexis is also able to be patient when necessary. She often vocalizes when she is on the commode and ready to come off, but if we cannot come immediately for some reason, she waits a couple of minutes before calling out again. This pattern of responses is called socialization and it is what any caring, decent parent does for his or her child. It can be argued, in fact, that socialization, even more than the capacity to reason at a normal level, is what makes us human.[18]

What else can we hope for and expect of Alexis? From the beginning, Joe and I agreed that if we could not help her very much to develop her mind, at least we could collaborate with her to keep the beautiful body she was born with as intact and functional as possible. We knew this would require a lot of work and that she would have to work with us if we were to succeed.

As I stated previously, Alexis' formal exercise program began when she was 9 months and 2 weeks old and it has not stopped since. Her neck muscles were very weak and flaccid so that she could not hold her head up for more than a couple of seconds at a time. Under the direction of the Mayfield physiotherapist Alexis started with seven 'sit-ups' three times a day. We would place her in a prone position (lying on her back) on the floor and, while holding onto her hands, slowly raise her to a sitting position. Her head would lag behind and we would stop halfway and say to her "head up, Alexis." Slowly she would adjust her head and we would congratulate her, raise her to an upright position and then gently lower her to the floor. It did not take long for her to make the connection between raising her head, and only then being raised to an upright position, before being lowered back down to a rest position on the floor.

This evidence of her ability to form a cause-effect relationship was a heartening sign that she was able to understand incoming signals from the world, at least at an elementary level. What was also encouraging from a physiological perspective was that she gradually got better at raising her head!

With further input from the Mayfield and Glenrose Hospital physiotherapists, and later school physiotherapists from the team of resource specialists in the Edmonton Public School Board referred to previously, we gradually developed a comprehensive 'range of motion' (passive exercise) program that encompassed every joint in her body down to her three finger joints and two toe joints.

When we, as laypersons, started this process 43 years ago it was still being frowned upon, with good reason, by most professional physiotherapists. Their belief was that the bone-cartilage-muscle-ligament support structure of the human body was far too complex and delicate to be manipulated by amateurs. And they were right in one sense.

It is very easy to do damage to joints when exercising them. But what is the alternative? The alternative in centre-based programs, at least in the days that I was exploring them, was for a professional physiotherapist to work with each client once or twice a week, often for as little as 15 or 20 minutes at a time.

The assistants who work with Alexis, spend up to an hour at a time covering the complete range of motion and we have routinely done this twice a day instead of once. Has it always been done right? No. We have an elaborate, richly illustrated exercise book and both real time and shortened video presentations. An experienced assistant trains each new staff person on how to do the exercises a minimum of three separate times before the new person is allowed to work alone with Alexis. Even then they are encouraged to do the exercises while working along with the videotape before trying to do them on their own. But still things can go wrong.

When we first started with an agency to maintain Alexis and two friends in our home under an adult, 24-hour funding model, a new staff person caused a permanent arm injury to Alexis. Either she had not received proper supervision—and I was not in charge at that point—or she just had that kind of disrespectful personality where she was going through the motions and wanting to quickly finish an unpleasant job (as she must have perceived it). In any case, she roughly jerked Alexis' right arm over her head without properly warming up the muscles first and severely damaged her rotator cuff. It has never been right since and Alexis has never had the same range of motion in her right arm as she has in her left.

How do I know it was the rotator cuff? After taking Alexis to conventional doctors and receiving no clear diagnosis or help I made arrangements to take her to Dr. Randy Gregg, a former Edmonton

Oiler who, since his retirement as a professional hockey player, has specialized in sports medicine. Sadly, by the time I got in contact with him Alexis' injury had become permanent. However, at least he was able to explain to us what had happened to her and to provide us with strategies for not aggravating the 'gravel' in her shoulder, so we would not make it worse when we did Alexis' range of motion exercises on her arms.

Because of the range of motion work that has been done with Alexis through the years she has the muscle strength and the flexibility to sit squarely on her buttocks in her wheelchair, as long as her trunk and hips are supported to keep her from sliding forward. Sadly, this is not the case for most cognitively impaired individuals with physical disabilities as severe as hers. That is why one generally sees them in reclined positions in tilt-in-space wheelchairs or their equivalents. These are chairs that lean backwards and raise the knees into a w-like position as in hospital beds so that the user cannot slide forward.

For years I looked with compassion, but also a sense of annoyance, at the individuals lolling in these chairs. Now Alexis, weakening with age, and the ongoing debilitating effects of her seizures and other physical problems, is in the same position. She can still sit up but is more comfortable leaning back. One of the many lessons I have learned through my journeying with Alexis is not to be too quick to judge others!

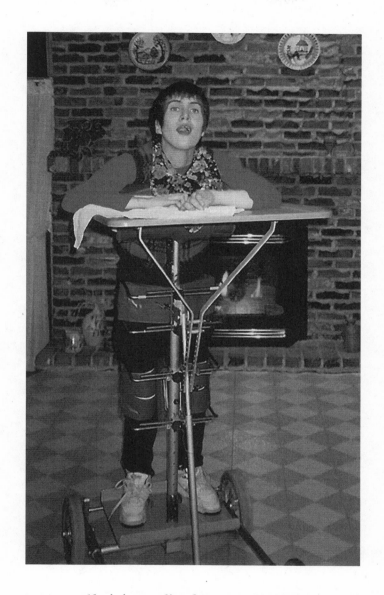

Alexis in standing frame, age 22, 2000

CHAPTER 42

The Standing Frame Story

As I have mentioned previously, Alexis' range-of-motion program was supplemented by the suggestions we received from Margaret George, based on input from the Philadelphia Patterning program. One invaluable exercise that we have always maintained since Alexis started on that program at age two is something Margaret called "the sleepy bear." It consists of pushing Alexis' shoulders in one direction and her hips in the other and then reversing sides. This exercise has helped to keep her spine and hip joints flexible through the years.

What the Glenrose physiotherapists added to Alexis' life was an emphasis on leg and foot development. From the time she was about two until she was 38, she was in a standing frame every day or second day for up to an hour at a time. In order to accomplish this, she has had to have what are known as ankle-foot orthotics, or AFO's. This is a leg and foot brace made out of hard silicone or plastic extending almost to her knees and cast to fit her legs and feet exactly. These AFO's keep her in the proper position for weight bearing and also maintain heel cord length so she can wear normal shoes. In order to maintain that position, we have also done daily heel cord stretches, leg stretches, positioning exercises, and toe mobility stretches with Alexis. Interestingly, a Glenrose physiatrist we consulted years ago asked us why we bothered to do the heel cord stretches since Alexis would never be able to walk, anyway! This is one of many examples I could provide as to why we decided long ago that we could not entirely trust professionals to provide the answers that Alexis needed. But that resulting lack of trust has cost me and therefore has cost Alexis too. The Standing Frame story provides a good example of this and I am sure the catch-22 position we found ourselves in with regard to its use has also happened to other families in our position.

Here is the story of the frame: its rise, its fall and its surprising resurrection! We have had the same wheeled standing frame since Alexis was 7 years old. It was adjusted by Glenrose technicians through the years to accommodate her growth and in the past 10 or 15 years we have returned there for assistance on several occasions because Alexis' left foot was raising up while in the frame. As a result, she was taking all her weight on her right leg and complaining more and more each time we put her in it. Finally, no more accommodation could be done, and we had to face the fact that Alexis was in more pain than she could or should bear while standing in this position. Although we well knew the importance of weight bearing to prevent calcium loss in the bones and to keep her 'neurological scoliosis'[19] in check, we regretfully concluded that we had to discontinue its use.

This was not an easy decision because the standing frame had added much to Alexis' life. Standing tall in it, even taller than the rest of us, I like to think she has a different perspective on life despite the fact that we have been told she cannot see. It keeps her back straight and checks the constant pull of the muscles that twist her spine into a modified c shape otherwise. It was her chiropractor who informed us that Alexis has a 'neurological' scoliosis because the spine itself had not yet been permanently distorted.

When Alexis is in a standing position, we are also able to use our heavy-duty massager on her back, providing valuable sensory input. The rest of the time her back is either blocked against the back of her chair, her bolster in bed, or the exercise or change table. It is therefore inaccessible to us and insensible to her. I believe that having

access to it so we can massage and stimulate it helps her to understand where her body is in space and to become aware that she even
has a back. The strong pulsing of the massage unit also goes some way
towards undercutting the unnatural pull of the muscles, thereby correcting, at least for a short time the 'neurological scoliosis'. After we
stopped using the frame, we still tried to use the massager when she
was lying on her side on the exercise table, but it was not the same.

There is another reason that the standing frame has been such a
gift to Alexis. Many times through the years I have put on a CCR
(Credence Clearwater Revival) tape or cd and swung her around in
the standing frame as we danced together. I can feel her following the
beat and sometimes I have even drummed her hand on the attached
tray as an accompaniment to the rhythm. Dancing is something special for me and I have always wanted Alexis to feel the music pounding in her blood as it does in mine. These dance sessions have been
some of our best times together when I have felt most connected to
her and I believe that she senses that and feels the same. There is
something special about having her at the same level as me when we
dance, and in her standing frame she has been my best dance partner
ever! With my husband, an accomplished but only mildly enthusiastic
dancer, I was never able to give into that same wild rhythm on the
dance floor.

For almost three years we parked the standing frame in our storage room and lived with this sad state of affairs, as if it was the end
of an era. Then something unexpected happened. I was seeing a
physiotherapist for my own persistent right shoulder problems and I
shared with him my concerns about Alexis' increasing spasticity since
we had stopped using the standing frame. On his invitation, Joe and
I brought Alexis in for a session, but I don't think he had realized
how serious her disabilities were and he had little to offer us in terms
of remediation. However, he told us that he knew of a specialist
physiotherapist who might be able to help her with the spasticity and
we promptly made an appointment with this individual.

During our first meeting with Pranjali, I told her all about the standing frame saga, why we had stopped using it, and how we were now seeing an increase in Alexis' spasticity and in her scoliosis. And this is the part that is hard to share here. All those years, when I had been seeing Alexis becoming increasingly uncomfortable with the standing frame, I had assumed that it was due to a rotation in her left hip that had in turn caused her left leg to retract upwards. I had seen this happen to several others in her situation. Therefore, my focus had been on accessing Glenrose technical assistance to adjust the frame in such a way as to accommodate the shortened leg. But no matter how many times it was adjusted her leg just seemed to keep shrinking upwards and the situation kept getting worse and worse until it was impossible to continue with her in the frame. But I was wrong.

After examining Alexis, Pranjali calmly informed me that the in-turned hip I had postulated was functional, not structural in nature due to the strong pull of the spastic muscles. Her own examination of Alexis led her to believe that maybe she would be able to use the standing frame again and she asked us to bring it along for the next visit. And therein lies another story!

Pranjali's next available appointment was at 10 AM on a weekday morning and that is never a good time for Alexis. Getting her up, dressed, fed and attending to her other personal care needs is a time-consuming process. Also, because of the size of the standing frame it was necessary to take two vans and the trip itself took 40 minutes. Joe left first with Alexis and the assistant and I followed him in our other van with the standing frame, since it is about five feet tall and non-collapsible.

When we arrived at the physical therapy centre, Joe helped me unload the standing frame from the back of the van and then went ahead quickly with Alexis since she was already a couple of minutes late for her appointment. I followed shortly but by the time I took the elevator to the second floor and headed up the long hall to the therapy centre they were already out of sight. As I went along, I noticed water on the floor and looked up at the ceiling to see if there was a drip. But then I noticed that the water proceeded in a long trail all the way up that long hallway. Suddenly, to my horror, I realized what had happened!

Several years previously I had placed Alexis on an Atkins modified diet on the advice of a group of nurses who had been researching its use in cases of intractable seizure disorder. I felt that I had to try this with Alexis as her seizures had become life-threatening at that point. The diet worked marvellously in controlling the seizures but at the cost of some devastating and permanent effects on bladder and bowel function. We had done what we could to remediate the situation and been successful up to a point, but Alexis still experienced bladder blockage on occasion. She would be unable to void for up to 12 hours at a time and when her bladder did finally let go, she would pass up to a litre of urine, three times the normal adult void.

On the morning in question Alexis had not been able to urinate when she was on her commode. On arriving on the floor of the physical therapy centre, her bladder must have reached its tipping point and nature had taken over! I searched frantically for a washroom to access some paper towels but when I finally located it, the door was locked. I headed for the therapy office and warned Joe and Charlene, her assistant, of what was happening. They had not even noticed. Pranjali gave them access to a private room where they could change Alexis into the fresh clothes we had brought along. Meanwhile I acquired the key to the washroom, accessed the paper towels and cleaned up the tell-tale trail. Just another day in the exciting life of the Pivato family!

Pranjali took all this in her stride and after that unfortunate beginning she was able to get Alexis into a relaxed enough condition that Joe and I and Alexis' assistant could lift and secure her in her standing frame. It was, of course, a shock for her since she had not been in it for almost three years at that point, and Pranjali used all her magic to work away the spasticity so Alexis could stand with reasonable comfort for about 15 minutes. We were elated! I gauged my own mood and realized that I had gone from dark despair to giddy happiness in a matter of half an hour. As Joe has always maintained, in our life with Alexis there is never a dull moment! And in retrospect I can appreciate the black humour in this scenario. Black humour has been an important soporific for us through our years of negotiating Alexis' life. And friends in the same situation as we are in have also found that to be the case. I remember a friend once half-bragging and half-complaining that her five-year-old, nonverbal and severely autistic son had been able to open a brand-new large bottle of mouthwash and dump the entire contents down the drain!

The positive result of the incident with Alexis described above—and one must always look for the positive—was Pranjali's suggestion that it might be easier for us if she were to visit Alexis at home to help the process of getting her re-established in the frame. Of course, she might have privately been thinking that it would also be easier for the clinic, but in any case, we were delighted with this offer!

Pranjali came to see Alexis weekly for several months and gradually we were able to re-establish Alexis full standing frame routine and to do so without undue discomfort to her. Pranjali also provided a workshop to train our entire staff on how to reduce the spasticity in Alexis' legs prior to her use of the standing frame and she reviewed Alexis overall range of motion program as well making various helpful suggestions and emphasizing the importance of proper head positioning.

The Pranjali story, touching as it is to us, is not unique in our life with Alexis. Through the years there have been others who have gone well out of their way to support her or to support us. I think it brings out the desire in people to help when they see how hard we are trying to build a positive life for our daughter and how positively she responds.

CHAPTER 43

Other useful therapy devices

Many of the rehabilitation devices used for Alexis through the years have only worked for her because her foot and leg alignment has been maintained through the use of the standing frame and daily exercises. The most successful of these has been her electric foot bicycle. Joe built a platform under the foot bicycle to raise it, and by removing her wheelchair foot pieces and tying her feet to the pedals with bungee cords, she has been able to pedal away on it for as long as she wants while sitting comfortably in her wheelchair. We usually set the timer for 15 minutes.

Joe and I remember dearly the first time we fastened her feet into this device and turned it on. The look on her face was priceless. As Joe said at the time, "She thinks she is pedalling to Red Deer!" (a small city 150 kilometres south of Edmonton). "She thinks she is doing it herself!"

The exercise this device provides for Alexis' legs and knees is very important. And I very much regret that we did not know of its existence (if, in fact, it existed) and acquire it much sooner, when her limbs were still young and relatively supple. We did have a mechanical foot unit but getting down on one's knees and turning the pedals for her did not appeal to our assistants for very long, or to me at all. I have bad knees and a short attention span!

As good as this device is for Alexis from a physical perspective,

I believe it is even more powerful from a psychological one. People as disabled as Alexis are used to having things done to them or for them—but never by them. The sense of self-efficacy she must feel, using her legs without a person leaning over her and moving them, must be powerful. It is noteworthy that she rarely complains when she is pedalling on the bicycle.

Another device that has worked well for Alexis is something called the 'back-to-life' machine. While lying on her back on her padded exercise table, the device is placed under her knees. It gently raises them up and down for the number of minutes pre-set by the timer. What this machine does that is so important is to stretch out her spine—the area of her body that is generally immobile and insensible to her.

A favourite device our assistants use with Alexis while they relax and eat their dinner is a leg and foot massager. Alexis' legs are inserted into this machine and it pulses back and forth against them and her feet at a controlled rate. If set too high, the resulting pressure can cause bruises, so we have experimented with finding the optimal level of pressure and length of treatment. Alexis' tolerance and enjoyment of the machine tell us when we have it right. It does have one drawback though. It is quite noisy!

Alexis also uses one of Dr. Ho's foot circulation machines periodically. This can only work because her feet are still sufficiently well shaped to sit directly on the footpads. Electrodes attached to her legs allow for some limited stimulation of the calves at the same time.

For the past 30 years we have also had a proper electro-muscle stimulation machine. This is more powerful and with the potential to cover more body area at once than either the Dr. Ho machine or the classic tens machine that physiotherapists often use for treating specific areas of concern such as a sore shoulder. Only licensed professionals are allowed to use these big machines and they are not sold to the general public because when used incorrectly they can do more harm than good. However, I was determined to acquire one for Alexis.

When there is no way to get direct verbal feedback from a person you are trying to help, you have little opportunity to know what intervention is or is not doing any good. What we have been told by various professionals is that there is some evidence that neuro-muscle stimulation used on the back muscles can delay or even reduce the progression of scoliosis to some extent. We have also learned that this type of stimulation can reduce spasticity, at least temporarily, giving her chronically tensed muscles a chance to rest. There have even been suggestions from one or two professionals that this process may ward off the onset of seizure activity, or at least reduce the intensity of a seizure.

After thirty years I cannot recall the qualifications of the woman who sold me our initial neuro-muscle stimulation machine by first purchasing it for herself and then passing it on. But I do remember that she was working in the area of alternative medicine and was well aware that this was not a legitimate transaction. To protect herself, she stripped off every piece of identifying information before selling me the machine and as a result I had great difficulty replacing the electrodes—the thin wires of which tended to break under constant use. I did find a source that could identify them from our existing ones and sell me substitutes but even that source finally dried up when they realized that I was not actually licensed to operate such a machine.

I found another source and we were able to keep the machine going a few years longer, but it finally broke down altogether. It was so old there were no replacement parts and we had to search out a new machine. After a year of researching, and with help from another professional in the field, a machine was finally identified that could do what we needed it to do for a price we could afford, and we again purchased it in this indirect manner. But it is so complicated that we have been afraid to use it. With the old machine we felt that, at the very least, we weren't doing any harm and were providing Alexis with a novel sensory experience, and at most it might actually be helpful in addressing one or more of the issues mentioned above. But the new machine is far more complicated and powerful than our old one and I was afraid that we might cause harm with it.

When Pranjali started coming for home visits we told her the story and showed her the machine. At first, she did not believe that it could help Alexis and even speculated that it might make her seizures worse. But the fact is that there is no clear clinical evidence to either support or refute its usefulness in ameliorating neurological scoliosis, spasticity or seizure activity meant that we felt obliged to at least try.

"It might add something positive to Alexis' life," I explained to Pranjali. "Can you please teach us how to use it properly so that at least we don't do any damage to her with it?" Finally, she agreed with me that under carefully controlled conditions, it was worth a try. We are beginning with neck and shoulder stimulation in the hope of correcting, or at least moderating, Alexis chronic head lag to the left. She explained that correct bodily alignment can only follow from correct head alignment so that is where we must start. Pranjali has pre-set the controls at a low level, to be adjusted upward if Alexis' response warrants it. If this works, we will then move on to doing some back stimulation in the hopes of at least partially ameliorating her neurological scoliosis.

Perhaps the real question underlying this chapter is: Why have we placed so much emphasis on machines and on meeting Alexis' needs for physical stimulation and rehabilitation as opposed to placing more emphasis on social and cognitive needs? The only answer I can provide is the following: what I look for primarily is a certain expression on Alexis' face that tells me she is engaged in the world. Direct physical interaction is what most often results in that expression.

Cognitive and Social Stimulation

We are coping with another issue with Alexis that has always been a problem to some extent but is much worse in recent years. Because of her unpredictable, and sometimes violent seizure activity, as well as her sudden bouts of non-breathing that can occur without warning, our assistants are no longer comfortable taking her out alone. As a result, it is up to Joe or me to drive them to various venues if Alexis is to get out. Since we are now retired this should not be a problem, but somehow it is.

We both have our own ongoing projects that occupy us, and we have no particular interest in attending most of the places that work best for Alexis except for the occasional Imax theatre presentation that we all enjoy. When I take her out, I often bring my computer and work on it in while Alexis tours the site with her assistant. That way I can quickly be at her side if there is a problem since we all carry cell phones. This works best in places like the zoo where I can sit in the café without paying an entrance fee and least well in places like Fort Edmonton Park where I must either huddle on a bench outside or pay a steep entrance fee to be able to use their restaurant as a place to work while having a coffee.

Once or twice a month Joe and I take Alexis out for dinner at one of the restaurants we have discovered through the years where her particular needs can be accommodated: a quiet corner where I can feed her discreetly (watching smeared food on her mouth and bib as she dribbles it out does not do much for the dining pleasure of other patrons), a handy electrical outlet not too close to the eyes and ears of others where I can grind up her food in our small Cuisinart machine, a peaceful atmosphere with no blaring music or loud, disruptive clients, and a patient and obliging server.

We have also been in the habit of taking Alexis to Mass every Saturday at 5 pm unless she is too groggy from a seizure or a nap that started too late, or is upset from one of her screaming seizure attacks. She seems to enjoy it. Our church, near the back, has several indented rows of pews to allow space for wheelchairs beside them. On good days we are able to access the end seats in one of those pews so we can park Alexis' chair beside us. However, it seems to be human nature for people to cling to the end seats and not everyone is willing to move to accommodate us.

Parking has been another issue. There are few people in wheelchairs in the church and those who do come are usually driven by DATS, the "Disabled Adult Transportation System" that is available in Edmonton. Yet, the dozen or so wheelchair parking spaces are always full. In the winter particularly, we struggle through the snow and ruts in the parking lot with the wheelchair and look at the sometimes tiny cars parked in the big wheelchair spaces. Many people, especially some older folks, have legitimate mobility issues and have therefore been granted a 'handicapped' sticker. However, if you are too disabled to walk more than a few steps on level ground, then it is unlikely that you would be able to manoeuver yourself in or out of a sports car!

In the church we sit near the back so if Alexis has a violent seizure or sudden screaming spell we can get out quickly and not disrupt the service. Some days Alexis makes it through the Mass with no problems and seems to enjoy it. Other days Joe quickly takes her out. He is better at calming her than I am because I tend to get tense and worked up.

A lot of times we sit outside the church in the reception area and look through the wall of glass windows and listen through the external speakers that don't always work. Before the Mass I go into the back pews and apologetically appropriate a set of the two hymn-books so I can sing along. The good thing about being outside is that we can relax. We don't have to worry about what Alexis is going to do next. Also, we can sit one on each side of her in chairs Joe appropriates from the adjoining committee room. Alexis likes having that close support on both sides and we feel that in general she just enjoys going out with her parents.

The server comes out to administer the Eucharist to us. Joe and I partake and then the server and I go through the same ceremony with Alexis. When she manages to swallow it without choking, we are both happy and relieved and deeply feel her success.

Wherever we sit it is quite clear that Alexis enjoys the music when it is good and puts her head down in disgust when it is bad. I call it bad when there is no noticeable tune and it comes across as more of a funeral dirge than a psalm. It is times like that I momentarily regret my conversion to Catholicism. The United Church in which I grew up always had lively music.

Since I like to sing and enjoy a good melody and particularly a good rhythm, this funereal type of music also puts me in a bad mood but invariably I find Alexis' head down responses amusing. I always recall Joe's classic assessment of our observations of Alexis: "She may be handicapped but she's not stupid!"

What I have described above has been our church-going pattern for the past 35 years, but not anymore! After enough experiences of uninspiring music, lack of parking and outer seat-hogging, Joe decided to do something about it. He determined that we should try out the new Sunday afternoon youth mass that had recently sprung into being at our church and it turned out to be a good idea. The Youth Mass is lively with a youth choir playing their own string and horn instruments to a much less crowded congregation and with ample handicapped parking available. It has proven to be a much better experience for Alexis and for us. But just a few months after we started on this new venture, in the spring of 2020, our whole country went into lockdown because of the pandemic and it came to an end. In July of 2020 our heavily populated church opened up again, but only by appointment and to a small number of parishioners at a time, so that part of our life is on hold for the time being. The risks of exposure outweigh the benefits of going, or any sense of holy obligation we might feel. We literally could not manage if one of us were to be infected and we then needed to send all Alexis' staff away while we went into isolation! And the horror of Alexis contracting Covid-19 is literally unthinkable!

Alexis' twice daily walks appear to be a source of pleasure to her, particularly when it is raining. Many times I have seen her coming back from her walk dripping wet but happy! I guess when you are locked in a world where you cannot see and cannot talk or understand most of what others say to you, the unusual sensation of rain on your face represents a refreshing change from your daily paucity of perception.

As long as the weather allows, Alexis eats all her meals on her screened in deck. She loves listening to the sounds of the birds and the squirrels and the swish of the wind through our tall trees. At this point of writing there is little else for her: no restaurant meals, church, or other venues. Even Rajan can't visit her on the DATS bus anymore. It is all just too dangerous because of the virus. But Alexis seems content enough. I am the only one who worries that we should be doing something more socially. However, who is to say what has meaning and value for her and what does not? We know she would enjoy some of the things she is currently missing but the risk we would be taking is just too high. And she seems content enough the way things are.

Alexis, Joe and Emma in Jasper by the Athabasca River, 2013

CHAPTER 45

The cart story

Alexis is quite well known in the neighbourhood from her regular walks in her large red cart. After she outgrew her infant 'Umbroller' stroller, basically a supportive sack, and then a larger, sack-like stroller designed for older disabled children, Alexis got her first wheelchair. But anyone who has had the pleasure of pushing a wheelchair around knows you cannot get too far with it outside unless you have access to a paved surface. One horrible early memory I have is of trying to push young Alexis in her wheelchair through the soggy grass of Hawreluk Park, Edmonton, during our annual summer *Heritage Days* celebration. The chair stuck constantly in the wet grass and threatened to tip over.

One summer when Alexis was about ten, our family was in Banff and we saw in the window of a camping shop an extended baby jogger designed for older children. We purchased it and it changed Alexis' life and ours. It gave her a degree of freedom she had never known before. For the first time we were able to take her for walks in the winter, the large wheels of the jogger easily slicing through the snow. We could also take her up and down the walking trails in our local ravine by tying a strap to the front frame so that one person could push the stroller while the other person pulled at the front as we worked our way up some of the steeper hills. With the stroller we were emboldened to take Alexis and our other children to the mountains for longer stretches of time. And just tooling around the neighbour-hood was much easier and faster than it was with the wheelchair, so we were able to go longer distances.

But Alexis continued growing and her feet hung perilously over the edge of the footrest—which was at that point so high in relation to her body that her knees were practically in her face. The husband of one of our assistants was a welder and he kindly offered to design and forge a new footrest that he then mounted lower on the frame so that Alexis' legs were once more in the proper position. This held us for a few more years, but the lightweight aluminum frame of the chair, the same frame that made it so easy to move around, was gradually wearing out.

One summer we were in Canmore, Alberta (a tourist town near Banff where we own a timeshare) when the front axle of the cart broke while we were strolling along the street with Alexis. Fortunat-ely, we were not out of town on any of the nearby mountain trails we liked to walk with her! It was not easy to get Alexis out of the jogger at any time as it was designed like the early 'Umbrollers', with a flex-ible sack in which an individual could sit much as they might sit in a beanbag chair that conforms to their shape. It was even harder in this case because the cart was now tilting precariously to one side, but together we managed to get Alexis out of the cart and strapped into the back seat of the van.

We loaded the cart in the van and went in search of someone who could help us, but the cart's frame could not be welded back together because it was aluminum, so garages had nothing to offer. We ended up at a bicycle shop where my husband bought a second-hand children's bike, removed the front axle and replaced the cart's broken axle with it by using plumber's grips. It worked quite well, but after that the cart always veered to the left when we pushed it. This meant that the driver of the cart had to constantly make correc-tions and resulted in many complaints from Alexis' assistants.

The cart was continuing to deteriorate, and we worried about what to do once it became unusable. Fortunately, a friend with an ambulatory daughter had a large cart to sell, a new type of cart that had only recently come on the market. We purchased it, but for the first time were presented with a new challenge. It was not a sack like its predecessors but a conventional cart that, like lawn chairs, was upholstered in a sturdy but very rigid fabric. It was inclined so Alexis could lean back, and it did have support straps, but with her pronounced scoliosis and tendency to slump to the left side, she could not sit comfortably in it, and when she had one of her increasingly violent hot screaming spells, she managed to thrust herself forward at a dangerous angle and could not easily be repositioned.

After considerable experimentation, we managed to raise the back straps enough so that she could not thrust forward too far, and we also found a memory foam head and shoulder shaped sleep pillow that worked to support her left side so that she remained in a comfortable and normalized position. I mention all this tedious detail just to point out the kind of flexible thinking required to cope with all the exigencies that go along with supporting an individual with such multiple and complex disabilities. It can be done. It just can't be done if you don't learn to think outside the box.

CHAPTER 46

Impulse buying—pros and cons

There are two other material items in Alexis' world that I have not yet mentioned—a hammock and a jet tub—that add to her leisure life. For years we have played off and on with the notion of a hammock, and I even purchased one when Alexis was young, but it never worked, and it certainly would have been dangerous to leave her in it unattended. Alexis herself did not feel safe in it and actually cannot tolerate being in a horizontal position on her back because she then tends to choke on her saliva. Thus, she immediately tensed up when placed there, the exact opposite effect to what we were hoping for.

One afternoon quite a few summers ago I was wandering around London Drugs, a large Edmonton drugstore chain, when I was stopped short by a novel hammock arrangement. Instead of being flat it was arched up in the back with metal sides holding the sack-like hammock in a firm position. These sides were so high that I could see immediately how Alexis could be placed in it with no danger of her falling out. Also, it was possible to stabilize the hammock against the frame to prevent it from swinging back and forth when loading and unloading, an important consideration.

In my younger, rasher days I would have purchased it immediately. I did that once, seeing a willow rocker in a store, a chair that seemed to have enough support for Alexis to sit in normally with no further adjustments or support ties needed. I hemmed and hawed for about two minutes but remained delighted and obsessed with the concept, so I bought five of them, one for each member of our family. My 'Alice in Wonderland' fantasy was that if Alexis could not sit in our chairs, we would all sit in hers! I visualized us relaxing around the fire in the evening rocking away in a little circle, equal and together for once as a family. It was a compelling picture.

But, when I got them home my husband was not equally impressed, to put it mildly, and as it turned out, Alexis could not sit in the chair without sliding forward into a dangerous and uncomfortable position, so my little dream went out the window along with the five chairs. I gave away some and returned the rest.

The same thing happened a few years later when I went sofa shopping. I came across an amazingly inexpensive black leather sofa unit with a high gloss finish that I thought would be reasonably impervious to Alexis' drool. It had a conventional sofa back with an extended lounge piece and a high arm that should prevent Alexis flopping over the side. I imagined her sitting there with her legs stretched out restfully in front, enjoying our company as we sat beside her perhaps watching a television show. Again, I did not consult my husband who generally managed to counter my more innovative suggestions, and in due course the sofa arrived at the house.

Joe took one look at the sofa and informed me that it would not work. I glared at him and managed to hoist Alexis out of the wheelchair and onto the unit. Standing behind it I was then able to easily pull her back so she was firmly placed against the back of the sofa with her legs stretched out in front of her just the way I wanted. But unfortunately, the reason I could adjust her so easily was because of its smooth, slippery surface. Within seconds she managed to slide all the way forward until her legs were hanging off the end. The sofa never worked for Alexis. It sat accusingly in the middle of our living room like a big, black monolith for several years until I managed to rationalize giving it away to a friend who seemed to be in need of it.

This time with the hammock I was not taking any chances, but as I tried to explain it to Joe on the phone, he had all the reasons why it would not work. I insisted that he come to see it however and would not take 'no' for an answer. This time I *knew* I was right. He arrived a short time later in not very good temper, took one look at the hammock and surprised me by turning to the salesperson and telling him that we would take it. He saw at a glance that it would work!

Alexis' response to the hammock was the same as her response to the electric foot bicycle. She felt the sense of her own power and it delighted her! Whenever she moves in the hammock—and she is rarely still—the hammock moves with her and I believe she feels like she is powering it herself! The fact that it arches up means that her head and upper chest are always upright, so she cannot choke on her saliva. She is completely relaxed in the hammock, as was Rajan when he visited.

Early on when Alexis was about 10 years old, we acquired a hot tub for her. I thought she would enjoy the jets and floating around in the warm water. But she never felt safe and for some irritating reason the water never really got warm enough to be fully relaxing. In a bath chair her head and shoulders were too far out of the water to keep her warm and in a life jacket we had less control of her unless we got in the tub with her. Eventually, we gave up and looked for a different answer.

The answer came to me one day in another store when I saw a regularly sized jetted bathtub. We purchased it and Joe ripped out the old bathtub we had installed on the main floor for her. Then he built a frame to mount the new jet tub on so it would be at a comfortable height for us or the assistants to bathe her and she has been using it ever since, about 20 years now. It is probably the single best piece of equipment for her in which we have ever invested!

However, there are many other pieces of equipment we have purchased through the years that did not work as we thought they might. Joe and I have each fallen into this trap at times. A lot of them have to do with our ongoing battle to provide Alexis with comfortable bathroom facilities when she is away from home. And that is the topic I will address next.

CHAPTER 47

The Travelling Bathroom Dilemma

A major chunk of my mental energy over the past 35 years has gone into solving the toilet access issue for Alexis and others in her situation when they are away from home. I am talking about any wheelchair-bound individual too disabled to do either a standing or seat-to-seat transfer to a public toilet, and anyone without the upper body strength and control to use any device for toileting purposes but a specially adapted commode unit.

We are fortunate in Alberta to have had a powerful advocacy voice to speak on behalf of individuals with developmental disabilities. But people in Alexis' condition represent a very small part of that population, perhaps one or two percent at most. They and their advocates are only a faint whisper when it comes to fleshing out favourite advocacy terms like access, dignity and inclusion. A fundamental need for all of us, labeled or otherwise, is access to private and clean bathroom facilities when away from home. But "handicapped" washrooms or washroom stalls in public places have virtually no meaning or value for individuals with really severe physical challenges.

Some families in situations like ours have solved the bathroom access problem by never attempting to toilet train in the first place, and just using the biggest and most absorbent diapers they can find for trips of any length outside the home. Others continue to toilet train at home and at school until the individual becomes too big for one person to lift. And many professionals believe that even attempting to toilet train children with such severe and complex needs is pointless.

The logistical problems are huge with Alexis and others like her. We are talking about people with no formal communication system and no physical capacity to help themselves. Yet I have remained fervent and obsessed with this toileting issue all these years. And I am sure it has caused some to wonder about my mental health!

When I ask myself 'why', two answers come to mind. Alexis' early positive responses in this area were the first sign to me that there really was someone there. And secondly, her slender, well-proportioned body, attractive face and pleasing personality seem to me to radiate a certain dignity. I do not want anything to take away from that dignity. At one point in the long, adaptive commode saga I even referred to the prototype that had been created as 'the dignity chair'.

Through Alexis' young years we devised various stopgap solutions to the toileting issue so we could take her places. One year, for example, the kind people at West Edmonton Mall allowed us to place her portable commode in their first aid room for the summer. As a result, Alexis was able to spend the best part of many happy days at the water park and the amusement park there. But that did not help us much when we wanted to take her elsewhere.

Joe tried to make special support seats that we could carry with us and place on regular toilets. At one point we even bought a porta-potty unit and he rigged up a support frame for it. All these devices were cumbersome and none of them could be carted around public venues easily or discreetly. Also, none of them made Alexis feel secure enough so she could function the way she did on her adapted commode at home.

The strategy to which we mostly defaulted was simply to never go any place with Alexis for more than two hours at a time. This placed severe restrictions on our social life outside the home, not only for Alexis and for us, but also for our other two children. I realized that we had to find a way for Alexis to maintain her toileting, and for the rest of us to still have a life!

One day, when Alexis was 10 or 11, I was on my way to a small town in Northeastern Alberta called Cold Lake, about 300 kilometers from Edmonton. At that time I was a psychologist for the Edmonton Public School Board specializing in the assessment of children with multiple and severe disabilities, and Cold Lake was within our catchment area.

As I drove along, I was mulling over the toileting issue for Alexis. I knew that one big problem was that she had to be firmly supported. Another was that with her low muscle tone she needed a toilet seat sized to her small frame that could keep her stable. I thought of various configurations, searching for one that would give her the same upper body support she had in her wheelchair and still be small enough to carry around with us.

As I pondered this conundrum, a proverb came to mind: *If the mountain won't come to Muhammad, then Muhammad must go to the mountain.* I realized suddenly that the only device that would give Alexis the support that her wheelchair provided and at the same time be feasible to carry around with us when we travelled was, in fact, her wheelchair!

My first thought after this epiphany was one of revulsion accompanied by a fear of social rejection. Who would use their chair as a toilet! It would immediately be perceived as grossly unhygienic. The *ick* factor seemed insurmountable. And my own sense of personal squeamishness almost caused me to dismiss the idea without any further consideration. But then I thought: *There is a way to make this a hygienic process. In fact, from the user's point of view it could be more hygienic than using a public toilet seat could ever be!*

I then allowed myself to properly consider the possibilities. People who are as disabled as Alexis cannot use a regular folding wheelchair with its cloth seating sling and back. They need those parts to be replaced by a specially adapted insert that provides adequate shaping and cushioning to support their poorly muscled bottoms, and with proper moulding and strapping to shore up their upper bodies.

These inserts sometimes come in one piece permanently attached to the wheelchair from which the original cloth back and seat slings have been removed. But sometimes, as in Alexis' case, they come in two pieces. Her wheelchair back is securely attached to the frame but the seat cushion slides in and out. I speculated that it could simply be removed and a toilet seat and shallow commode unit attached underneath. Then it could be replaced and the top of the wheelchair seat would never come in contact with the commode unit so there would then be no hygiene issue.

So where did that bring me? I wondered. If some clever person could put such a chair together as I had conceived, then all we would need to do was to find some way to conceal the commode unit and Alexis could present herself with as much dignity in public as any of the rest of us. Now just two problems remained. Who could I get to develop such a unit? And how would we handle the lifting and transferring problem? It is not as if public washrooms had private change tables, except small ones for babies, that we could use.

Then another thought occurred to me: Alexis was due for a new wheelchair as she had outgrown her existing one. This was always a three-stage process. First there would have to be an assessment to determine if she actually needed one. Then the wheelchair would have to be chosen and ordered. And thirdly, one of the seating specialists at Glenrose Rehabilitation Hospital would need to design a new seating insert for her. All I would have to do would be to convince this specialist that the seat had to be removable, a commode unit had to be installed beneath it, and the wheelchair itself needed to be a fully reclining unit.

I had recently seen a wheelchair that reclined to a completely horizontal position. If we could get one of those chairs, we could then use it in that position as a change table for adjusting Alexis' clothing. After that we could simply take out the seat cushion, raise Alexis to an upright position and, voila, she would be sitting on her commode unit! Time passed, and when Alexis' appointment came up we met with Peter Jarvis, the Glenrose orthotics technician assigned to prepare Alexis' seating insert.

I described my idea and the rationale behind it to Peter with the same eager passion I always employ when I think of a new way to improve Alexis' life and the lives of others like her. Sometimes it seems to turn people off and sometimes they buy into it. I never know in advance which way it is going to go, so these meetings are always nerve wracking. Through the years this adapted wheelchair project has been particularly problematic. I am always afraid that in trying to sell the idea of it to those who might actually be able to make it happen for the not insignificant number of people who could benefit, I will turn more people off than on with my zeal.

But back then, more than thirty years ago when Alexis was 11, Peter was enthusiastic about the idea and did his best to make it happen. He located a version of the reclining wheelchair I had identified, measured Alexis and got to work. The chair, like most wheelchairs, was a folding one. That meant it had crossbars underneath to provide the necessary structural support and to allow it to collapse for storage during transport. As I had been dreaming on my way to Cold Lake that day several months previously, I had not considered that!

The problem seemed insuperable, but Peter came up with a solution. He had available some very specialized equipment because custom-made trunk supports were still necessary at that time for people in Alexis' condition, and they were all molded individually to achieve a proper fit. Peter moulded a pot in the shape of an egg timer that fit snugly but easily between the crossbars and then he cast it in durable plastic.

The next problem was the toilet seat. Alexis is small and she was very small in those days. Peter cast one to fit her out of soft rubber that allowed her to sit comfortably and conformed readily to her body, providing maximum support. Unfortunately he sprayed it with black, waterproof paint, and every time Alexis used it she came away with black bits of paint on her bottom!

The trunk support was created with the same level of skill and competence as the other wheelchair adaptations so it fit Alexis well and provided maximum support. She was happy and comfortable sitting in her wheelchair proper as well as on the commode version, and because of that chair we were able to travel as a family and expand our horizons for the first time. I should mention that by that time we had installed a wheelchair lift in our van and were able to transport Alexis in her chair instead of transferring her into the car seat and then storing the chair.

For the next three years Alexis travelled freely. The only problem we had in attending to her bathroom needs in public washrooms was that most handicapped stalls were too small to allow the wheelchair to recline in order to adjust her clothing. But we did find a few in the city that were large enough, allowing us to go to a few more places outside the home than had previously been the case!

One thing about life with Alexis: there is always a new challenge to be met. After three years she outgrew the wheelchair and we had to start over with a new one. This time we were able to acquire a chair that did not collapse—so no cross bars. Also, the reclining portion was hydraulic, not manual, so it was a lot easier to raise and lower, an important point since she was now becoming too heavy for us to lift up the back without considerable effort when it was reclined.

The chair seemed ideal and, as the technician worked on the necessary modifications, I dreamed of how easy it was going to make our life. But, as I have said, life with Alexis is never simple. This chair had a new problem: it did not recline fully. That factor, combined with Alexis' increasing leg length, meant that it never really worked as a change table. When we laid it back it was still in a low sloping position. By the force of gravity, Alexis would then slide down the chair until her feet were hanging off the end and it became difficult or impossible to reposition her. This meant that we always had to have some substitute for a change table when we wanted her to use her chair as a commode. I came close to breaking many an infant change table in various restaurant and store washrooms by trying to balance Alexis' then 80 pounds on them so we could prepare her for using the commode. And this is not to mention what I did to my back in the process! The situation was untenable, so for the most part we were back to square one. And Alexis would not have qualified for a new government chair for at least another five years at that point.

One day I was at the wheelchair store where we always got our lifts fixed and was talking to the technician about the adapted wheelchair problem, describing how important it was for Alexis and other people in her position to have this facility. He was another person who saw the merit in this idea, and he had a few suggestions to offer.

"We have dozens of old wheelchairs in the back that were returned when people did not need them anymore and they are just going to end up in the scrapheap. You can have one of those if you want and then I could modify it for you."

Soon he came trundling in with a large wheelchair with a high back, clearly an older model—and not a recliner. I looked at it doubtfully.

"It would be way too big for her," I said.

"I can make it work. I need to cut out the crossbars anyway and then reinforce it along the sides for added strength and also pull it in, so it is a little narrower."

"Then we can use a bedpan that would be easier to carry around than a pot!"

"Oh, I have a better idea still!" he responded. "This chair is wide enough to fit over a toilet. We should be able to eliminate the need for a bedpan in most circumstances!"

"Wow!" was all I could think to say, suddenly imagining what it would be like to have an almost normal life with Alexis when we went out. "But it is not a recliner. What about the change table we need?" I asked.

"I can cut the bars holding the back up and replace them with latching hooks that can be easily undone. That way the back can fall flat and function as an effective change table and then be raised back into a vertical position and latched."

After a pause, I asked: "But what about the seating insert? The one she has now is too narrow to fit in this chair and she will not qualify for a new one for a long time."

"How distorted *is* she?"

"She has a scoliosis."

"How bad?"

"Bad enough that her wheelchair back has to be modified but not nearly as bad as some."

"How about her hips?"

"The left hip joint is slightly rotated but she can still sit on a regular cushion."

"We have level one seating specialists who work here, and I am one myself," he told me proudly. "I'll go talk to the other guys."

"I don't know," I said. "What about stability? Structural integrity? How could we travel with it in the car? Would it be safe if we got in an accident?"

Actually, I did not say any of those last things. In those days I was not thinking along those lines. I was thinking of *getting* Alexis a life, not of her *losing* it because of a poorly constructed wheelchair!

"Let me talk to my boss and do some thinking and then I'll get back to you," he said. "But it would help if I could meet Alexis."

"I'll bring her in when I pick up the lift tomorrow. Will you be working?"

For some wonderful reason the two technicians he spoke to were also intrigued by the challenge of building such a chair and anxious to help Alexis. That store had been our go-to place for many years in terms of ordering and fixing Alexis' various pieces of therapeutic equipment, so they made it seem like something of a family effort. They wanted to do it in their spare time and would only charge us for the cost of the extra equipment needed to modify the chair and construct the seating insert. The very next day I brought Alexis in for a fitting and they were able to work from the dimensions of her existing insert so that saved a lot of time and trouble.

Well, in due course we did get that new chair with the new insert for a very reasonable amount of money—about $1500 if I recall. That chair, covered in an odious pink vinyl that I had romantically chosen in an impulsive moment, served us quite adequately for a couple of years. We were thrilled and delighted to be able to contemplate taking Alexis places again without having to worry about toileting!

But of course, I should have known it was too good to be true. On my very first venture into a public washroom with Alexis using the new chair I realized the fatal flaw in the technician's idea.

We were of course using the handicap stall because that is the only public washroom stall large enough to lower the wheelchair back so we had a change table. After I had done this, pulled out the seat cushion so Alexis was sitting on the commode unit, raised the chair back to an upright position and adjusted the support straps so she felt comfortable and secure, I then ceremoniously angled the chair to slide it over the toilet. But the wheelchair would not fit over the toilet!

Never having occasion to actually use the toilets in the handicap stall for her since we always had the commode pot, I had not observed what was now painfully obvious: toilet seats in handicap stalls are raised two inches or more above the level of regular seats to accommodate disabled people who have trouble getting into a full sitting position. And that was the end of that idea!

Fortunately, the technician had installed a frame to hold a bedpan since I had explained to him that we sometimes had to go off-road when travelling where no toilets were available. Luckily for both of us, I did have the pan with me in a bag slung from the back of the chair. Why such foresight, since foresight is not one of my strengths? It was because of that maxim we had learned to live by. *Where Alexis is concerned, always assume there will be roadblocks.* That is to say, never take anything for granted!

Despite this setback, the lack of direct toilet access was really only the lack of an aesthetic and timesaving luxury. It was not the lack of a necessity. With this chair we were again able to travel freely with Alexis. And we did. In 1998 we had purchased a timeshare in Canmore near Banff and every year thereafter we took Alexis there for a week, stopping in Red Deer on the way down to attend to her washroom needs.

The Information Centre there has two private handicap accessible washrooms so Joe and I could work together to do the lifting and toileting. In the case of the pink reclining chair it worked like a change table, so in that sense there was no transferring involved. However, returning the chair to an upright position with Alexis in it was quite a struggle and required two of us to manage it—one to hold Alexis in place and the other to lift.

We went on like this for a while and then we purchased a timeshare in Mexico. We took Alexis there for the first time in 2001, and then every year thereafter until 2014, 13 times in all, two weeks at a time. The reason for the longer stay was that it was so traumatic to take her there on the plane that it took us two weeks to recover enough to make the return trip!

During our first and only trip to Mexico with the pink chair, a careless baggage handler just tossed the wheelchair out of the cargo hold onto the tarmac and bent it all out of shape. The chair was made of aluminum. The main source of structural integrity, its cross bars, had been removed and then reinforced elsewhere by a well-meaning amateur who was not an engineer, so it was not surprising that it was unable to withstand rough treatment.

While we were in Mexico, we were able to manage with the bent frame as Alexis was lightly dressed and we were travelling on manicured walks at the resort. But back in the Edmonton winter the wheelchair quickly warped further as we made our way along snowy walks with Alexis wedged into the chair in her bulky winter clothing.

The chair went from difficult to dangerous in a short time and we were forced to revert to her previous chair for safety reasons. I did try to have the chair fixed but because of the soft aluminum from which it was constructed this was not possible. We did receive some insurance compensation from WestJet, and I set out to find another solution that would enable us to maintain our new, freer lifestyle with Alexis that had ended all too quickly.

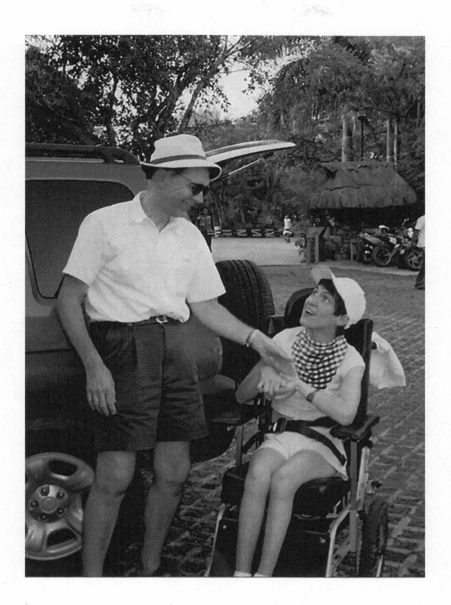

Joe and Alexis, February 2008. Alexis in the Dirk Kos wheelchair before beginning jeep trip from Playa Car, Mexico to Belize.

*Alexis and Joe, on the Catamaran in Mexico before
setting off to sea, March, 2013*

CHAPTER 48

Let's start again—from scratch

Through my connections at the public school board I had become aware of the work of a man named Dirk Kos who adapted equipment to meet the needs of children with physical disabilities. I procured his contact information and gave him a call. I described our situation to him and what we were looking for and we arranged a meeting time.

Dirk came to our home and met Alexis and we saw at once that he was a kind man and a practical man. He was intrigued by the challenge we presented to him and set out to develop a prototype. His idea was that he would build a new wheelchair entirely from scratch with a built-in commode tailored to Alexis' size and particular needs. It seemed likely at that point—Alexis was then 22 years old—that she had reached her full adult size.

The chair Dirk developed for Alexis was nothing short of wonderful! It was compact, lightweight and perfectly balanced. It was a "rigid, upright" chair. That is to say, it did not lean back and it did not collapse. Hence, there was no need for crossbars beneath the seat. Alexis at that point weighed about 85 pounds and was 5'3" tall.

Dirk installed a drawer glide system under the seat designed for a conventional bedpan to fit into it. After use, the bedpan pulled easily out from the back for emptying and cleaning. He also put a narrow skirting around the wheelchair seat in the same black vinyl upholstery he used for the rest of the chair. This effectively concealed the bedpan so we could just leave it in place when we travelled with Alexis. This feature alone made our life considerably easier!

By the time Alexis reached her mid 20's, she had grown some more, and the lifting was becoming more difficult. Despite this we went to a lot of places with Alexis in that chair. Sometimes we used lifting belts to stabilize our backs in order to lift her safely. At least, my husband did, always more cautious and farseeing than me. I was usually in too much of a hurry and too impatient to bother and I have permanent joint damage as a result to remind me of the error of my ways.

There were many awkward bathroom moments in various 'handicap' washrooms along the way in terms of trying to negotiate Alexis onto baby change tables she had long since outgrown so her clothing could be adjusted, securing her there with one hand while removing the seat cushion over the commode with the other, lowering her safely onto the commode and then later repeating the process in reverse: 4 lifts and transfers in all. This was always very time and labour consuming and resulted in many back and muscle strains.

There were other times when not even these inadequate facilities were available and we had to park on some country road when travelling and then roll Alexis in her chair out of the van—we have always had a 'Swinger Lift', made in Edmonton, that allows us to unload her in her chair from the side of the van in a space as narrow as three feet. No other van lifting system that I know of can be operated in such a narrow space but still people will park closer to us than that despite the fact that we are in a handicap parking space and that we have a sign indicating wheelchair unloading in the side window.

Anyway, once we got Alexis out of the van in these situations, we had then to lift her back onto the floor of the van, adjust her clothing, remove the cushion from the chair and place her on her commode. Then all we needed to do was wait and hope that no well-meaning person would come along, see our stopped van and wander over to ask if we needed assistance!

Once in Mexico we were foolhardy enough to rent a jeep, lift Alexis and her wheelchair separately into the back and drive down to the neighbouring state to visit an ocean-side park there. On that occasion we had to lift the chair out on the rocks above the pounding surf for Alexis to perform her necessary functions and by the time we returned to the resort, Joe, who had done all the necessary lifting, had a very sore back.

I think the worst bathroom adventure I ever had with Alexis was in Calgary, however. We were visiting the famous Calgary Zoo and I had telephoned in advance to check out if they had private handicap washroom facilities. I was assured that they did and that they were quite roomy. We were driving there from our timeshare in Canmore quite early in the morning and by the time we arrived Alexis was indicating in her nonverbal way that she needed to use the facilities. I hunted them out while the rest of the family went off to see the sights as our time frame was quite limited. But the washroom was not what I had been led to expect.

It was a long narrow room with no baby change table and little room to turn around. There was a sink with a narrow counter right inside the door and barely enough room for the wheelchair to sit beside it. With some negotiating I managed to get Alexis up onto the counter where I had placed the large changing pad I always carried with us. The trouble was that the counter only extended about a foot from the sink, and this meant that the middle of her body was draped over and drooping into the sink. I steadied her with one hand while reaching down with the other hand to remove the seat cushion from the wheelchair and that was when the trouble started. Her head flopped off the counter and the rest of her body threatened to follow.

Because of the confined space, I did not have enough leverage to regain full control and realized that I would eventually lose the battle. I dared not reach down to unlock the wheelchair brakes so I could push the chair out of the way, and even if I could have done so

I would have had no way or retrieving it after. I was well and truly stuck and in the meantime Alexis, feeling the insecurity of the situation, was working herself up into a full-fledged panic at which point I knew I would lose all control.

The situation was very dangerous, and I had to have help. I managed to get the door open and call to a woman for help, but she seemed to be the slow moving, timid sort and could not wedge her way in. I was standing right in front of the door because the sink and counter, with Alexis half on and half off, were right there.

Finally, a man passed by and I knew that it was muscle that was needed if I was to resolve this incident without Alexis being injured. I begged him to help me and as he wiggled in, he grasped her fallen head that I had let go of so I could move from the sink area to the short counter and support the rest of her. Together we worked to get her stabilized. I had covered her up the best I could because of course she was completely undressed ready for toileting when this happened, but I realized that if I had to choose between modesty and safety I would have to choose the latter.

Once we got Alexis back in place, I asked the man to stay while I finished dressing her—I had at that point lost all intention of placing her on the commode. Then I asked him to help me get her back in the chair. By that point I was trembling uncontrollably and was too weak to do much of anything. I don't know what he thought of all this, but I knew what I was thinking. I was thinking that this was the last straw. Something had to be done!

After we were able to wiggle our way out of that wretched washroom, and Alexis and I found her father, I don't remember what happened. I only know that on that day I vowed to myself that I would find a better solution to meeting Alexis' toileting needs and that relying on inadequate and non-existent change tables was not going to be part of that solution!

Over the next few months I sulked and fretted and thought. Then one morning I woke up thinking that since there was no way to carry around a change table, we would just have to eliminate the need for one. And since lifting and transferring over and over made a very simple process very complicated and time consuming, we would have to get rid of transferring altogether. And since the only place Alexis felt really safe and well supported was in her wheelchair when we were away from home then maybe that is where she would have to stay. In other words, all the lifting and dressing and undressing and toileting and cleaning would have to take place *in* the wheelchair.

The all-in-one wheelchair

S**ome people keep** their problems to themselves. Some people are nice and go through their life acting like counsellors and social facilitators to others. That is to say, they always politely ask how others are doing and follow up on the comments they receive with further questions of the person sharing with them. I never developed that particular skill.

When I have something burning in my brain, I either don't want to talk to people at all or else I talk obsessively about my issue when I am in conversation. Thus, I had scattered my wheelchair combo preoccupation around to everyone I thought might be a sympathetic listener or might have the faintest interest in such a project. As a result, I experienced people literally walking away from me at social gatherings once I launched into my monologue!

People I shared with in the developmental disabilities field patted me on the back and told me what a good idea it was, but then either changed the conversation as they could offer no way to go forward from there or directed me to somebody else who might have some relevant information to offer, either in terms of funding or in terms of refining the concept. But they definitely did not want to hear about my project a second time around! In this way I gradually advanced my knowledge base in the general area at the cost of an ongoing narrowing of my social circle.

Although I probably wore out my welcome with a lot of people, I did acquire some interesting pieces of information along the way to add to my slender store. One of the most important of these was the disabled Seniors issue. I was made aware of the large number of people who came into extended care settings continent and in two weeks were rendered incontinent.

'How can that be?" I asked a nurse in one such setting and a recreation therapist in another. "Why would that happen?" The answers I got ranged from overwork to lack of adequate facilities. The frontline staff in this type of setting, I was told, consisted largely of low paid workers. There was barely enough time to handle the basics for their patients: feeding, dressing, bathing and changing people who were often in such a disabled condition that they could do nothing for themselves. How could they handle regular toileting sessions on top of this?

Even when they did try to meet the toileting needs of such patients, a cumbersome floor lift had to be found and wheeled over, and then two care providers (an Occupational Health and Safety requirement in Alberta) had to remain in attendance while the person was hoisted up, transported to their bedroom, lowered onto their bed to be undressed, then hoisted up again and somehow transferred to a toilet in their too small bathroom, or to a commode unit in their crowded bedroom.

Anyone who has ever tried manoeuvring a floor lift in tight spaces will know how difficult this is. And after all that effort, the care providers were often too late. The patient had already made use of the diaper, so they simply changed them and returned them to their previous setting. This would be frustrating enough but there was another problem as well, a psychological one.

These patients were often sad and lonely, and feeling as if they had been abandoned by those closest to them in their senior years. The result was that they did whatever they could to garner a little care and attention from the care providers, the only people they had more than fleeting contact with during the long, dreary days. Thus, some of them made unnecessary demands for bathroom assistance, when what they really needed was simply attention.

While I was still mulling over in my mind the horror of this, I was chilled even further by some additional information from people I had met who worked in the homecare field. They told me about the people they had known as clients who had lost so much of their physical functioning that they could no longer transfer to a regular toilet even with assistance, but who desperately wanted to remain in their own home. They told me about the spouses, sons and daughters who wanted to keep them there but finally had to give up because of that one issue—the toileting issue.

Everything else could be managed: meals on wheels, home care nurses to visit for regular monitoring and medication administration, care providers to do light housekeeping and give baths. All of this could be taken care of because it could be done on a preset schedule. Only toileting assistance could not be provided in that way. And, quite apart from the deep anger and compassion I felt over this injustice, what else I realized was that there was potentially a large market for the type of chair I was proposing!

The marketing issue was a very important one if a wheelchair such as I had in mind was ever to be developed and mass-produced in sufficient quantity so it could sell for a reasonable price. I knew that that market did not exist among individuals with severe developmental disabilities. As mentioned previously, many, or most parents, did not even attempt toilet training under these circumstances. But seniors who had enjoyed a normal life into their later years and then found themselves so severely constrained that they could no longer handle their personal needs independently were the ones most likely to purchase a chair such as this—a chair that would give them back their freedom and their dignity.

About this time, an example of this type of sad situation hit close to home. My Aunt Hildur, my mother's sister, was the closest family that my brother and I had left. She lived in the Vancouver area, was widowed and without children of her own, and was becoming increasingly dependent on us. After several unfortunate incidents we knew that we had to convince her to move to Edmonton where we could better support her, and that was no easy task. Finally it was arranged, and I flew out to Vancouver and accompanied her back on the plane to take up occupancy in the apartment we had arranged for her and her cat. But this carefully planned out scenario was not to happen.

As we debarked from the plane in Edmonton, my aunt had a severe seizure. An ambulance was called and she was taken to hospital where she continued to have seizures and suffered more loss of physical capacity. After several weeks in hospital she was discharged to an Extended Care hospital where she was to remain for the last few years of her life. There I saw firsthand exactly what I had been told about. Within two weeks of arriving there, my high-spirited, quixotic, fiercely independent aunt had been placed in diapers!

With all of this in my mind I thought I could not wait any longer. I had to find out if the idea I had been mulling over for a long time could possibly work. At that point, I was teaching graduate courses at Athabasca University on a continuing contract basis. I was part of an interdisciplinary program in the arts and humanities and as such I could apply for a research grant if my project was seen as worthwhile and within scope. My goal was to design a wheelchair with a built-in lift, a lifting sling that would allow clothing to be lowered and raised in the lift position, and a built-in commode—and that was what I needed the grant money for. But in order to access the grant money I needed first to carry out a relevant research project to demonstrate the need for such a device.

I thought it would be unrealistic for me to suddenly insert myself into the seniors' healthcare field and request access to seniors or their families who found themselves in this position with regard to bathroom access. I had absolutely no background and therefore no credibility in that area. I would have to approach this challenge from a different perspective. And I knew what that perspective would need to be.

I was still in contact with many of the children I had worked with and known in the early years of the GRIT program, and I had already conducted two other research projects with that population previously, so I had considerable background information. I contacted the early GRIT families and got preliminary approval for their children to be involved in my proposed study. I then prepared questionnaires for each family to complete and went through the necessary ethics review at my university so that I could carry out such a project under their auspices. Since I was actually a member, and later the chair, of the Department of Humanities and Social Sciences Research Ethics board at that time, I understood the process, so this part was not too difficult for me.

The basic research question I was posing was this: Had equipment been available to make the toileting procedure less labour intensive and more portable could your child have attained continence? As it was, I knew that only two of the original ten, Alexis and one other girl, were still using a commode.

What the research results[20] indicated were that nine of the ten individuals whose parents were interviewed could have been toilet trained if logistics had made that process feasible! With this information I was able to establish that a real need existed, and that developing a chair that could meet this need would be of both social and financial benefit. I applied for and received a small research grant from Athabasca University to help me to bring such a chair into existence.

A team of Calgary engineers developed the first chair. It consisted of a crane-like system with removable, storable parts that was built into an Invacare Reclining Wheelchair with anti-tip bars on the back wheels that had to be used whenever the lift was in operation to prevent over-balancing. The chair worked well but was somewhat awkward and cumbersome. However, proof of concept was achieved. That is to say, I now knew, and could demonstrate, that it was possible to build a lift into a wheelchair in such a way that it could operate safely.

Heartened by this, I applied for and received a second research grant from Athabasca University to further refine the model. Dr. Jonathan Tyler of Tyler Engineering, the Edmonton engineer I chose to work with on this new project, took one look at my prototype and declared that he could design a model with the lifting parts built in that would be far more streamlined and elegant and, most importantly, much easier to operate than what I had.

I purchased a second-hand Quickie Rigid chair for a good price, but it was much too large for Alexis. Jonathan was able to reduce it in size and when the new chair was finished it was all that he had promised: lightweight, small and easy to manoeuvre, but solid and perfectly balanced. The lifting arms flipped down the back of the chair when not in use and were completely unobtrusive. In short, it had all the attributes that the Dirk Kos chair had had but with the additional benefit of a built-in lift.

Joe was not equally impressed, however. To conceal the toileting component of the chair, Jonathan had fashioned a large stainless steel drawer under the seat holding the receptacle. The receptacle he had chosen, in the interests of elegance and his idea of normalization, was a stainless-steel salad bowl. Joe and I took one look at it and knew it would never work. And the chair with the huge drawer was anything but discreet. Some might speculate that it housed a powerful battery for operating a power chair but the lack of electrical wiring on the arms would quickly discount that notion.

Once we got the chair home, Joe removed the drawer and modified the guides so a bedpan could be installed. The steel border was left and it concealed the pan from three sides. To hide it from the back, Joe fashioned a black leather skirt that matched the leather on the seating insert. We were then ready to use the chair out in public and on our annual trips to Mexico and Canmore. But we quickly realized there was another problem for which Jonathan was not responsible.

All this time I had been focusing on designing a functional chair with a built-in lift and commode. And I had naively purchased so-called 'toileting slings' that were supposed to provide the magical answer for that part of the operation. The first prototype chair, with the crane-like apparatus, had lifted Alexis high off the seat so there was plenty of room to manoeuvre and to do the necessary clothing adjustments for toileting purposes. But Jonathan's more streamlined model only lifted Alexis a few inches. In that tight space we could not manipulate the net lifting sling sufficiently to remove her trousers and underwear for toileting. And replacing them afterwards was even more difficult. At that point in the process I realized sadly that I had made a fatal error.

It was summer then and our son and his family were visiting us. I explained the problem to him and demonstrated Alexis in the sling. He looked at his sister and immediately saw the problem. "You are on the wrong track, mom. A cloth sling will never work. It pulls her legs together and that can't work for adjusting the clothes. You need a hard sling that allows them to remain apart."

"But how?"

Together we got to work. I knew certain things from what background I had in neuro-anatomy and my knowledge of Alexis' physical condition and how her spastic muscles worked. Marcus knew other relevant things from his background in math and physics and his understanding of mechanical processes. What we came up with together was the following.

To lift Alexis or fragile, elderly people with the proposed hard sling we would have to distribute the lifting pressure, i.e. pounds per square inch. And where we needed to place most of that pressure was on the largest and sturdiest bones in the body. Those bones are the backbone and the thighbones. This is what we decided to do.

The back of the wheelchair would have to be reconfigured so that it would lift up with the individual fastened to it, their spine then taking most of their weight. Fastened to the chair back would be a foot wide, flexible belt that would not place too much pressure on any one of the ribs as it was secured in front when in use. Ribs are bent and flexible, incorporating much cartilage so they can easily move in and out to accommodate their respiratory function. This makes them weaker than most of the bones in the body and more easily broken.

The legs would need to be lifted by the use of steel bars extending out from the arm rests and ending in thickly padded loops that could be fitted over the legs just above the knees. These loops would support the rest of the occupant's weight and the empty space between the base of their spine and their knees when in the lift position would be ample for easy clothing adjustments.

We took these ideas to Jonathan and he got to work. He removed the original lifting bars and rigged up the back of the chair so that it could raise and lower. He rebuilt the armrests so the lifting bars could extend and retract from them. Padded loops were then hooked onto the bars in the extended position and removed before retracting them. We needed to carry them along separately in Alexis' backpack but that was not a big issue.

Finally, the revised chair was ready, but of course there was then another problem—there always is! The belt Jonathan had chosen to meet the requirements I had given him, i.e. minimal pressure on the ribs, was elasticized and as soon as Alexis was raised in the new device her bum slipped down because the pressure of her weight caused the elastic parts to extend. Still, this version of a lifting sling was much more workable than its predecessor.

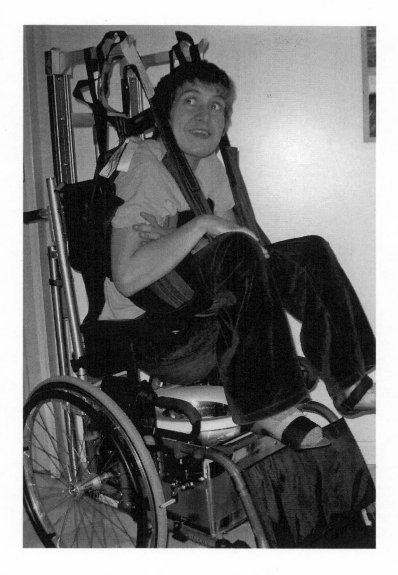

First prototype of wheelchair/lift/commode unit,
by Tangent Engineering, 2013

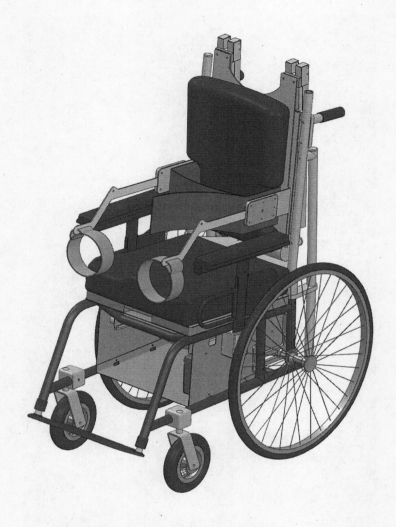

Second Prototype of wheelchair/lift/commode unit,
by Tyler Research Corp., 2015

CHAPTER 50

Starting all over again

When we first got the new chair, I marched it and Alexis around to various groups and individuals, proudly demonstrating how it worked. One occasion I remember is a presentation that Alexis and I did at a disabilities conference. She is attractive, as I might have mentioned a couple of times. And on this occasion she was elegantly dressed, sitting tall in her chair and smiling sweetly. She cooperated beautifully as I raised her up in the lift, removed the seat to reveal the commode unit beneath, replaced it and lowered her back down. I introduced her as my research associate and the people in the crowd smiled indulgently.

On that occasion, Alexis was pretty, poised and pleasant and, like any proud mother, I secretly took credit for all three qualities. *There are other people with equally severe disabilities, sprawled and misshapen in their wheelchairs—and then there is Alexis,* I thought to myself smugly. But in my life experience, hubris has a way of catching up to you.

As I mentioned previously, Alexis continued to deteriorate through her late 20's and her 30's and by the time she neared her 40th birthday we noticed how much Alexis' scoliosis had increased. Also, her neck was becoming contracted due to increased spasticity and she was slumping more and more to her left side and dropping her head down. Thus, she was no longer comfortable in the rigid upright wheelchair we had worked so hard to adapt for her, and we had to return to the Glenrose Rehabilitation Hospital for help. I knew what she needed— although I could hardly admit it to myself.

The day of our appointment came, and I asked the occupational therapist who was assessing Alexis' seating needs if she could author-ize a tilt-in-space wheelchair for her. When this chair is reclined, the front of it raises up, placing the client in a comfortable 'w' position with knees raised and supported, much like what happens when you relax in a recliner chair. All the other people I knew who shared Alexis' level of physical disability were already in these chairs or ver-sions of them and I had always been secretly proud that Alexis could still sit upright. Like I said, any little act or thought of hubris on my part always seems to backfire!

The Quickie Tilt-in-Space wheelchair was approved but we had to pay almost half the cost ourselves because only the longer, heavier and clumsier version made by another manufacturer was fully covered. When I asked about building a commode unit into the new wheelchair, as had been done by Peter Jarvis so many years ago, I was turned down. The pressure on the Glenrose Hospital Seating Clinic to provide necessary equipment adaptations was so high, and resulted in such a long waiting list, that they could not consider any extra options.

I did convince the seating specialist to create the chair insert in two parts so the seat portion could be easily removed. My secret thought was that Joe could figure out a way to put in a commode unit himself since he has solved many technical problems relating to Alexis' equip-ment through the years. But I was told sternly that the chair could not be tampered with in any way or we would be responsible for the full cost of reimbursement should Alexis pass away and the chair need to be returned. Given her deteriorating health that was a real possibility at that point, so I was too intimidated to even try.

What I was also thinking, though, was that it was the tilt-in-space chair that was really needed by the very disabled seniors who could benefit from a built-in commode unit and lift. Therefore, even if Alexis had been able to continue comfortably in her rigid, upright chair, further refinement of that model would not benefit the senior population with their fragile bones and less efficient circulation. And, as I said previously, that was where the market was.

As soon as we got the new tilt-in-space wheelchair home, I arranged to take it to Jonathan Tyler, the engineer who developed the commode/lift system in her upright wheelchair, so he would have the opportunity to thoroughly examine it and determine if a lift and commode unit could be built into it without interfering with its specialized tilt mechanism. After his evaluation he explained that it could be done, but he would have to start from scratch, redoing all the specifications. He could do the job for me all right—but it would cost approximately $100,000! And this did not include the cost of providing a new tilt-in-space wheelchair for him to work on, an additional $4000 to $5000.

By this point in the wheelchair saga, Joe and I had contributed far more money to the two projects to date than the university research grants had been able to cover and we knew that we could not deplete our retirement funds by an additional $100,000, since we were at or near the age of needing it for our own purposes. We decided that Alexis would have to use the new tilt-in-space chair in which she was comfortable, and we would have to restrict her outings to short jaunts not requiring a bathroom break. What we did not say out loud, although we were both thinking it, is that Alexis might not need it that much longer anyway. Her increasing weakness, spasticity and fatigue were ominous signs, consistent with the warnings about a significantly foreshortened lifespan for her that we had previously received from the three neurologists.

I did try to argue that we were on the verge of a break-through at this point with the chair and if we ever succeeded it would help many, many people—not just our daughter. But Joe has never been particularly interested in supporting my larger humanitarian concerns in this area. He is interested in helping his daughter and thinks, quite justifiably, that that is enough of a challenge for anyone. Without his help I knew I could not succeed.

It was a very sad situation. After all we had been through with the chair issue, we were effectively back to square one with no built-in lift and not even a built-in commode unit. We were in the same position with regard to meeting Alexis' bathroom needs when away from home as we had been when she was ten—except it was worse because she was bigger, more spastic, and more deformed than she had been then. But I was not ready to give up and decided to make one last try.

Our provincial government had established a new technology research branch. Albertans were increasingly aware that we could no longer rely so heavily on oil royalties to sustain our various services as we had in the past and must make more focussed efforts to diversify our economy. It occurred to me that this might provide me with an opportunity to push for research funds to further develop my adapted wheelchair prototype. I could make an argument not only for the humanitarian benefits of such a device but also for the potential savings to the taxpayer, since less staff time would be involved in the toileting process in Extended Care settings. Also, it would help more disabled seniors to remain in their homes longer. That in itself would result in significant savings to the province. I could even argue for the ecological benefits: less non-biodegradable diapers in the landfill!

I soon arranged a meeting with a representative of this technology research area and explained my idea, asking about the possibility of funding to allow for further development. I was told that such funding would have to be siphoned through a special branch and could not come from the government directly. There was a process involved. First, I would have to incorporate as a business in order to be eligible to receive government research grants. Also, I would have to attain a patent for my product. Only at that point would I be able to apply for a feasibility grant to pay an expert to evaluate the wheelchair's marketability. And *only* if that panned out would I be considered for a larger research and development grant.

I was of retirement age myself at that point and the last thing I wanted to do was start a business, but something kept driving me forward and I did incorporate as Alexis Enterprises, and I did get a North American patent under that name. In due course Alexis Enterprises was approved for a $20,000 feasibility grant. I was then directed to choose a company sub-contracted by the government to explore the marketability of proposed new products.

A newly hired individual, who was also new to Edmonton, was assigned to my case. I provided him with the list of the contacts I had already made who had expressed interest in the project, all experienced people in the area and some in senior positions in other Canadian hospitals—but he did not follow up on this information.

Instead he relied primarily on consulting with administrative and nursing personnel in various Edmonton hospital settings who were used to handling the toileting issue in their own ways, some being pretty dehumanizing in my opinion. I don't know how he described my wheelchair to them and doubt that he even fully understood how it worked and the potential financial savings it might create. In any case, these people were reportedly unable to see the point of my project and this effectively meant that I could not proceed with an application for a $50,000 research and development grant. Instead, I was advised to approach various wheelchair companies to see if they would buy my patent. I did approach some, but with no success.

Still, I hang on stubbornly to the patent, renewing it when necessary and paying an accountant annually to keep the company duly registered, all money down the drain it would seem. Joe has been very patient with me clinging to the remnants of my seemingly hopeless dream. I think he is hoping that one day I will finally be ready to give up, and I am getting close to that point.

I console myself with the knowledge of all the failed inventors who have gone before me and who had perfectly good products that were later brought back to life by others along the road.

CHAPTER 51

Feeding Alexis

Like most people with severe cerebral palsy, Alexis has big challenges with chewing and swallowing food. In past eras, she most likely would have died as a child after frequent bouts of aspiration pneumonia caused by inhaling food particles had critically compromised her lung function. But that happened mostly to children in institutions who were being "bird fed" by inexperienced, constantly rotating staff. We were warned early on about the danger of feeding Alexis in a supine position or feeding her any food that could be swallowed wrong and clog her airway, and so she has lived, and to some extent thrived.

Joe and I have worked hard to maintain a diet for Alexis that is healthy, tasty and of the right texture to swallow easily. And, as mentioned previously, when she was still very young, considerable effort went into developing her tongue muscles with the aid of the 'therapeutic mouthpiece' so she could manipulate the food into the right position in her mouth for safe swallowing.

Fortunately, Alexis has always had a hyperactive gag reflex, so she is quick to cough and sputter, violently expelling offending food particles if they threaten to go down her throat the wrong way. Not everyone so severely affected has this final line of defense. Unfortunately, she has had for most of her life a troubling tendency to 'up-chuck' thick wads of mucous wrapped around food, often losing whole meals in the process. This has been very upsetting to both her and us but has not tended to lead to aspiration.

In recent years, two changes have occurred with Alexis' eating problems. Her swallowing issues have become worse so her food must now be even more finely pureed than previously, and we need to be very careful not to disturb her concentration while eating. On the positive side, Alexis' 'upchucking' spells and associated red, itchy face miraculously stopped when the Valproic Acid that she has been taking for seizure control since she was 18 months old was gradually reduced to one quarter of its previous level and replaced by other medication.

Valproic Acid is known to be very irritating to the stomach lining, but the big medical fear has been its well-known toxicity for both liver and kidney function that has resulted in several deaths since its introduction in the 1980's. Fortunately, Alexis' ongoing testing has never revealed any damage to those organs, and neither us nor her doctors through the years made the connection between this drug and her allergic reactions and upchucking bouts until they gradually slowed and stopped as the dosage was lowered. Side effects are a serious issue with anti-convulsive medications, as with other drugs, and there are many examples in the literature.

Eating is one problem; drinking is another. I have always been able to get Alexis to drink, often with minimal spillage, but to do so the two of us practically have to fuse into one being, and that is not something I can expect in the relationship between her and her assistants. I stand on the right side of Alexis while she is upright in her chair with the tray on and her hands restrained. I then hold her head firmly at exactly the right angle, place a bell shaped, plastic Tupperware glass with just the right pressure on her lower lip, carefully sense the moment when her lips purse in anticipation and her body tenses slightly, meaning she is ready to intake, and then tilt the glass up. After that I must judge when exactly enough liquid has gone in by the rate and rhythm of her gulping. I then tilt her head forward to ease swallowing, but at just the right moment so she does not open her mouth and drop the liquid onto her bib.

This intense process of reading her body language and sensing her rhythm is not something that is easy or even possible to completely teach to her assistants. They must develop their own rhythm and relationship with her built on the gradual development of mutual trust. They must realize that she is capable in this area if it is handled correctly, and she must realize that they have the ability and the will to proceed properly.

About ten years ago Alexis lost this trust. We were going through a period of staff transition and many new people were trying to get her to drink without having the necessary competence. Finally, Alexis quit responding altogether to the point where even I could not succeed. She literally clamped her mouth shut whenever the glass was raised to her lips.

Alexis' family doctor referred her to a gastroenterologist who strongly recommended a feeding tube. Neither Joe nor I were comfortable with that option and Joe in particular refused to even consider the idea. His argument was that eating was one of the few pleasures Alexis had in life and we could not deprive her of it. He did not buy the counterargument that we could use it just for drinking, maintaining that it was a 'slippery slope'.

We then went to the 'swallow clinic' where specially trained staff tested Alexis with various thicknesses of barium-laced liquids while x-raying her throat. She choked on all of them so there was no solution to be found there. We took her home and decided we would have to find our own answer—as has so often been the case when new problems with Alexis have arisen.

I wondered if, given her good tongue movement, a jelled liquid might work because she would not retain it in her mouth until it liquefied, as would be the case with many of her peers. I purchased some Knox gelatine powder and used it to jell a 50-50 mixture of low calorie cranberry juice and water. It worked like a charm and soon she was taking in six cups of this a day for a total of 120 calories. She relaxed, we relaxed, and her assistants relaxed.

I then retrained all her assistants on how to handle the drinking process correctly and eliminated all environmental distractions, like people talking nearby or even lively music. Alexis learned to trust us again and to drink liquids in small quantities. But she still has the six cups of jelled juice a day that Joe faithfully prepares for her and we still keep careful track of her fluid intake.

One of the drinks Alexis particularly enjoys is her occasional glass of either 4 ounces of beer or 2 ounces of wine when we take her out to restaurants for a meal. More would not be wise because of possible interaction with her seizure medication. Joe and I laugh that she never seems to spill these drinks as she does others!

We have purchased multiple food processors through the years and done much experimenting to achieve just the right texture of the various foods we give Alexis while retaining their nutritional value and taste. We have also made a conscious effort to maintain Alexis at an appropriate weight by limiting the amount of starch and sugar in her food. Excess weight would be a burden for her in terms of moving her body with her limited muscle strength and it would also make it harder for us to lift and manoeuvre her as needed. This in turn would place further limits on her life—where she could go and what she could do.

As a baby, when Alexis was ready to start on solid foods, I pureed various foods and stored portions in ice cube trays that could then be quickly warmed up in the microwave. As she grew older, I explored other food options to make her meals more interesting. A favourite early lunch stand-by was actually developed by her brother when he was about 5. Marcus needed a prop for his current fantasy life at that time, which involved a baby Martian. But the thought of carrying some kind of doll around offended his sensibilities. I always tried to help him with this type of dilemma and decided to make something sufficiently otherworldly to not be seen as too girlish, but I am no seamstress.

My father had given me a large bedspread with a broad, maroon fringe, the sole function of which seemed to be to gather dust! I removed it from the coverlet and coiled it up like a length of rope. Then

I tied bits of string around the middle and upper sections to create a waist and head and sewed a large black button on the head portion for an eye. Voila: one baby Martian that our son carried with him everywhere for about a year!

Once Marcus had his baby Martian, his next concern was what to feed him. He asked me for some tofu and a banana which he mixed together with a fork, mashing it finely, with a little help from me. Satisfied, he informed me that this would be something his baby Martian could manage. I immediately saw that it was also something Alexis could manage! My modest contribution was to grate in carrot for extra nutrition for both of them and Marcus soberly agreed that this was a wise idea. This tofu/banana/carrot concoction became a great addition to Alexis' diet and a quick and handy solution when we wanted to take her out over the lunch period.

Since Alexis and baby Martian both had the same diet, except for Alexis' 'allergies', Marcus and I had many discussions about appropriate food combinations over the next year or so until the baby Martian phase passed out of his life. It was just one of the many areas when, as a little boy, he expressed concerns about Alexis and searched for solutions to her various challenges. Gradually, however, he came to realize that there were no real solutions, only ways of coping that only worked temporarily at best.

One day when he was eight, he came to me and said: "Alexis is never going to get any better, is she, mom?" And after that he seemed to stop trying to help her except when specific issues came up where he felt he might have some answer. An example was when I was muttering away about steps she could not access with her wheelchair and how many places she could not visit as a result. He went away and came back a short time later with a drawing of a wheelchair with caterpillar treads.

Meanwhile, I was moving on in the endless struggle to keep Alexis gastronomically comfortable and well nourished. I have mentioned earlier the introduction of the 'therapeutic mouthpiece' and how much that helped to activate her tongue so she could manipulate the food in her mouth more efficiently. However, she never did learn to use her teeth effectively so pureed food remained a necessity. As I have also said, there were frequent bouts of upchucking of mucous laden food and itchy red cheeks, and much face scratching on her part generally accompanied these bouts. We had to protect her eyes by keeping her fingernails ground right down, and wiping her face continuously with a cold, damp wash cloth, and then using cortisone cream on it to stop the itching when she had these bouts so she would not scratch. At times we even had to tie her hands briefly to prevent eye damage until the cortisone cream could take effect.

In addition to the stomach irritation caused by the valproic acid, Alexis also had some food allergies. Gradually we identified the cause-effect relationship between the introduction of certain foods and the red, itchy face episodes. The offending foods included dairy, citrus, tomatoes, rice, corn and parsley. This pretty well eliminated the Italian diet the rest of us ate so I had to carry on making her meals separately. I remember feeling sad and bitter that we couldn't even share with her something as fundamental as the foods we enjoyed on a daily basis. And Joe and I wracked our brains for ways to circumvent these limitations. One of his solutions was to make the very non-Italian black bean chilli that they both liked, substituting lots of sweet red peppers for the tomatoes. It worked!

Somewhere along the line we realized that Alexis could tolerate cream but not milk and she could handle aged cheese like parmesan but not regular cheese. This at least made Fettuccine Alfredo possible, an Italian break-through! What else we noticed was that she never seemed to be allergic to anything expensive. Avocadoes, asparagus, radicchio lettuce, papaya were on the non-allergy list while cabbage, turnips, ordinary red lettuce, and oranges, for example, were not. She dribbled water and juice all over herself but, as mentioned, rarely spilled a drop of the beer or wine we occasionally offered her in small quantities—unless it was of inferior quality! We inferred that there were personality factors affecting the oral intake problem, but that only made us happy because it suggested to us that there was a real person still locked inside the shell that Alexis had become before we ever met her.

We struggled on through the years in our efforts to feed Alexis nutritiously and ensure that she had enough fluid. Often we failed but occasionally we succeeded in adding a new and interesting item to her diet. This is called intermittent reinforcement and it helped to keep us going!

Compounding the intake problem was the exit one. Cerebral palsy does not just affect the striated muscle tissue in arms and legs and neck and back and shoulders. It can also affect the smooth muscle tissue that lines the gut. In Alexis' case it seemed clear from the time she was a baby that something was wrong with her elimination process. Peristalsis, the snake-like twisting of the intestines that allows food to pass through, was definitely slower and weaker for her than normal.

Initially, we handled this problem with suppositories, but neither Joe nor I were comfortable with that solution. We thought they were disruptive, invasive and unnatural, and I worked hard to find another answer. I succeeded—until much later in her life when a new crisis changed everything, but I will get to that later. What I did with Alexis' diet was to add significantly more fiber and fluid. We settled on two portions of green vegetables, one of red or orange, and a portion of protein for dinner. Breakfast was always whole grain cereal and juice, and as the years passed the fiber increased and the juice decreased to be replaced by water or plain tea. Lunch might be a sandwich, but with homemade bread consisting of whole grains and nuts and seeds ground up. The filling always included a little protein (lean sliced ham or canned tuna or salmon or soy cheese of different kinds) and the sandwich was lined with two pieces of lettuce and often a generous chunk of sweet pepper.

For many years this dietary regimen worked well. All events related to eating and metabolizing and eliminating excess food were relatively normal and I began to forget that Alexis ever had a problem. That must be the reason that I finally agreed to place her on the

Emma Pivato

modified Atkins diet when her seizures became so severe that no medication seemed able to control them any longer. This was the method for controlling intractable seizures being proposed by a group of specialist nurses at the University Hospital in Edmonton.

As I have said elsewhere, the Atkins diet worked marvellously to control her seizures but had a devastating and permanent effect on her digestive process. Specifically, it led to such medically serious impaction that she had to be hospitalized twice, and her entire lower bowel was so stretched out of shape that for the first time in her life we had to resort to permanent invasive measures to make evacuation possible. In addition, her chronically swollen bowel exerted sustained pressure on the bladder (which lies right next to it) causing so much urinary retention that it too was stretched out of shape.

After the second bout of severe impaction requiring hospitalization, neither her colon nor bladder was any longer able to work normally. Initially, Alexis had to be catheterized and subjected to one strong chemical enema after another. Finally, through radical dietary changes and the introduction of Restoralax twice daily, we were able to help her regain partial control of these functions. She is no longer catheterized, and enemas are a thing of the past, although she still experiences periodic bouts of painful urinary and bowel retention. The use of Dulcolax, a harsh chemical suppository that we used daily for almost a year after the crisis period, is now only necessary occasionally, once or twice a month at most.

The amount of pain this bladder and bowel condition has caused to our formerly healthy and energetic daughter, because that is who she was despite her severe cerebral palsy, is unconscionable and I have blamed myself again and again for not following my initial instinct to avoid the modified Atkins diet and for not having sufficient respect for the efforts both Joe and I had put forth to sustain her on a healthy diet suited to her needs for so many years. I should never have tampered with it. But truthfully, the seizures she was having prior to the diet were so life-threatening that it really was a catch-22 situation.

296

During this bad period in Alexis' life, one of the graduate psychology courses I was offering at Athabasca University was on behavioural self-management. This was a lab course involving independent research projects of personal interest. One brave student chose to set up an experimental design introducing a variable he hypothesized might help to ameliorate his own chronic constipation issue. I say brave because all data collection was kept on a site open to all students in the class so they could critique each other's designs and data collection methods.

After collecting two weeks of baseline data the student introduced his independent variable, a new cereal on the market called 'Skinny B' that functioned to draw water into the gut because of the chia seeds it contained. As the weeks passed his data postings indicated that this intervention was having a positive effect on the dependent variable: his constipation problem.

I followed this student project with interest and one day while out shopping I saw the magic cereal in the grocery store and purchased it. After a week of introducing it into Alexis' breakfast regimen I could see that it was making a positive difference and we have been using it ever since! However, it is quite pricey, and I resented paying the cost. I grumbled about this one day to Juliana on the phone from Toronto where she lives. She immediately went out, bought a package and methodically disassembled it. Then she sent me an email with the recipe: 2 parts chia seeds, 2 parts hemp seeds, 1 part buckwheat.

I went along with this recipe faithfully for a number of years, carefully grinding the buckwheat so it would be fine enough for Alexis to eat safely. But then one day I realized that it was primarily being included as filler, and so that the product could be advertised as gluten free. I knew that, despite her history of digestive upsets, Alexis did not have gluten intolerance because I had her tested for that. And she needs a regular source of insoluble fibre as well as the soluble fibre the chia seeds provide. I decided to substitute bran buds for the buckwheat and added it in equal amounts to the chia and hemp seeds as the buds are puffed up, taking twice the volume per gram as the buckwheat. This new formula works even better for Alexis than the original one and is a lot easier to put together.

What is it like to cook for Alexis—for her and for us? From her perspective, she has been condemned to a lifetime of TV dinners. We make all her evening meals in advance and then freeze them in microwavable containers. But what that also means is that we retain quality control and do not expose her to the vagaries of inexperienced, opinionated or just plain inadequate home cooks.

What is a typical dinner for Alexis? In her oblong plastic supper container measuring about 4 x 8 inches she has four separate items in equal portions: one meat or fish, two green vegetables and one red or orange vegetable. But where is the starch, you might ask?

Achieving just the right texture for the various food items Alexis consumes is key to preventing her from aspirating while eating. Yet all food items do not produce the same results with the same food processing techniques. Some can be readily ground up in an efficient, high-speed processor like a Cuisinart or high-powered Braun. Others, like beans or asparagus, require more intense processing as in a Vita-mix blender or a Magic Bullet machine.

Some vegetables have the right consistency on their own and others require the addition of broth or water to achieve this. Others, like zucchini or spinach, have too much water even when we stir fry or bake them, and that is where the starch comes in that keeps Alexis' diet balanced.

One of our greatest culinary discoveries in our ongoing food saga with Alexis was processed potato, the kind you find in boxes at the store that can be magically turned into instant mashed potatoes. Normally I avoid processed food, but these precooked and dried potatoes have been a Godsend to us. I simply beat a small amount into overly liquid food when it is still hot to achieve the correct texture.

As with many other aspects of Alexis' life, my processed potato need led to an interesting experience. One day I rushed into a grocery store to replenish my supply and was pleased to find some boxes on the shelf because they are not always available. I approached the checkout counter with a relieved look on my face and the clerk, a seasoned woman of middle years, regarded me with barely concealed contempt. To her I must have appeared as the epitome of the lazy housewife! I left the store wondering how often we judge people without knowing their full story.

Well, I have digressed. Back to asparagus! Certain vegetables like asparagus and green beans are so fibrous that even the most efficient food processor will not deal with them effectively for our purposes. That is where the role of the Vitamix, a liquefier with the energy of a lawn mower, comes into play! After much experimenting, I have found that the best way to deal with asparagus, for example, is as follows: after washing, break the tough part of the stems off and cut an inch or less only off the most fibrous ends. However, if the asparagus is young and supple enough you may not have to discard any of them at all, making preparation both easy and economical. Microwave the spears until bright green, 3 to 4 minutes, and then process in the Vitamix machine until they turn into a sloppy liquid. Microwave the stems in a covered dish until soft, 3 to 4 minutes. Then add them to the asparagus liquid in the Vitamix and blend until fine, which takes only seconds. The mixture will still be quite sloppy, even though no water has been added. And this is where the potato flakes come in. Remove the mixture from the container and place it in a large bowl. Then add the dried potato, a teaspoon at a time while beating vigorously. Stop at least ten seconds between each addition, as the thickening does not happen immediately, so you need to proceed judiciously. Even after that it will thicken further as the potato flakes soak up the water. But the potato flakes will dissolve and absorb better if the mixture is still hot so the whole process is a delicate balancing act—like our life with Alexis in general! Add seasoning to taste.

These are some of our food adventures with Alexis. I could elaborate further because I have much to say on the particular type of food preparation but perhaps that is best left for a separate project.

CHAPTER 52

Running 'the business'

Long before **I** reached the age of career decision making, I knew that I never, ever wanted to run a business. I did not want to be obliged to interact with people every day, or to be a 'boss'. I wanted to be alone, with my family and my books. Bookwork was what I was good at, not social stuff, not physical stuff; work, not play.

In my adult professional life I worked for others, primarily as a psychologist and later on as an academic. I brought to those tasks my strengths and my weaknesses and carried out my various duties and obligations to the best of my ability and according to my work ethic.

But once Alexis came along, I was cast into a second life and a second career. I became a businesswoman, running the very serious business of creating a place for her in the world. In my first life, others managed me. They dealt with whatever strengths, personality quirks and limitations I had to get the best out of me for the good of whatever business they were running. Because that is what good managers do—and most, but not all of my managers, were good and effective in their role.

In my new, second life I have become the manager. I must deal with staff quirks and their strengths and weaknesses to get the best out of them. I must be very careful what I say and not "blur boundaries." That is, I must not share with them anything that will weaken

301

my own position of authority, but at the same time I must share on relevant issues that help to improve team spirit and encourage them to invest in Alexis. They cannot just work by blindly following instructions. They must be able to believe in Alexis and understand why the program is set up the way it is. They must form a real relationship with her and the rest of the team, and recognize when she is feeling happy and satisfied and when she is not and when the team is working well together and when it is not.

All Alexis' assistants, whatever their background, are carefully trained and oriented by senior staff members and me after hiring, and then closely monitored. But occasionally we make a mistake and hire somebody who talks the talk but does not walk the walk. Alexis always knows sooner than we do. They don't have to do anything overt. But by little delays, by continually misunderstanding her communicative intent, by disrespecting her in subtle ways she quickly becomes alienated and uncooperative. It is quite clear to us that Alexis has a definite sense of her own worth and dignity and place in her home. And it is my responsibility to ensure that she will not be obliged to interact on a regular basis with someone who will undermine her sense of self.

All of this is a delicate process and it can be quite exhausting at times. It is not something that comes naturally to a person who was raised the way I was. But, on the upside, it has forced me to grow and to develop into a more socially adept person that I was previously. It has also obliged me to push through my own feelings of inadequacy because there is simply no time for them. The phrase, 'suck it up', has a lot of resonance for me.

That is not the only positive part of the picture, however. Just knowing all these people through the years who have come to help us with Alexis has been a very rich and satisfying experience. Of course, there has been the odd bad apple, but some truly wonderful people have come along from time to time and that has more than balanced the others out. And the vast majority have worked conscientiously and methodically with Alexis to carry out the program for her that we have developed.

I am grateful to the government of Alberta and its developmental disabilities funding arm, Disability Services (PDD), where I have also had the privilege of working with some great people. Without the financial support we have received and the flexibility we have been given in hiring staff and running our own program, Joe and I could not have done what we have done. And without the advocates who came before us and lobbied hard for the level of financial support we have here in Alberta it never would have happened!

Alexis on her exercise table, visiting with her nephew, Xeno Couroux, age 3 (during his Wonder Woman phase!), 2018

Alexis with her nieces, Aziza and Leila Pivato, summer, 2017

CHAPTER 53

God, friends and others

What about God?

We belong to the Roman Catholic faith and attend our church regularly—except when Alexis has a bad spell or we are too tired from dealing with her bad spells or it is Christmas or Easter, the two most important days of the ecclesiastical year. Why do we miss those days? Because all the people who don't come to church the rest of the year crowd in on those occasions and there is too much noise, too little oxygen, and no easy escape route for when Alexis has one of her seizures. In other words, there is no room for Alexis on those days so we do not attend either.

How do we feel about our faith? For Joe it is easy to just attend when we can, and not worry about why or whether or not we are doing enough. It is part of his Italian culture and he grew up in that tradition in Canada. Also, Joe's high school experience in Toronto was as a student at St. Michael's College School, a Catholic high school run by the Basilian Fathers. They taught him that he should use his critical faculties when dealing with religious questions.

For me, a convert, it is more difficult. I take the church requirements more seriously. Yet, at the same time I have a conflict. Of all the people who Joe and I have come to know through our academic and professional training and careers, few are believers in God. It is hard to be going along a different path than those whom we respect and value in other areas and to pretend it is all a matter of personal choice. And what makes it even harder for me as a convert to Catholicism is to buy into a firmly delineated set of rules and a culture of subservience when I have spent a lifetime seeking out the answers to my own problems.

What about others?

When a child with a profound disability joins your family you become a handicapped family. You become 'the other' and are perceived to be outside the mainstream. I know this not only from my own experience but also from the experiences of fellow parents in our situation. This reality has coloured our life in all sorts of ways.

Through the years Joe and I have hosted many dinners and various parties for people we know through our respective work settings or have met casually in other contexts. I like to cook and we are comfortable entertaining in our own home because we can have Alexis there. She is not at the table; that would be too awkward. But she is somewhere near, working through her program with her assistant.

But what we have both noticed is that we are rarely invited back. We have asked ourselves why and have concluded that just as people feel uncomfortable visiting a dying friend or acquaintance in the hospital, many people feel uncomfortable when observing our situation. In both cases they do not know what to say.

But then I had a second thought. Maybe it is not just that people we know outside the disability world are feeling like they don't have anything in common with us. It is also that we have become so involved in Alexis' world and all the moving parts in it that must be constantly dealt with to keep it in balance that we don't have much in common with them either anymore. And I also know that not everyone likes to cook and entertain as much as we do. So the occasional pleasant evening together is great but maybe that is enough!

There is also another way of looking at this. We have a lot of social interactions that other people do not have—and the pandemic of 2020-2021 has really brought that into focus. We have been very enriched by the people Alexis has brought into our lives and have formed many good relationships with other parents or professionals dealing with disability issues or with former staff members who have formed a connection with us and have chosen to remain in our lives.

Our Home-Within-a-Home Board members, mostly former staff members or other parents, meet with us and Alexis every three months to trouble shoot and to upgrade her program plans. And then there is Elena, my senior by a generation and someone very close to my heart. She also uses her superb sewing talents to mend and adjust Alexis' clothing as needed and routinely sends home special culinary treats for her when I visit.

As for the rest of our social life, we try to take Alexis different places, to share what we can of our own interests and experiences with her. But there are many barriers apart from the obvious physical access ones. There are operas and symphonies we would like to attend with her because she really does appreciate good music. But the one time we tried that, I ended up in the lobby with her, watching the performance on a large screen TV because she made too much noise in the theatre. So much for our $100 tickets!

Of course, there are some venues like the zoo that we can access together with Alexis any time in the summer. However, once a year is generally enough for us, although she is happy to go multiple times with her assistant. Apart from our city museum, a few family restaurants and our church, the only other venue that seems to work for us as a family, i.e. one that meets both our needs and our daughter's needs, is the Imax Theatre at our local space sciences centre.

The Imax theatre is tiered, and we sit right at the top at the back in the 'handicap' section. It has a handy access door behind us so we can quickly leave for a few minutes if Alexis becomes too noisy. Its unique sound quality holds a special interest for Alexis and engages her far more than regular movies. But the new films we would be interested in seeing only come around a few times a year. That leaves a lot of unfilled time

What about Alexis' friends?

Does Alexis have friends? Can she have friends? Or do we just pretend … playing the normalization game? She has always seemed quite comfortable with Rajan and sometimes there has appeared to be some connection between them, although that may be wishful thinking on our part. Other 'friends' facing similar challenges also visit from time to time but her reactions toward them seem more muted except for Trevor. He has his own very significant limitations but he can walk around and he talks to her, a few words at a time in his slow, deep voice. Perhaps because Alexis cannot see she responds more intensely to voices and we have observed that to be particularly the case for low male voices like her father's and Trevor's. Maybe this is one reason she seems so comfortable with Rajan, listening to his vocalizations and at times vocalizing back because he also has a deep voice.

What of other friends who visit with us and Alexis from time to time? Alexis sometimes appears to recognize them but mostly I think she just appreciates having a few minutes to socialize with somebody other than her parents and assistants. There are exceptions, however. She is more responsive to our friend, Lissi who has been faithfully coming to our home to cut Alexis' hair for the past 25 years and has developed a good relationship with her. And when we put on the video of Alexis' former assistant, Manu, doing the exercises with her, Alexis turns towards the sound and appears to be paying close attention. Manu returned to India in 2012 after working closely with Alexis for five years and using her professional training as a physiotherapist to develop Alexis's motor strength and flexibility as much as possible. And it seems like Alexis still remembers her!

Sadly, Alexis' brother and sister live so far away that they can only visit rarely. But because of the pandemic we are now having regular zoom visits with them which Alexis sits in on and appears to enjoy.

What is friendship, really? According to the Stanford Encyclopedia of Philosophy, 2017 revision, *"Friendship ... is a distinctively personal relationship that is grounded in a concern on the part of each friend for the welfare of the other, for the other's sake, and that involves some degree of intimacy."* Can we realistically attribute these capacities to Alexis given the profound extent of her disabilities? At one point, when she was younger and the seizures had not yet done all their damage, I honestly felt that she was capable of a certain level of empathy. Now I no longer sense that.

Many times through the years I have felt that the deepest relationships Alexis has are with her assistants. And that is where she seems capable of showing the most discrimination. They work with her day after day and she is soon able to discern whether or not they are sincerely engaging with her or just going through the motions. She has 'told' us again and again through her behaviour when things are going right and when they are going wrong. And a number of these assistants have described to me how they feel that they have a real relationship with her, can even talk to her about their problems when they do not feel safe to talk to anybody else about them. So I would say, that insofar as Alexis has any genuine friends in the full and proper sense of the word it would be her assistants.

CHAPTER 54

The mothers who won't quit

I **started the** 'Mothers Who Won't Quit' group a few years ago. A half dozen of us who are still closely involved in our adult children's lives meet monthly to discuss our current concerns, to support each other and to call each other out when we are going down a wrong track. These sessions are very intense at times, and just to put my own story in perspective I would like to briefly share some other stories with you. I am doing so with the permission of my fellow group members.

I will start with Kathy Talwar, Rajan's mother. When Kathy's close friend, Penney, died of cancer a few years ago, she left behind five children with special needs. Although she was single, Penney had adopted these children as infants or toddlers and raised them together as a family. Before she passed away, she asked Kathy to take care of them when she was gone and to keep them together, but Penney did not leave a will.

After Penney died, Disability Services (PDD) took over, as it was their legally designated responsibility to ensure that the now orphaned two children and three dependent adults and their financial assets would be kept safe. On the day of Penney's funeral, the three adults were sent to three different homes in widely separated parts of Edmonton and the surrounding area. The two juveniles were placed together in a foster home in Edmonton until the case went to court.

Then the home Penney had built for her children and altered to accommodate the two who were in wheelchairs was sold, along with the furniture, adaptive equipment and toys that could not be used in their new temporary settings. The proceeds were placed in trust until such time as the guardianship and trusteeship of Penney's five children could be legally determined but guardianship was being contested by others with competing interests.

Undaunted, Kathy and her two daughters Kiran and Anjulie attained legal support to assist them in gaining guardianship. It was their dream to reunite the five siblings in honour of Penney's wishes. But it was a long process and Jesse, the older of the two juveniles who was then fifteen, was not willing to wait. Four months after Penney's death he ran away from the home in which he had been placed to live with Kathy and her husband, Prem. Because of his age the court determined that he had the right to choose where he wanted to live and he was not returned to the foster home.

For the younger child it was a different story. It was eleven months before Kiran and Anjulie Talwar finally gained legal guardianship of Leanna. She and Jessie then went to live with Kathy's two daughters full time in the new home they had purchased to accommodate them.

After 2 years and 3 months and 5 court trials, and after much money spent on lawyers and some unpleasant confrontations, Kathy finally succeeded in acquiring legal guardianship of Penney's three dependent adult children. Kathy and her husband had purchased and modified a home directly across the street from the home of their daughters and Penny's two younger children. Finally, the three adults and Kathy's son, Rajan, were able to move in to what Kathy dubbed as "Penney's Place," and after this long struggle Penney's children were united once more.

As Kathy has shared her story with me through these years, I have been constantly awed and surprised by her tenacity, her determination to succeed against all odds, and the outstanding support of her two daughters, Kiran and Anjulie, to ensure that this could happen.

The whole story did not fit with the Kathy I had once known—and I told her so. She just looked at me and said, "I've grown up a lot in the past 20 years, Emma." Kathy is the perfect example of how circumstances can force us to become better than we are. I have personally experienced the same phenomenon through my own life struggles with Alexis.

I have to end Kathy's story on a sad note. Within three years of Penny's family being reunited, two of her five children, both in their thirties, passed away. Death at this age for people with severe to profound disabilities is quite common, but at least Kathy has the satisfaction of knowing that because of all her efforts to reunite them they were able to spend their last three years with their other siblings and they died surrounded by family.

One of the women in our group, Carla,[21] is not a mother at all. She is the sister of Bethany who contracted encephalitis when she was 16 and suffered extensive brain damage. Bethany's mother cared for her as long as she could but eventually had to place her in an institution and Carla moved on with her adult life. But she was always haunted by the thoughts of Bethany living away from family. They had been exceptionally close to each other growing up.

By this point Carla was nearing retirement age and living in Edmonton. She and her husband, Jeremy, entered into a series of long talks and Carla did much fervent praying on the subject. Finally, an answer emerged. They would build a new home, a duplex of sorts with Bethany on one side and them on the other. They bought a property, tore the existing older home down, struggled to work around various zoning laws because of the unusual design of their duplex, and worked hard to sell their original home so they could finance this new one. In addition, funding and staffing had to be arranged for Bethany who was living out of province. But somehow they succeeded and have now been living next door to each other for several years.

Again, this is a story where I could hardly believe it could happen, knowing all the roadblocks that had occurred along the way.

When I expressed this to Carla, she simply replied "I didn't do it; God did it." This is an interesting aspect of our group. All the women involved in it are quite religious.

Mary Jo Gariano has been a friend for a long time—since the early GRIT days although she was the parent who would not enrol her disabled daughter, Angela, when we were so desperately looking for members that first year! But GRIT still managed to move on and two years later her second disabled daughter, Sarah, joined the GRIT family.

Mary Jo has five daughters in all, and two of them share the same neurodegenerative disorder that over time has left them fully dependent. She and her husband, Tom, have been running their own agency for twenty-five years now, and the girls live together in a home that they provided for them. Once every month they go to their parents' home for the weekend. Tom and Mary Jo also take them around to various evening events and travel with them during the summer, going to the mountains occasionally and more often to their cottage at the lake. When she was young, Mary Jo had other plans for her life but she has made a career out of looking after her girls.

Ruth Hyrve has a daughter, Laura, who can actually walk, albeit with some difficulty due to her cerebral palsy. Laura lives at home with her parents and is assisted by staff day and night because of her very severe seizure disorder. Ruth makes sure that Laura is out every day at one venue or another and she and her husband have travelled extensively with Laura, even taking her to New Zealand for a year.

Ruth Bisson has a son, Trevor, in his 40's and also ambulatory. He and his two roommates are fully supported by staff. To make sure that Trevor's needs were properly met Ruth purchased a home for him in 1994 and established her own agency to handle both residential and day programs. In the process, she helped a large number of people with disabilities and supported their families along the way. A few years ago Ruth realized she was reaching a point where she needed to turn operations over to another agency, but she is still closely involved in the workings of Trevor's home for the benefit of him and his roommates.

Marty Cender, Brandi's mother, also attends our group occasionally, when she is not travelling around the world. As I have already mentioned, Marty's husband, Richard, passed away a few years ago but Marty still lives in the upstairs apartment of the house they built for Brandi and her roommates, and she still takes Brandi out in the evenings the way Richard used to do.

This is our little group so you can understand why I do not believe that what Joe and I have done is all that unique. We have simply played the cards we were dealt to the best of our ability, similar to the stories of many different people in many different circumstances throughout human history.

CHAPTER 55

Has it been worth it?

On January 30th, 2018, we celebrated Alexis' 40th birthday. No medical expert who has dealt with her through the years ever believed that she would make it that long. Should we have been celebrating or not? Alexis has endured a cruel twist of fate and as a result has only been able to live out a tiny fraction of the life she might otherwise have enjoyed. And, in order to give her even that minimal life, four other lives have been significantly impacted.

Was the decision we made when Alexis was 9 months of age to keep her with us and do the best we could by her the right one? Or was it just a blind act of hubris that in the end has cost us all too much? We will never fully know the answer to that question. I can see how everyone else in our family might have had quite different lives without the daily time and energy consuming pressure of Alexis' care, and without the frequent drama of her seizures and other problems. But I can also see losses it would have meant for each of us, quite apart from the monumental loss to Alexis if she had never been able to experience a normal family life.

I think that Alexis' siblings are kinder and more concerned about others than they might have been without her daily presence in their lives when they were growing up. When I marvelled to my older daughter at what a patient and effective mother she is, considering my memories of being preoccupied and not very present for her when she, herself, was young, she surprised me by her reply. "I learned that from you, mommy: how patient you were with Alexis and how you kept trying new things to help her." When I asked my son why he gave up a successful career in theoretical mathematics to virtually start over in an applied area using mathematical modeling to shed further insight on selected social justice issues, his reply also surprised me. "Pure math is beautiful, and I love it mom, but I wanted to do something that would make a useful social contribution."

I have asked my husband to answer this question himself, and I will end this story with his remarks for he has worked as hard or harder than I have to give our daughter a life with some meaning and value in it.

Emma and Alexis at Lake Kananaskis, near Banff, Alberta,
during the summer of 2014

Alexis' 40th birthday with 4 candles and 40 guests

Joe Speaks Out:
Life with Alexis

⤛⤜

I **am the** father of Alexis. Her mother, Emma, asked me to write a few words about how living with Alexis may have changed the course of my life over the past forty years. As is evident from the chapters in this book, life with Alexis has many difficulties and many rewards. Alexis has kept us close as a family.

I was raised in an Italian-Canadian family with parents who were stay-at-home people. Their focus was their house, which they tried to make as comfortable as possible, and their garden. Gardens require daily attendance and many hours of work. So, I grew up with these values of regular work habits. When I married Emma, I brought these values and habits into our daily life.

These work habits have been very useful in our life with Alexis. Her daily needs require constant attention so that the expectation of routine and work is re-enforced. Because my work schedule at Athabasca University was flexible, I was able to do my part in assisting with Alexis and helping Emma with many different family chores.

All my life I have been a doer. I would much rather work on a problem and find a practical solution than talk about it for hours. For example, Alexis likes to eat outside in our backyard, so I found a suitable gazebo to fit the deck outside her bedroom and attached it directly to the house so that she can enjoy her three meals next to the garden among the sounds of birds and the squirrels. It has mosquito netting to keep her safe from our Alberta pests, and since it is against the house on two sides it remains sheltered from the wind. It has a strong metal structure so she can use it even when the weather is rainy or windy. We all enjoy seeing her outside in her world of natural sounds. We sometimes forget that Alexis is blind and lives in a world of sound.

Over the years Alexis gave me a perspective on people with disabilities or those who are physically different from 'normal' people. We have a Eurovan with a wheelchair lift and so can take Alexis places such as the Edmonton Space and Science Centre, the Edmonton Zoo, the Alberta Museum, to our church and to the occasional restaurant. She likes to eat different dishes. We have taken Alexis to Mexico's Mayan Riviera 13 times. She likes to ride in the catamaran over the warm salt water.

On our Home-Within-A-Home Society website I wrote the page on the quality of life that we have tried to develop for Alexis. In addition to helping Alexis enjoy life to her full potential, it is also a matter of social justice for people with severe disabilities. This social justice question is also reflected in some of my research work on ethnic minority writers. These are writers in Canada who often have been excluded by literary journals or publishers because of their ethnic origins, cultural differences, or even odd sounding names. By promoting these marginalized writers at conferences, in my literature courses, in literary journals and with my books, I have been able to help change the perceptions about what constitutes Canadian literature. Italian-Canadian authors are some of the beneficiaries of my efforts in this area.

University professors are able to do considerable travelling in order to do research and speak at conferences. I was able to do my share of these activities, but not as much as I might have liked because I felt I needed to stay home to help Emma work with Alexis.

During my 39-year career at Athabasca I had fives sabbatical leaves, but only on one of these (1984-85) were we able to move as a family to another city for the duration of the leave. This required elaborate arrangements: Emma, Marcus, Juliana and I moved to Toronto for the academic year while Alexis stayed in our house in Edmonton being cared for by a young family.

During other research and study leaves I went off by myself, spending two weeks in Italy on one occasion and a month in Wollongong, Australia on another in 2004. When I was holder of the Mariano Elia Chair in Italian-Canadian Studies I went to York University alone for the academic year. In 1991 I was Canadian Visiting Fellow at Macquarie University in Sydney, Australia for four months. Emma was not able to come with me even for a short visit. I often thought that when the family was still young, we could have spent a sabbatical year in Italy, but that was not to be.

I spent most of the time in my research and study leaves working at home. I had to focus my creative energy on projects that I could carry out and complete from Edmonton. I sometimes wonder if by focusing on projects in one location I may have gotten more done than if I had travelled around to different university settings. Writing, after all, is a solo occupation.

On one occasion I was made aware of the politics of death. In 2009 Alexis was in an Edmonton hospital from February 2nd to 18th. One morning when Emma and I were speaking to the nurse at the ward counter about Alexis' stay and when we could expect to take her home, one of the attending doctors spoke up and said, "Don't worry about taking your daughter home, you can leave her here. We will take care of her." Alexis had been placed in the geriatric ward at the end of a long hall where old people were waiting to die, some quite alone. Instead, we had members of our staff stay with Alexis during the day and I did some night shifts during that very cold February winter. I remember that Dixie, one of Alexis' new young assistants at the time, did some as well. Her mother drove her again and again to that south side hospital from their home on the northern edge of the city.

After two weeks, Alexis came home with us and has been a healthy young woman for years since. To me our work with Alexis has been worth it. We have given her a life with many pleasures and have given ourselves a rich and interesting forty-three years to date in the process. Personally, I have no regrets.

By the time I retired from the university in 2015 I had published 10 books on Canadian Literature, and I completed another one on Comparative Literature, which was published in October of 2018.[22] Maybe Alexis helped me to focus on doing the work rather than flying around from flower to flower.

As I write these last words I remember my mother who died at age 64 and so missed seeing many of the achievements of her grandchildren. Her father had come to Canada in 1904 and worked for many years as a stonemason in Northern Ontario and planned to bring his whole family to Canada after he fought in WWI. It was not to be, but in 1952 we came to this country and have benefited from all the riches it has to offer. And Alexis has enjoyed it as well.

Joseph Pivato

Epilogue,
March 31, 2021

⸎

On December 22nd, 2020—five months after this book was accepted for publication, three days before Christmas, and in the middle of the Covid-19 epidemic, Joe and I received some life altering news. Our Alexis is not who we thought she was. She is not the way she is due to Rubella damage during pregnancy or trauma at birth. At most those are only compounding factors. The primary reason underlying her profound level of disability is a genetic disorder. This disorder, labelled CACNA 1E, is so rare, we were told, that only 30 other people in the world have been identified with it to date—and none of them have lived beyond age 25 at this point in time. Its very existence as a separate disorder was only realized in 2018 and so little more than that is known about it at present.

I sent in an application for testing of Alexis to the Genetics Clinic in Edmonton many years ago, so long ago that Joe and I had forgotten all about it until we were contacted in the summer of 2020, after finally coming to the top of the wait list. We provided some additional information to add to the long questionnaires we had earlier completed, and some basic genetic testing was then done, the kind it is possible to do in Edmonton at this time. But Alexis came back negative with no genetic disorders being discovered. Subsequently, we were asked if we wanted to pursue advanced genetic testing and we agreed to do so.

On September 11th of 2020 Joe, Alexis and I each contributed several vials of blood at a local lab and these samples were sent off to a specialized genetics lab in Finland for analysis, one of the few places in the world where this complex level of analysis can be done. It was the results of this testing that we heard about in December.

What is CACNA 1E and how does it manifest? We were told that it disrupts the flow of calcium to the brain cells and this in turn leads to epileptic encephalopathy, an intractable epilepsy so severe and unremitting that it results in more brain damage and ultimately death. CACNA 1E is not an inherited genetic disorder and no similar markers were found in either Joe's genes or mine. But it does perhaps explain why Alexis has those frightening spells of non-breathing which have appeared up to this point to be unique to her among all the many other people, both disabled and non-disabled, whom we know and who have epilepsy.

Joe and I were both stunned by this revelation that Alexis has a serious and life-threatening genetic disorder, and I had a particularly difficult time coming to terms with it. Why? Joe actually felt a sense of relief in finally having an answer and in knowing that there was absolutely nothing we could have done differently, either before or after her birth that would have changed the outcome. But I have been feeling something that has taken me several months to even begin to understand—and I am still not entirely sure exactly what it is.

Looking back, it seems to me that I have spent the bulk of my adult life struggling and striving to help Alexis be all that she can be—to improve the quality of her life against all odds. And at some level I know that I have done so. Yet, when I consider all this effort in terms of her diagnosis, it seems rather futile to me now. How, after all, can you fight a missing gene? And more than futile, perhaps it has been destructive to the rest of us in the family. Should we have listened to that initial specialist who recommended institutionalization? Alexis would be long gone by now and maybe largely forgotten.

Many friends and doctors through the years have told us so and I do believe that without the level of care we have provided for her that would indeed have been the case.

But we did not opt for institutionalization or even for a more reasonable position of keeping her with us but not making her the central focus in our lives. We have accepted the resulting limits that this choice has placed on us. That was our choice—but in making it we also chose limits for our other children. What about that? What about all that we took away from them in the process? What about the lost music and language lessons, the lost opportunities to travel with them and experience the cultural and geographic richness of other countries together? What about the lost time we could have spent nurturing and supporting them—making them strong in the face of the world? Was it right to do that?

I have asked them that question and Marcus and Juliana have both given me the same reply.

They claim to not feel cheated over whatever they may have missed out on and they state further that growing up with Alexis, observing her struggles and our efforts to meet her needs was its own form of enrichment that has served them quite well in their adult lives. I suppose I must take their answers at face value although I know that you can't miss what you never knew in the first place. Also, I suspect that they could hardly have answered otherwise, knowing how it would have affected me.

All I know is that the choice we made back in November of 1978 to keep our daughter with us and to help her to be the best she could be was the only one we could have made at that time. This is a choice that all parents in our situation have to make and I have known many parents through the years and have seen many different choices. In the end, I guess, we all have to be true to ourselves. I am who I am and Joe is who he is and we are in the situation we are in. That situation is a privileged one in many ways and it has allowed us to make a choice that not everyone similarly challenged by such circumstances would be able to make. Whether or not everyone in equally privileged circumstances would choose to make it is another question, but that is not for me to ask.

What I *can* say as a final word is that we all seek out meaning and purpose in our lives. That is the human condition. In our case a large chunk of that meaning came to us and our older two children through Alexis. We did not have to look for it. By accepting the challenge she presented and dealing with it the best we could we really have been enriched, and continue to be enriched, in the process. And so has Alexis … and no belated diagnosis can change that!

Joe, Emma and Alexis Pivato—2018 picture for our church directory

*Alexis at the Blue Chair Café responding with delight
to a folk music group, 2018*

Afterword,
by Alvin Finkel

❧

In 1981, about three years after Alexis was born, a fellow staff member at Athabasca University said to me one day: "I think Joe and Emma are obsessed with Alexis. They're ignoring their other two children and themselves. Emma has thrown away her career."

This outburst surprised me, and I began defending the Pivatos, but I was quickly cut off. "Well, I suppose I am defensive," she said, "because I gave birth to a handicapped child like Alexis some years ago. But I gave her up to an institution because I didn't feel that I could do justice to her and my three older children."

There is no answer to that. Not everyone is in the same position mentally or materially to make sacrifices when life throws a particular challenge at them. But that conversation with my co-worker did make me wonder what life was really like inside the Pivato household.

At work, Joe did make reference to how Alexis was doing occasionally but mostly he was focused on teaching and scholarly issues and seemed as laid back a person as you could ever hope to meet. I saw Emma from time to time at parties and she seemed an ebullient person, always happy to debate almost anything and in her own way, spoiling for a friendly fight. Much of her conversation certainly was about Alexis but it was more focussed on her frustrations with dealing with 'the system' than on the work involved with Alexis herself.

I thought that I had a pretty good handle on Joe—he was a

bookish stoic with a wry sense of humour and just accepted whatever sacrifices in his private life were required to accommodate his younger daughter's needs—but found Emma a touch enigmatic. When she did return to work, she did seem happier than when she was focused solely on the home. And what she brought to her work seemed to be the same feistiness and defense of her clients that she brought to her efforts to integrate Alexis into the schools and the larger community.

In their home it was clear that the Pivatos arranged everything around Alexis's needs. Joe and Emma threw a lovely welcoming party for my older boy when my ex and I adopted him in infancy in 1986 from St. Vincent and the Grenadines. I remember thinking ungraciously about how happy I was that my baby boy was like the Pivatos' two brainy, older children, not Alexis, but also marvelling at how happy Alexis seemed throughout that party and how healthy and strong she looked for an eight-year-old who could not speak or even sit up on her own.

I did not think I would ever have personal experiences that would help me understand the Pivato household beyond the surface. But as fate would have it I did. In 1990, my former wife and I adopted our second child, a baby boy who seemed perfectly normal until he was seven years old. At that point he was diagnosed as suffering from Foetal Alcohol Spectrum Disorder (FASD), which in his case was manifested in paranoia, violent rage, extreme social anxiety, and unbelievable rigidity in almost all things.

Overnight our lives changed, and my younger boy's needs became the organizing principle of our lives. Our work lives, social lives, and the ability of our family to function all suffered but in ways that we often could not explain to others. We were too busy putting on brave faces and my academic career, which was in high gear, became a crutch in a life so compartmentalized that I sometimes wondered if I was one person.

Throughout those turbulent years of my son's childhood and youth, I felt lucky to be a privileged university professor who could organize my time to deal with all the people in 'the system' who needed to be dealt with and with the unpredictable character of my son's days. I could not imagine how an ordinary working or poor family with a child like mine could continue to function or be able to give such a child the intensive support required.

Although Alexis in so many ways is different from my son, ... *and along came Alexis* seems a familiar story to me. Here is Emma with her third child, and she has suspicions early on that something is amiss. But when a preliminary diagnosis of "severe developmental delay" is given, she is devastated. Emma's PhD thesis was on gifted children and she did complete it, but almost immediately abandoned work in that area to focus her scholarly and professional interests on disability.

The seizures that Alexis suffered, like my son's long, uncontrollable tantrums, became a constant reminder of how fragile Alexis's life was. The seizures and non-breathing spells seemed to weaken Alexis's strength and cognition. Figuring out what foods she could tolerate and what outings were possible also became ongoing challenges. Meanwhile Emma developed GRIT, Gateway Residential Intensive Training, an intensive, home-based program designed to meet the developmental needs of children like Alexis. She found other families whose children faced similar challenges and successfully lobbied government officials for provincial funding in order to cover operational costs.

At the same time as this was happening, Emma was putting together the book, *Different Hopes, Different Dreams,* stories from Alberta families about their experiences raising a child with developmental disabilities. It became a resource for parents and well as for students and professionals in the special education field.

From the completion of her PhD in 1980 until 1984, Emma's work with Alexis and children with similar issues was all unpaid work. She re-joined the labour force in the fall of 1984 as a school psychologist in Toronto while there for Joe's sabbatical year. For both funding and health reasons, Alexis remained in Edmonton that year, cared for by her GRIT assistant and her new husband, a minister and aspiring lawyer.

After the rest of the family returned to Edmonton the following summer, Emma's focus was on ensuring that Alexis and others in her situation were included in regular classrooms in publicly supported schools. But there were also challenges in terms of finding activities in the community that Alexis could enjoy and the ongoing struggles that her various health issues created. Throughout the book, there is a conversation occurring between mother and daughter that reflects Emma's efforts to communicate in every way possible with a daughter who could not talk to her in the ways that parents normally talk to their children.

Alexis was 42 years old as Emma reached the end of her manuscript, ... *and along came Alexis*. Thus, Emma and Joe had experienced issues that arise at different ages and stages for someone with complex intellectual and physical challenges. This book will offer hope, but not of an unvarnished sort, for parents in similar situations. The point is always to be searching for those ways in which children like Alexis and my son can have their basic physical, mental, and emotional needs met while still finding ways of integrating their lives with those of everyone else as best you can.

At the same time there is the need to carve out spaces in one's life for fulfilling goals, both in terms of work and pleasure, beyond being a faithful servant to the needs of a high maintenance offspring. Where there are other children, their needs also need to be considered. It's not easy. And while Emma and Joe remained committed to their marriage throughout all of the challenges and sometimes chaos that her book describes, the divorce rate for couples with one or more severely disabled children is incredibly high. Their social lives were restricted and Emma's work life, at least, proved different than what she had envisioned.

On the other hand, Emma became a detective storywriter, fashioning stories that involved the lives of people with various disabilities and their families. Readers of this book will see a detective mentality at work as Emma, faced with the limitations of her younger daughter, searches out clues for who and what can help to make

Alexis's life happy and healthy despite her deficiencies. This should be an inspiration to others who also have special needs children or who work with such kids professionally, or indeed just those who have friends or relatives whose lives have been at once blessed and cursed by the challenge of having kids who will never be "launched" into independence. Those children, and later adults, call out to the entire community for understanding, patience, and love.

Alvin Finkel, Ph.D.
Professor Emeritus of History
Athabasca University*

*Alvin Finkel has published widely on world history, with a particular focus on social policy and labour. Notably, his most recent book (at time of writing) is entitled *Compassion: A Global History of Social Policy* (2019).

Acknowledgements

Thank you to all the following:

My daughter, Alexis, for pushing me ever onward.

My friends and family for providing the necessary encouragement and flattery to keep me going.

Dr. Alvin Finkel, for writing such a thoughtful and perceptive afterword.

Colleen Hermanson, Kathy Talwar, Debbie Appleby, Marisa de Franceschi and Juliana Pivato for their helpful editorial comments.

Mary Jo Gariano, for suggesting the title for this book.

Gary Clairman, for his thorough, patient and sensitive editing of the manuscript.

David Moratto, for his impressive artistry with the cover picture of Alexis' ravine, taken by Joe.

The staff at Super 8 Motel, Leduc who make me so welcome when I retreat there to write.

Barb Reid, executive director of the GRIT Program, for updating me on their current operations.

And, most of all, to my husband, Joe, for his never-ending support, critical input, and direction.

About the Author

Emma Pivato, B.A., M.A., Ph. D, is a retired academic and psychologist who is currently working on her next volume in the Claire Burke murder mystery series. These books incorporate a rich variety of characters with various developmental disabilities and/or a range of personality quirks and issues. But whatever their state or condition these characters band together from time to time to work on the different mysteries that face the main protagonists, Claire, her daughter Jessie and her neighbour and good friend, Tia.

Emma also has a long history of advocating for people with intellectual and physical disabilities and has published a number of articles in this area as well as several on other aspects of intellectual and personality functioning of particular interest to her. Her previous book, *Different Hopes, Different Dreams*, an edited work encompassing stories from various families raising children with cognitive deficits, was first published in 1984 with a revised and updated second edition appearing in 1991.

At the website, emmapivato.com you can find further information and a variety of pictures illustrating family life with Alexis. Emma's blog at this site shares her current research activities including her progress on a specialized cookbook for people experiencing chewing and swallowing difficulties entitled *Gourmet Puree: What to do if you can't chew!*

Endnotes

1   When my daughter, Juliana, read this section of the book she pointed out that the Rubella vaccine was not available until 1969 so I could not have received it as an 8-year-old child. Yet this memory is very real to me and I argued mightily for my version of the truth until she showed me proof. Obviously, it must have been some other vaccination that our class received that day. But false memories start like this: extreme emotional distress, often for long periods of time, and, in my case, a characteristic tendency to blame myself when things go wrong. Before this happened to me, I did not believe that false memories could be this powerful and real. Now I do!

2   Severe Developmental Delay—In 1998 when Alexis was initially diagnosed, this was the nomenclature of the day. However, current DSM-5 categorization lists Alexis' level of disability as F73, Profound. Specifiers for inclusion in that category involve the following: "The individual has very limited understanding of symbolic communication in speech or gesture ... may understand some simple instructions or gestures ... expresses his or her own desires and emotions largely through nonverbal, non-symbolic communication ... enjoys relationships with well-known family members, caretakers, and familiar others, and initiates and responds to social interactions through gestural and emotional cues. Co-occurring sensory and physical impairments may prevent many social activities ... as well as functional use of objects. The individual is dependent on others for all aspects of daily physical care, health, and safety ...."—*Diagnostic and Statistical Manual of Mental Disorders, 5th Edition. (DSM-5)* p. 33.

3   Disability Services is the larger provincial category under which PDD, Persons with Developmental Disabilities is placed. The mandate of PDD is to provide the funding and supervision of support services designed to meet the needs of adults throughout Alberta who were either born with or subsequently contracted various levels of intellectual impairment before the age of 18. Despite efforts to homogenize services throughout the province there remain various differences in how this mandate is applied. In Edmonton we are particularly fortunate to have had some creative and farseeing administrators who have introduced a level of flexibility into program administration that has resulted in an enhanced lifestyle for many individuals receiving their service.

4   The Gateway Association for Community Living, as it is now called, is "... a family resource centre and an employment resource centre that provides education, family support, mentorship and inclusive employment. It is our mission to assist the community to understand disabilities." https://gatewayassociation.ca/ Retrieved January 14, 2019.

5   When I first became involved with disabilities organizations, brain damage sufficient to impair intellectual functioning was called 'mental retardation' and that was the name in use in the Diagnostic and Statistical Manuals of that time (DSM-III and DSM-IV). The DSM (*Diagnostic and Statistical Manual of Mental Disorders*) is the major reference manual in use to describe mental disorders of all types in the Western hemisphere.

However, parent advocates found this term demeaning and chose to use the term 'mental handicap'. It had for them a more positive connotation since physical impairment was better understood and accepted by the public at large than mental impairment and the word 'handicap' had become associated with physical impairment.

The online dictionary defines handicap as "a circumstance that makes progress or success difficult." One could certainly argue that this more accurately reflects the situation of a person with a cognitive limitation than 'mental retardation' since by suggesting the slowing of intellectual development the implication of the latter term is that there will be a later catch-up—and brain damage does not go away.

The negative connotation that had attached to 'mental retardation' soon transferred over to 'mental handicap', however, and advocates then began talking about 'challenges' and focusing on strengths rather than weaknesses. 'People first' became the new buzzword and there was a move away from labeling and objective evaluation. Many disabilities support groups across the country, including Gateway and the Alberta provincial association, changed their names from an association for the mentally retarded to an association for the mentally handicapped to an association for community living within the span of two decades. And our provincial association is now known simply as 'Alberta Inclusion'.

Finally, when DSM-5 was released in 2013, the term 'mental retardation' disappeared forever, replaced by 'intellectual disability'. "Intellectual disability (intellectual developmental disorder) is a disorder with onset during the developmental period that includes both intellectual and adaptive functioning deficits in conceptual, social and practical domains." (DSM-5, p. 33).

This term is straightforward and descriptive, as it should be. But the reason given for replacing the previous term, 'mental retardation', by the psychiatrists and psychologists who developed the DSM was not that it was inaccurate but that the term 'mental retardation' had picked up a negative connotation.

Ref: *Diagnostic and Statistical Manual of Mental Disorders, Fifth Edition (DSM-5)* (2013) Washington, DC; American Psychiatric Publishing

6 Pivato, Emma (2018) "What is it to be Human?" in De Gasperi, G., De Santis, D. and Di Giovanni, C. (Eds), *People, Places, Passages: An anthology of Canadian Writing,* Montreal: Longbridge Books.

7   Handicapped Children's Services is now called Family Support for Children with Disabilities.

8   Hypsarrhythmia is a form of disorganized brain activity indicating a lack of the normally paced and consistent relationship between signal and response on an EEG report. It most frequently appears in infants where it can be a temporary reaction to a high fever and is referred to as 'infantile spasms'. When it persists, as in Alexis' case, it is an ominous sign of moderate to severe neurological damage and other causes, such as birth hypoxia or uterine infection during gestation or some genetically based structural abnormality, are generally found to be the triggering factor. (Monrad, Priya. (2018) "Paroxysmal Disorders" in Kliegman, R., TothBrett, H., Bordini, J. and Basel, D. *Nelson Pediatric Symptom-Based Diagnosis, Elsevier Health Sciences.*

9   Frankl, Viktor E. (1963) *Man's Search for Meaning: An introduction to Logotherapy.* New York: Washington Square Press.

10 PDD stands for Persons with Developmental Disabilities, the Alberta government department established to monitor and fund the necessary support services for persons with developmental disabilities in the province. It is now called simply 'Disability Services'.

11 On January 7th, 2020, at the age of 41 years, Kent DeFord passed away after multiple bouts of aspiration pneumonia. At the time of writing those of us who knew and loved him are all still grieving his loss.

12 'Dependent Handicapped' was the official category in use at that time by Alberta Education to designate funding support level for school-aged children, so they applied it to our pre-school children as well.

13 I was Dr. Pivato at that point, but no medical professional has ever taken that appellation seriously!

14 Very sadly, Joe's mother passed away in May of 1984. Thus, Joe's dream of spending an entire sabbatical year with both his parents was never to be realized.

15   The Boston Process Approach considers the types of errors clients make in answering neuropsychological test questions and the process they go through to reach the answers they provide.

16   This was termed a 'glow light'. Designed as a toy for children, the entire end of it lit up and flashed. We had discovered it at the Edmonton Exhibition when we saw another child playing with it. His father explained to me that they had purchased it there, but it had been the very last one available. In my single-minded focus on doing everything I could to improve Alexis' life I managed to convince him that she needed it more than his son and he sold it to me. I don't know now how I could possibly have felt justified in doing that, and as it turned out Janni got a lot more pleasure from it than Alexis! Notably, this was the case with many of the things we bought to provide sensory stimulation for Alexis.

17   Bruce Uditsky was then, and remained until recently, the director of Alberta Inclusion, previously known as Alberta Association for Community Living.

18   For a discussion of this see the article listed in footnote 6.

19   Neuromuscular scoliosis affects the ability of people with severe cases of cerebral palsy, as well as certain other neuromuscular conditions, to exert the necessary level of muscular control over the spinal vertebrae.

20   Pivato, Emma (2009) Breaching the Last Frontier: Dignity and the Toileting Issue for Persons with Multiple and Severe Disabilities, in *Developmental Disabilities Bulletin, 37, 1 and 2.*

21   The names in this story have been changed at the request of the contributor.

22   Joe is often too humble about his publications. I will list some of them here:
    - After our stay in Toronto in 1984-5 he published *Contrasts: Comparative Essays on Italian-Canadian Writing* (1985), which became a seminal book for ethnic minority writing.
    - During his stay at Macquarie University in Australia in 1991

he produced *Echo: Essays on Other Literatures* (1994), a selection of his own articles on ethnic-minority writing.

- In 1998 he edited *The Anthology of Italian-Canadian Writing.*
- He co-edited and contributed to the journals: *Canadian Literature* No. 106 (1985) and *Canadian Ethnic Studies* 28.3 (1996).
- He also co-edited and contributed to the volumes *Literatures of Lesser Diffusion* (1990) and *Comparative Literature for the New Century* (2018).

In addition, Joe has edited separate books on Caterina Edwards, F.G. Paci, Mary di Michele, Sheila Watson, Pier Giorgio Di Cicco, and George Elliott Clarke.

MARQUIS

Québec, Canada

MIX
Paper from
responsible sources
FSC® C103567
FSC
www.fsc.org